Affectioi

MW00532889

The Civil War Letters of
William R. Jackson and his Wife Julia

"The Busy Office Of A Cavalry Quartermaster"
Photo from *The Photographic History of the Civil War,*
The Decisive Battles/The Cavalry, Volume 2
Patriot Publishing Company, Springfield, MA
1911

Transcribed and Edited
by
Cheryl Jackson Baker

ISBN 978-0692339329

Copyright © 2014 Cheryl Jackson Baker
All Rights Reserved

For Misti,
Fellow lover of
history and
books —
Enjoy)!
Cheryl J Baker
Nov. 2017

Dedication

This book is dedicated to my parents, B. Jean Obee Jackson and Theodore Ernest Jackson, from whom I learned so much, not the least of which is the appreciation of the written word.

"A written word is the choicest of relics. It is something at once more intimate with us and more universal than any work of art."
Henry David Thoreau, Walden

Preface

"To whom much is given, much is required," Luke 12:48[1]

Many people - friends and strangers alike - have told me how lucky or fortunate I am to have found these Civil War letters of my great, great-grandparents, William Robinson and Julia B. Williams Jackson; however, I feel that is a huge understatement! Even after all these years, I find it difficult to describe what I felt that October day in 1997 when I came upon the old box holding these letters. Elation, surprise, and sadness come close... but words fail when I attempt to recount my feelings as I held the box and read my father's handwriting on the masking tape across its lid: "Civil War letters of W.R.J. 1862-1864." Actually William and Julia's letters covered a span of five years (early 1862 through 1866) and even include letters to and from my great-grandfather, Theodore, written later in the nineteenth century. The box which held the (now) 150 year old letters in their original envelopes is about 10 inches square and 3 inches deep and is made of heavy cardboard with a paper covering that has the look of leather. With three of its dark brown sides having two stars embossed on them and its beige, hinged lid displaying a gold U.S. seal, it certainly doesn't appear to be just an ordinary box.

Unfortunately, all those times our late father, Theodore Ernest Jackson, shared his stories of our ancestors from Huron County, Ohio I had listened only half-heartedly. Because so often I was busy with my work and/or family, I could remember some but not all of his stories, and just ask anyone who knew him - our dad was known for his jokes and stories! He was knowledgeable about many things and so many times since his death one of my four siblings[2] or I found ourselves thinking *"if only we could ask dad..."*

Dad was born and raised in Palm Beach County, Florida, along with his older brother, Richard. Their father, William *Richard (later changed to Randal)* Jackson, moved with his parents and older sister, Marguerite, from North Central Ohio to South Florida in the late 1800s or early 1900s. My sister and I were cleaning dad's old house, where he'd moved in the late 1960s; this was the same house *his* father and mother had lived in from the 1940s until their deaths. This house *and these letters* had survived Florida's hurricanes as well as the high humidity in several decades without air-conditioning not to mention paper-eating insects. Later, while reading through other papers of our father's, I found a letter from his mother, our Grandmother Eve, written to an autograph collector in hopes that she might sell these "old Civil War letters." Fortunately, for us, the collector was not interested.

Our three brothers (Teddy, Randy, and Kit) were at work when Deborah and I were cleaning dad's house but soon heard of my find. Teddy and Randy later excitedly approached me about the letters. We three oldest, these two brothers and I, sat reading various letters in turn, first amazed by the fact that they were *Union* letters as our dad acted like such a *Rebel* sympathizer that his house even had a doorbell that played 'Dixie!' We were fascinated by the elegant handwriting, details, and emotions within these letters. Although Randy, known as the Civil War buff, felt he should have them, Teddy, our oldest brother, stated with his air of authority, "Who is really going to <u>do anything</u> with them? Cheryl's our family historian." So it was that I ended up with the personal letters and Randy was given those papers or letters that looked "official" or related to military matters.

Once home in Tennessee, I immediately set to work on this epistolary project determined to *"do something with them."* As I removed each letter from its original envelope (most already had their stamps removed and the postmarks are illegible), I carefully unfolded and copied each of the originals and then stored them in archive safe materials in a bank vault. Subsequently, I began the daunting yet enjoyable task of transcribing - from the copies - these beautifully scripted letters. Each one was different and since they were not in any particular order, each revealed various details about its author, the war, or other family members and friends named in the letter. It was as though I'd emptied a 1000 piece puzzle from its box and now could begin to put those pieces together to create a clearer and larger picture. I couldn't help but feel grateful for this opportunity to view my ancestors' personal thoughts and feelings as well as information about their daily affairs. As I read each one of these personal missives, I felt, at times, as though I was eavesdropping on intimate conversations, especially when I came upon the more intimate love letters of Julia and William (July-August 1864). Since I have always enjoyed receiving and writing letters myself and since letter writing is fast becoming a dying art, it was not lost on me just how special these letters were for so many reasons. They had not only survived the weather and insects, but also were not sold or thrown away as one or another ancestor of ours moved or passed away.

Therefore I first want to express gratitude for my ancestors who saved these letters and am also grateful to so many others who have helped me finish this project:

Virginia "Penny" Carlisle d'Armand, a volunteer with Sons of the Revolution at the East Tennessee History Center in Knoxville, Tennessee, helped me with reading some of the fanciful handwriting. With her help, I was able to decipher words and script no longer used today. Once the transcriptions were complete, I began to focus my energies on researching these over 150 letters (not all included in this book).

Thanks to June Shawver, a woman from Huron County who I met online, my brother Ted and I were able to meet our third cousin, Ray Heck and wife, Carolyn, in 1998, when we visited our ancestors' home and North Central Ohio for the first time.

Ray, who is the great-grandson of one of William and Julia's daughters, has allowed me to visit their home, the "old home place" in Monroeville, almost every time I am in the area doing research. He and Carolyn showed us papers they had in Ray's grandmother's handwriting about the family tree. Ray's family tree and stories he'd heard matched those of our dad's stories and handwritten family tree.

Mary L. Stewart, with St. Paul's Episcopal Church (Norwalk), helped early on with information about the Williams (Julia's) family. Also helpful were Jamie Ebert, Superintendent of Norwalk's Woodlawn Cemetery, and Kenny Balliet, of Bellville Cemetery. The latter was especially helpful with finding information on the Jacksons who are buried in Bellville's old cemetery.

Mary Carabin and the staff at Fireland's Historical Society's (F.H.S) library in Norwalk, Ohio have been extremely helpful each time I visit and in answering my every email or phone request. Whether researching William's regiments, Julia's family, or specific people mentioned in any of the letters, the volunteer staff at the F.H.S. library have been invaluable and I can't thank them enough for their help with this project.

Likewise, the staff and volunteers at the Ohio Genealogical Society were very helpful during my brief visits to their excellent four year old facility in Bellville, Ohio. It was here that I found most of the information on William's family.

Peggy McClintock of The Camp Nelson Heritage Center told me a few tidbits about "Mrs. Scott," mentioned in several of the letters and has also been good to respond to my emails or phone calls.

The friendly and knowledgeable staff at our own wonderful local library (Blount County Public Library) in Maryville, Tennessee, have been extremely patient and kind with my every request, sometimes even getting *almost as excited* as I am about "the book" project! They have been especially helpful with computer searches and obtaining hard to find books. I am blessed to have them and my Friends of the Library (F.O.L.) volunteers in my circle of support!

I feel tremendously blessed with not only the above named but also so many others who have been so kind to listen to me through the years as I spoke passionately about these letters. Kate Clabough, a local writer, deserves special mention as she has many times offered her time, advice, and expertise.

My "long standing friend," Nancy Vrooman, deserves a special note of thanks for her keen eyesight and attention to detail, not to mention time and patience, with help on this project; from transcribing some of the letters to editing-her help has been invaluable! Apologies abound for my not naming *everybody* who has listened and encouraged me throughout the years, but for fear of omitting someone, just know that if you are one who listened to me, read some of the letters with me, offered your advice and other help, I appreciate you so much! I hope you all realize just how valuable your support has been to me through all the years of my work on this project.

Our two children, Matthew, and Megan have had the questionable "advantage" of hearing so many stories about William and Julia; like their maternal grandfather, I enjoy telling stories as well. Phil, my husband of 35 years, has been especially patient with my stories and musings not to mention *researcher extraordinaire*! His culinary expertise kept me well fed especially on the long days of writing or editing!

Phil, Matthew and Megan as well as daughter-in-law, Emily, have been my editors of choice and generous with their time. Their encouragement has kept me from quitting many times; their belief in my ability to finish this book outweighed my belief a multitude of times and for that, I will be forever grateful! My sister, Deborah, has never wavered in her support and encouragement with this project so deserves special mention as well.

I thank *all* my siblings for entrusting these letters to me and for believing I would "do something with them." Even though Teddy and Randy both passed away in 2012, I know they believed I could and would finish this book and for that, I will be forever grateful.

Thanks to *all the above*, we now have a glimpse into the life of a Union Quartermaster, William R. Jackson, and his wife, Julia, who was home in Ohio with their five children, making the most of the frightening and lonely times while separated by our nation's Civil War, "The War of Northern Aggression," or "War Between the States." By whatever name we call it, it was war and as General William T. Sherman said several years after this war ended: *"War is Hell!"*

Preface Notes

1. The Holy Bible Revised Standard Version (RSV, New Testament) p. 74.

2. Teddy (Theodore Richard Jackson), Randy (John Randal Jackson), Deborah (Deborah Jean Jackson Duck), and Kit (Christopher Harlan Jackson).

TABLE OF CONTENTS

Introduction.. **xi**

Chapter One **1**
From Monroeville, Ohio to Kentucky, Tennessee, and Alabama

Chapter Two.. **45**
Outfitting the Seventh

Chapter Three **51**
Hoping something will turn up this spring to bring this thing to a close.

Chapter Four... **117**
Camp Nelson and Fear Filled Times on the Home Front

Chapter Five **143**
"Home Is No Home Without You"

Chapter Six **201**
The War's End

Epilogue **239**

Glossary **245**

Persons of Interest.. **249**

Bibliography **271**

About the Author **277**

Introduction

"The histories of the Lost Cause are all written out by 'big bugs' generals and renowned historians,...But in these pages I do not pretend to write the history of the war... Of course, the histories are all correct." - Sam Watkins, *Co. Aytch*

We may never know why William Robinson Jackson decided to join the Third Ohio Volunteer Calvary (O.V.C.) in November 1861. There is nothing among these letters to show that he had heard any "clarion call" as so many on either side of this conflict said they had heard. It was six months after the War of the Rebellion, also known as "the Lost Cause" (and about 28 other names), had started and most likely many of William and Julia's neighbors were joining the Union effort in response to Ohio's call for "75,000 troops." Men were answering ads such as this one:

Once More to the Rescue
Our Country Needs More Soldiers!

...began the ad printed in *The Norwalk Experiment* in the latter part of September 1861.

Attention Cavalry to Arms Ye Brave!

read another, with promises of a finite term of enlistment of as little as six months or as much as three years, pay of $13 or more per month, depending on one's rank, and a bounty of $100 at the end of the war. In December of that year, the same newspaper placed an ad showing which states had met their quotas of Cavalry men, with Ohio having raised a total of 6000 men in six different Cavalries. Not only did Ohio provide six Cavalry regiments but she supplied more than 260 regiments with over 300,000 men total - third in numbers to New York and Pennsylvania.[1] Two days before Christmas of that year, there was a list of the organization of the Third Ohio Cavalry, its officers and staff who were then in Camp Worcester, in Monroeville; William R. Jackson was listed as "B.Q.M. appointed Nov. 4, 1861."[2]

Beliefs were so strong on either side that it had come to this: a war that at first was thought might be short lived but would actually see over 600,000 killed in battle, mortally wounded, missing or dying from disease before it would come to an end four years later, in April, 1865.

The 1860 census names William, aged 37, as Assistant Marshall of his small town and also as "farmer." He and his wife, Julia, had bought the land where they lived from Julia's parents, James and Sarah Hunt Williams, who lived in nearby Norwalk, Ohio. William and Julia's twins, Fannie and Julia, were ten years of age, with younger sisters, Florence and Lillian, listed as five years old and eight months, respectively, on the 1860 census. My great-grandfather, Theodore William, was three years old at the time of that census. Julia and William's oldest, Charles Benjamin, was absent from this census because sadly, in 1853, at only seven years of age, he had drowned.[3]

At the time the war began, William's parents, Benjamin Jr. and Nancy Robinson Jackson and many of his nine siblings, were living in Bellville, Ohio, a town about 50 miles southeast of Monroeville in Richland County. As evidenced in William's and Julia's letters, the town was spelled 'Belleville' then. According to Bellville's history, the spelling change occurred while Dr. Abijah Beach, married to William's oldest sister, Elizabeth, was the Postmaster. In 1872, the name was again changed back to its original spelling by order of the Post Office Department.[4] Both Benjamin Jr. and his father, Benjamin Sr., were veterans of various wars, with Benjamin Sr. having served in the Revolutionary War. In the "Declaration in order to attain the benefit of the act of Congress of the 7th of June 1832," obtained from the National Archives' Veterans Records, Benjamin Sr. is listed as 81 years of age. Later in this document his birthplace and birth date are listed as Morris County, New Jersey, March 5, 1750, respectively.

Benjamin Jr., also born in New Jersey, moved to Ohio in 1815 and to Richland County in 1825. One newspaper article about his death states "he built the first frame house and the first brick house in Bellville and was always one of the leading businessmen in that place."[5] Benjamin Jr.'s signature, as Judge, is on several documents found at the Ohio Genealogical Society in Bellville. Benjamin Sr. appears to have moved to Ohio to be with his son and family soon after the younger Benjamin moved there.

Huron County, where Julia's parents settled, is in the part of Ohio known today as "The Firelands." The "Fire Sufferers' Land," as it was once called, was land given by the State of Connecticut, in 1792, to the citizens of nine towns whose homes and private property were destroyed by fire during the American Revolution. This half million acres was at the west end of the Connecticut Western Reserve in Northern Ohio. Since Connecticut had no money at that time to give these petitioners, who had lost so much during the Revolutionary War, they gave them land grants instead. Most of the actual "sufferers" had already rebuilt their homes, moved to other locations or died by the time the land was secured through a treaty in 1805. Therefore, many who actually moved there were heirs of the original "sufferers" or people who had bought from land speculators; up until then, the land was inhabited mainly by Native Americans. Later settlers agreed to its final name change, "The Firelands."[6]

Julia's father, James Williams, was also born in the state of New Jersey and moved to Ohio in the early 1800s as one of the new pioneers in the Firelands. According to one lengthy article found in the *Fire Lands Pioneer* of October, 1874, "this area of the country was one vast wilderness." Since James was apprenticed in law but "the litigating period had not yet arrived among the settlers," when Julia's father first arrived, he began life in Ohio "in merchandizing." Later after moving to Norwalk, the new county seat of Huron County, he was appointed as the "first Clerk of the Court of Common Pleas and of the Supreme Court of Huron County." Printed in this same issue of the *Fire Lands Pioneer* is an article on Julia's mother's death: "Mrs. Sarah Matilda Hunt Williams: relict of the late James Williams, Esq. died in Norwalk, August 25, 1871 in the 80th year of her age." The seventh daughter of Major David Hunt, of Jersey City, Sarah married James in 1813. Raised a Quaker, Sarah decided at age 22 to join the Episcopal Church, most likely because it was her husband's church. Records from the local libraries in Norwalk show two of Julia's older siblings, Louisa and Theodore, as being the first children baptized in Norwalk's St. Paul's Episcopal Church.[7]

Julia, born in 1824, was one of eight children, seven who survived to adulthood. Theodore, her older brother and the author of one of the letters (June 3, 1862), was a prominent businessman and owner of a store in Norwalk. Julia writes of him and several other siblings in many of her letters. His letter to her, written while she was at Pittsburgh Landing, Tennessee, helping to nurse William back to health, is one of seventeen letters in this collection written by other family members or friends. Even being an officer with better living conditions than the soldiers, William was stricken with "bowel complaint," one of the effects of poor living conditions and hygiene, contaminated water, and food.

Though I thoroughly enjoyed reading these letters that were transcribed by late 1999, family and career concerns kept me from working on the letters for ten years. Since retirement and returning to work on the book, I have been able to re-visit North Central Ohio four more times.

Living within a day's drive of Huron and Richland Counties, I have visited actual graves, read copies of the original newspaper articles, microfilms etc. but found that even these primary sources have conflicting information. To make matters more confusing, in Julia's letters, "the children" are often referred to collectively, but most of the time, referred to by nicknames and not as they were listed on census records. To confuse matters even further, William had a sister named Julia and both had sisters named Sarah and Caroline; ironically both also had sisters named Henrietta who died young. With many of their friends also having similar names, it was challenging trying to figure out to whom William or Julia might be referring in each letter! I attempted to identify most of the persons named within each letter and was successful with a large percentage of them. Those identified are noted in the "Persons of Interest" Appendix.

Once the letters were transcribed and saved on floppy disks (as that <u>was</u> the technology of the late 1990s), I began to research terminology, the Civil War, and Ohio's part in it as well as the movements of the Third and Seventh Ohio Volunteer Cavalries, the two regiments in which William served. The information on the floppy disks was transferred later to modern day technology (thanks again to my husband, Phil) and the transcribed letters are now saved in several locations. The originals will be donated to the Rutherford B. Hayes Presidential Center in Fremont, Ohio. There they will be available to not only our family but the general public and researchers as well. For clarity, those words, abbreviations, or phrases in the letters that are not commonly used today, are included in the Glossary.

In most of the letters, punctuation, including capitalization and periods at the end of sentences, was non-existent; therefore, I added capitalization, punctuation or changed spelling mainly when necessary for clarification of a sentence or flow of a letter. I also have chosen not to write "sic" after every misspelled word or grammatical error. Since Julia and William, like many of the people in the North, had the advantage of at least six to eight years of education, major spelling or grammar errors are few. If a letter or word seemed to have been omitted, I placed the omission within brackets (including words written using shorthand) but I did not omit a letter in any of the letters' misspelled words. When William's writing often made "corps" look like "corpse," I chose to give William the benefit of the doubt and assume it was a flourish in his handwriting. Where a page was torn or a word smeared or otherwise illegible, I have placed an ellipsis. If a word was indecipherable due to handwriting or when the initial letter was clear but the rest of the word was not, I have placed a line (_____).

Expecting mostly love letters in this large collection, I found instead that Julia's letters are filled with news of not only her health and the children's but also of the state of their land, their animals and other family members and friends. One of her letters included the names of as many as thirty people! In most of her letters, she mentions the hired help as well as several neighbors in their small township. Like other wives left alone in both sides of the conflict, she seemed to be handling the role of primary caretaker of their home as well as could be expected and most of the time, was fortunate enough to have had another female living with her to help with cooking, cleaning, sewing, and the children. Julia also wrote of males who helped with the farm chores traditionally done by men. One of these men is a Negro nicknamed "Ben." First mentioned in William's letter of February 9, 1863, he is sent to Ohio apparently to help at the Jackson's farm. Julia writes kindly of him at first, but later is clearly upset with Ben and even writes in one of her letters, "I wish he was dead." As hard as it is to read Julia's angry and derogatory language, I have chosen to maintain authenticity and have not altered the original content of any of the letters.

Julia's letters of 1862 are filled with pleas to William to come home, and "not to go any further south" for she fears he will be "consigned to some Southern fever." Her fears, of course, were not unfounded; as mentioned above, William did become ill and even in the early part of the war more men were dying from disease than from battle or wounds incurred in battle. In the Third O.V.C. alone, a total of 59 men were killed or mortally wounded and 235 died from disease, during their term of service. In the Seventh O.V.C., the second regiment William joined, there were a total of 28 killed or mortally wounded and 201 who died from disease.[8] Besides the unsanitary living conditions, there were other reasons for such large numbers of soldiers succumbing to and dying from disease. Germ theory, sterilization of surgical equipment, and treatments, such as antibiotics, were not as well-known at the time. The physical exam for entering recruits was often so haphazard as to allow men to enlist who were already infirm or ill. In fact, some accounts report these examinations so lax that it is estimated that as many as 400 women, dressed up as men, were able to fool the examining doctors and thus signed up as soldiers on one side or the other![9]

In her letters from the last two years of the war, Julia's tone seems to change to one of pride and compassion for William as he continues with what he feels is his duty. Although she continually presses William as to when he will come home to visit or when she and at least a few of the children can come to him, she also praises him for his perseverance and work with the Seventh O.V.C. Since officers were allowed to go home or to have their families come and stay with them for extended periods of time, long breaks in the letters are assumed to be times when they were together at home in Ohio or with William in his "camp." As evidenced by some of the letters, the twins who were the oldest, and sometimes all three of the oldest girls, would stay with another family member or friends for long periods of time; at those times, Julia often went to visit William with the younger children and sometimes by herself, leaving the children with hired help or other relatives.

Julia almost always started her letters "Dear William" but varied the closings in her letters, using 'affectionately' or 'affection' in over half of them. None of her letters included full dates; rather they were as vague as 'Thurs. morn' or 'Sunday Eve.' When her letter included the day and the date, such as 'Sunday 18,' or 'July Thursday 14' my task in placing the letters in chronologic order was made easier, especially with the help of two websites.[10] Context clues were helpful in letters where Julia wrote of a recent battle or details about the weather, such as snow or extreme heat.

William's letters, like Julia's, are mostly written in ink, but some are in pencil and often smeared. His almost always had the month, day, and year at the top of the letter. He usually wrote in paragraphs, unlike Julia whose letters were often one long paragraph, no matter the length of the letter! As a quartermaster, he was often far from the fighting so was usually safer than many of the other officers and soldiers, but his life was certainly not without danger or concerns. Most of his letters, however, seem to avoid those details that might add to Julia's anxiety. He often describes his camp or, when in a hotel or house, his more comfortable accommodations. He writes Julia about his responsibilities or duties and almost always inquires about the children or bids Julia to give them his love and kisses. He often mentions their pet cat and horses and even closes with terms of endearment for them, as in his letter of August 15, 1862, "kiss Pussy real hard for me." His letters almost always end with "Your affectionate husband, Wm" (with 'affectionate' and 'husband,' being written partially with shorthand symbols). Although William also came from a large family, he doesn't mention them as much as Julia mentions either of their families.

In general, these letters of William and Julia Jackson not only reveal details about the life of a Union Quartermaster in two different Cavalry units but also that of those left at home, doing the best they could as they waited and prayed for the safe return of their loved ones.

Introduction Notes

1. Cavalry regiments - from Reid, Whitelaw, *Ohio in the War Her Statesmen, Generals, and Soldiers, Vol. 2*; Cincinnati: Moore, Wilstach & Baldwin; 1868, pp. 5-6: "In the course of the war Ohio furnished two hundred and thirty regiments: besides twenty-six independent batteries of artillery, five independent companies of cavalry, several companies of sharp-shooters, large parts of five regiments credited to the West Virginia contingent, two credited to the Kentucky contingent, two transferred to 'United States Colored Troops,' and a large proportion of the rank and file for the Fifty-Fourth and Fifty-Fifth Massachusetts. Thirteen were cavalry."

2. *Norwalk Experiment* ads recruiting for the Third O.V.C. were printed weekly from August through December 23, 1861, with the last listing the staff and officers of the Third O.V.C. William was listed as Battalion Quartermaster in the Second Battalion.

3. After having heard the story of "the child" of William and Julia's drowning in the creek from both my father and Ray Heck, I was able to find an article from *The Sandusky Register* with the help of volunteers at www.familysearch.org. See 'Charly' in the Persons of Interest appendix.

4. Information about Bellville's history is mainly from Thomas Hauck's *Bellville Defining An Architectural Identity in Ohio*; The Ohio State University Department of Architecture, Columbus, Ohio: The Ohio State University Press, 1975.

5. Specific information on Benjamin Jr. came from several sources at the Ohio Genealogical Society in Bellville but mainly from Richland County, Ohio abstracts, Common Pleas Court (May 1829-1831).

6. Information about Huron County and the Firelands came from the Firelands Historical Library and Museum which has copies of original newspapers, and W.W. Williams' books, *The History of the Fire-Lands Comprising Huron and Erie Counties Ohio*, 1879, and *The Firelands Pioneer*; Norwalk, Ohio: Firelands Historical Society, 1900, as well as many other books about Ohio in the War.

7. Baughman, A. J. *History of Huron County, Its Progress and Development*, Vol. 1, p. 53; Chicago: The S.J. Clarke Publishing Company, 1909.

8. Dyers, Frederick H. *A Compendium of The War of the Rebellion;* Des Moines, Iowa: Dyers Publishing Company, 1908.

9. Though the number of women who actually dressed and fought as soldiers has been debated through the decades, the most frequently quoted estimate is 400. For more on this topic, see Elizabeth Leonard's book, *All the Daring of the Soldier: Women of the Civil War Armies*; New York: W.W. Norton & Company, Inc., 1999, pp. 310-11.

10. Online sites with calendars back to the Civil War period and earlier include the following: www.copleys.com/calendar and www.timeanddate.com/calendar (accessed November 2014).

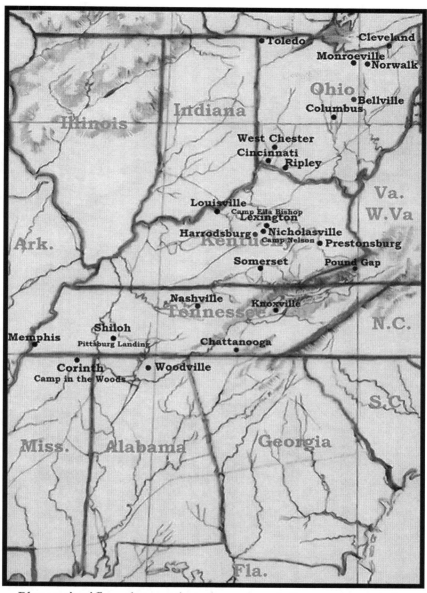

Places significantly mentioned or where letters were posted.
(Created by C. Stephen Badgley, BPC)

Chapter One

From Monroeville, Ohio to Kentucky, Tennessee, and Alabama
March-September, 1862

Special Orders No. 1
Headquarters District of the Ohio Nashville, Tenn., March 28, 1862.
II. The Sixth Division, Brigadier-General Wood commanding, will put itself en route on the Columbia turnpike to-morrow, the 29th instant. Colonel Barnett, with the reserve artillery, will report at once to Brigadier-General Wood, and will accompany the Sixth Division...
By command of Brigadier-General Buell.

Oliver D. Greene, Assistant Adjutant-General[1]

The Confederates' surrender at Forts Henry and Donelson, which earned U.S. Grant the moniker, "Unconditional Surrender" Grant, [2] was very recent news when Julia wrote her letter dated "Thurs. morn." The Third Ohio Volunteer Cavalry and others in the Union ranks, as well as civilians all over the North, were reveling in this victory in Tennessee.

The peace at Shiloh Church in southwest Tennessee had yet to be shattered. William's regiment was moving west and south from Nashville to what would become known as the first major battle of the war with total casualties from men killed, wounded, or missing estimated to be nearly 23,750, about 2000 of them Buell's. General Thomas Wood, discussed at length in William's letter of April 28, was with his Sixth Division when he came upon the Third O.V.C. which "took the advance of Gen. Wood's division," marching toward Camp Shiloh.[3]

In March, 1862, when this first section of letters begins, William had been away from Camp Monroeville for only a few months. Perhaps in the early days of his absence, neither William nor Julia wrote to each other regularly. Or perhaps they had not yet begun saving their letters. William, being an officer, had already made at least one visit home and Julia makes reference to this in one of her ten letters in this section, "It is six weeks tomorrow since you left and long, long weeks they have been." Like so many people in both the North and the South, the Jacksons may have thought the war would be over in a matter of weeks, then months, and were just beginning to realize the extent of this conflict and the importance of saving their letters. Handwritten letters were one of the few forms of contact with their loved ones from whom they were separated. Besides sending these letters by "the cars" (train), neighbors or friends would sometimes deliver some of the letters in person. There was also communication via telegrams sent by the now extinct electric telegraph system; however, due to costs, the latter was used infrequently by William and Julia and most likely used only for emergencies or especially good news.

The Sandusky Register and Norwalk Experiment were two of the papers Julia and her friends and family might have read in order to stay informed of war news. Norwalk also had The Reflector. Monroeville had The Spectator in their small village of almost 1300[4] and sometimes Julia sent William articles from these papers so that he could read news of their friends or family in other regiments. William and other officers or soldiers wrote letters to the various newspapers in their hometowns and these were almost always published.[5]

Julia's letters in this chapter are mainly filled with news about their children as well as their extended families and neighbors. She tells William who she's paid money to for which debts, how she is dealing with his absence and extra work at their home, and how all the family miss him so! Her second letter (March 7), like many of the letters, is written on both sides of a sheet of paper roughly 8x10 inches and folded in half. She seems to not even have room for her usual closing as she squeezes in last minute thoughts sideways and upside down on the first page. As with so many commodities during this war, paper was in short supply and what was available could be costly. In her letter of April 17, Julia begins by letting William know she is glad to have received his "long looked for letter" but complains creatively about not receiving letters from him often enough.

There are only seven letters from William in this first section and two are apparently drafts or letters he thought best not to send! One, written April 26 to his father-in-law, has many words and whole sentences crossed out as he is clearly angry over Julia's April 1 letter about an upsetting visit to her parents' home in Norwalk. This particular letter from Julia is not only her longest letter but also the longest in the entire collection. Another unsent missive of William's, written April 28 to "Friend John," seems to be in defense of the actions of certain regiments that participated in the Battle of Shiloh.

Also on April 28, Major General Halleck writes to his assistant-adjutant general as part of a Special Field Order: "The commanding general is satisfied, from his own observation and from reports of others, that the sick list is greatly increased by the defective cooking of soldiers' food. A company officer will be detailed to inspect the food at each meal and to see that it is properly cooked, and field and general officers will give this their particular attention."[6]

Shortly after this edict was issued, Julia's fear - that William might become ill - is realized. Due to William's illness, Julia goes south to help nurse him back to health. While in Tennessee, Julia receives a letter from her brother, Theodore. In this letter, one of two in Chapter One authored by someone other than Julia or William, Theodore writes about news at home and strongly encourages Julia to have "Will" come home with her as he says "he will of course be unfit for duty and would recuperate much sooner at home than there."

Whether or not William went home is unknown, but he did recover and in August, his battalion, along with the third battalion of his regiment, was sent into Alabama to guard a part of the Memphis and Charleston Railroad. In his two letters from there, William describes the countryside and tells colorful stories of the people native to the area. He warns Julia to "be somewhat guarded in your praise..." of a particular officer (August 15, 1862); Bruce Catton also wrote of this particular incident, a "problem in discipline," in one of his books.[7] In May, Major Paramore, one of the leaders of William's regiment, was facing a court martial, in fact, over an incident at Corinth (Mississippi). William's discharge from the Third O.V.C. in September, 1862, was not, however, due to a problem of discipline; rather he was listed as "supernumerary." No longer needed by the Third, he resigned and made a brief visit home.[8]

The Third O.V.C. went on to fight at several major battles, including Perryville, Stones River, and Chickamauga. This unit of Cavalry from the Buckeye state did go "further south," in fact; they were in Macon, Georgia at the war's official end. Those fortunate enough to have survived turned over arms and horses under orders from General George Henry Thomas and then reported to Nashville for "muster out." A short time later, closer to home for most of the soldiers, in Camp Chase, Ohio, "the regiment was paid off and discharged on the 14th of August, 1865, having served four years, lacking twenty days."[9]

Monroeville Thursday Morn {1862}

Dear William,

I went to the depot last evening through the worst storm we have had this winter thinking to see Hellen, as she had written to her Father that she would be on the cars, but we were all disappointed, the old gentleman felt it, I think they do not like it her staying so long. I saw Mr. Probert who had just come through so my stormy trip was not all for nothing, the snow had drifted all afternoon. they said there had never been such a day known in Sandusky. The storm was from the north east but not very cold but the "wind blew as t'would blown its last" you could not see three rods. I told Calligan there was only one man in this world that I would have taken such a walk to have heard from. Mr. Carbine took it upon himself to send in a bill of $9.55 to me by a boy requesting me to send the money by him. I sent word back that if you owed him anything you would pay it when you come home. I will send you the bill that you may see the style of it. there are no articles specified & I am sure I have not got anything since a year ago last summer. don't you think I ought to have sent it {inserted above the line "the money"} back by the boy. I concluded Bond or Ed Fish had been giving advice again. I hope I shall have no trouble with wood. the man told Johnny he didn't think he should bring any more than the one load. I went to see John Hill to have him bring several loads before the roads broke up. M_____ said he would tell him. I wrote a long letter Sunday but feel as if it was very doubtful about your getting it as all that I have got from you have been so long in coming. the one you wrote with a pencil and did not finish or direct which was dated 15th came Tuesday & the one dated 14th came Wednesday. the contents were much the same. Dora looks puny the others are well & expecting some present by Hellen. I am not very well myself. My head troubles me & am very nervous, my hands tremble so I can hardly sew. I shall take this letter to Norwalk as Mr. Probert called before I had written it. I supposed that he would take the cars here but he takes them at Norwalk. I did not wish to detain him. I send you the Register to show you how the capture of Donelson was received & the Experiment to show you the dab at your horses. I hope from all the victories there you may not have to go into action or be detained long from home.

Ever Sincerely Yours, Julia J.

~ 5 ~

National Hotel Louisville Mar 2 {1862}
Sunday Eve

Dear Julia,

I sent you a lot of things and a pkg of money by John Bennet who left here Saturday noon by boat - The last end of the letter was moved up in very great haste by me as I was very much engaged in fitting out the Regiment for a march to Bowlingreen. We received orders to leave Sunday. On Saturday it snowed and stormed all day & all knight and we had a goodeal of thunder during the night and has rained incessantly all day to day. The Regiment moved five miles out of Louisville, there is some of them camped in Tents, some in barns and a good many in a long roap walk* and the officers in farm houses and some in a school house. You can not imagine a worse day than it has been. I found that we would be short of forage and started after dark and am now at the National hotel where I shall leave early in the morning-I omitted to say in my last that Will was doing very well-

Oh! the confusion in getting the Regiment and 40 teams across the ferry today and the hollowing whipping and swearing at mules.

Co. L Capt. Flannagan started with three teams & before getting on the ferry one mule kicked entirely clear from the wagon and got away from them and they had not succeeded in getting it at dark. Another team broke the wagon tongue. Another is stalled on the levy on this side and some six or eight are stalled in or near the camp and so it has been all day.

I got my supper at one of <u>Darwins</u> kind of KY farms. It is a beautiful country where we are now and we have most of the way to Bowlingreen a good stone road.

I will write you from every point I can and that will be often because we are near the Louisville & Nashville RR most of the time.

I hope the children will feel satisfied with their presents. I had to do every thing in a hurry & how do you like your dress.

If Hamilton should make a call for it pay him $75--Kiss all of the children.

Your affect{ionate} Husb{and}
Wm R. Jackson

*Roap Walk (rope walk) - A long, low, narrow building, shed, etc. in which ropes are made. This building along with other large buildings and even private homes were often used to house officers.

Monroeville March 7{1862}

Dear William,

I received the box of presents & money by John Bennet. We were all very much pleased at being so <u>bountifully</u> remembered. I went to the Bank the next morning & got some of the bills changed for smaller ones, out of which I paid the two Martains, Murphy, & Pickard & Carbine & Simmons which took just forty dollars. I did not know hardly what to do about paying Hamilton as you did not say anything about him with the rest, but had spoken of it before, so as you told me to use my judgement, & I had told him that I would pay him some I went to his office & handed him $50 & saw him credit on the lease. There is $80 & 8¢ more he's due including the interest. I told him I would pay him more when you got the rest of your pay. I went over yesterday & gave mother ten & Theodore ten, which leaves me just $100. Bill Prentice asked me if he was to look to me for what we owed him. He said it was a little over $12. I asked him if he had given us credit for pasture. He said no. He would like to apply that on a note he held against you, of his & Stebbin. I told him I knew nothing about it, and would do nothing till I heard from you. I wish you would tell me what to do. There is ways enough for my money to go. John Slinker is hauling me six cord of hickory wood which I shall have to pay $2.00 a cord. I have been out to day to find hay or straw for the horses. Oat straw is three dollars a <u>load</u> & hay 9 dollars a <u>ton</u>. John Hamilton said he would bring me straw Monday for that price. If you can advise me in your next letter what to do about such things I wish you would. The sow that had the first pigs died last week. We are feeding the pigs in thin mush. Turner did not take any. Johnny took the other in that pen. I think the one in the lower pen would have died but I had him let them all out & feed them more. Your Father, Caroline & Walter came up last week & staid all night with me. They brought Aunt Mira's remains up to New Haven & found the services were to be the next day. So they came here & left in the early train. They all had been very anxious to hear from you, especially your Mother. Your Father came up to Shelby when the Regiment passed through there, to see you & would have come up here but they told him you was in Washington. I told him every thing you had done, how much you had made, & every thing I could think of & he was much pleased. The Dr & Elizabeth could not leave home on account of Libby. They are looking for trouble there. Will has got a nice boy. Tell him he is an <u>improvement</u> on his Father. Eliza is very smart. Old Terry beset Father in at Bennets about you he said every thing he could think of. He would like to know where you put that twenty five hundred dollars. Father said he guessed there was no such amount he knew there was & it was not in the Bank so his wife must have it, & she advised him not pay ~~what~~ his debts. Father told him he had never enquired any thing about it but he was sure I had not got it. I think Henry ought to <u>know</u> how he is talking & if he has the right feeling he will stop the <u>old fool</u>. I see his regiment is in Bowling Green. I went to see Theodore about what had better be done with it. He said he had just loaned

$25.00 for ten percent. I told him I wanted it to bring as much as we were paying him & then it would help to liquidate that. He said he would look around & tell me & I could write to you & see if you approved of whatever it should be. I was sleeping the other night & thought I heard you call me & raised up in bed & answered you so loud that it waked me. Your attitude & dress & voice were so perfect that it seemed all day as if it had been really so I thought you came to the bed room door as you used to in the morning to waken me & I said what. Yes. It troubled me for fear that something had happened to you or you were sick. Your letter from the hotel I got Wednesday night after you wrote it. You must be at your journeys end by this time. The children wonder you don't say anything about coming home. Fannie cried very hard thinking about it & Jule says what's the use it won't bring him a bit sooner. They were all delighted with their presents & Old Johnny gots out of bed to bring it up so I gave him the gloves. Perhaps you will blame me but it was a bad night. My dress could not have suited better & I think you bought it very low. I will send by F for trimming. The weather is cold & snow is on the ground. Tell me first how to direct my letters. I feel as if it would be a long time before you will get this. I hear John Brown is coming home soon. You seem to have the whole Regiment to see to. Where are the other QMs Mrs. Zahm is expecting him this next week so I hear. I have not seen her since the morning in Dennison did he pay her fare to you & how much is it if she should offer it to me This is full & consequently <u>I must stop</u>. Have you any idea when you will come on or <u>shall I meet you in Louisville</u>. Hellen thinks it would be nice I have paid Johnny $4.00 & he wants me to pay Father some rent for him I paid Lucy $5.00

A photocopy of the first page of this letter is shown as an example on the next page.

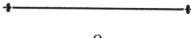

it & Julia say's whats the use it wont bring him back
sooner, they were all delighted with their prior cents
& old Johnny got out of bed to bring it up so I gave
him the g[il?]dols perhaps you will blame me but it was
a bad night, my dress could not have suited better
& I think you bought it very low, I will send by J
for trimming, the weather is cold & snow on the ground
Tell me just how to direct my letters I feel as
if it would be a long time before you will get this

Dear William _____ Monroe ville
this is full _____ March 7
hope you any idea when you will come _____
shall ____ would be nice ____ in Louisiana I Helen thinks is

received the boy of
presents & money by John Bennet
we were all very much pleased at
being so bountifully remembered
I went to the Bank the next
morning & got some of the bills
changed for smaller ones, out of which
I paid the two Martins, Murphy,
Pickard, & barber, & Simmons, which
took just forty dollars I did not know
hardly what to do about paying Hamilton
as you did not say any thing about him,
with the rest, but had spoken of it
before, or as you told me to use my
judgement, & I had told him that I
would pay him some, I went to his office &
handed him $50. & saw him credit on
the lease, there is $80 & 3 cents more

I hear John Brown is coming home soon, you seem to
love the whole Regiment to me to, where are they other D M's
three Johns is expecting him the next week so I hear I have not
seen her since the morning as I painted tea to pay for the gd
such that it if she thinks you it for me

Monroeville March 17 {1862}

Dear William,

The last letter I recd from you was mailed at Munfordville Sunday & I got {it} Thursday which was much sooner than the one you mailed from Bardstown. Mrs. Zahm's came Saturday night, Helen's Tuesday morning & mine Tuesday night all mailed the same time. Since I got your last I have felt very uneasy to hear how you got over the bridge & over the rest of the bad roads. There was a large masquerade party at the Hall last Friday eve & while there Zahms telegraph came. Josephine & I read it. She felt bad her mother was not there. I questioned a while in my own mind wether I should go home & cry all night or respect your feelings & stay & dance after the masquerade closed & I concluded "discretion was the better of valor" so I stayed till Calligan & wife came home & had a nice time. Perhaps you would like to know what my rig was. It was a scotch maid lassie short plaid dress, slippers, the strings crossing many times around my ankles & lying quite high, a turban made of my plaid scarf & three black plums, my long gay scarf pind on the shoulder, & tied under the other arm. Helen said it was the handsomest & most becoming dress in the room. They all said how young I looked & Miss Ward said I did not look more than fourteen & I must write to you that she said so. How I wished you was here. They took in $34 which goes to the Soldiers Aid Society. The children are very impatient for you to come. Can't you give some encouragement. Dora said last night "Mother every night when I say my prayers, I say O Lord take care of my Father while he is gone". Judy is at home with earache. The rest are well. I wrote a long letter thinking you would get it at Bardstown & hope you did. The baby wrote one too. I hope you will get all my letters.

I went over & <u>settled</u> Josh Waily Friday. He told Johny to shut up the horses & calves that they could not run any longer. I told him I had a deed to enough land here to pasture all my stock & Father reserved pasture for my cows. You ought to have seen him back down. Maybe they will <u>all</u> find out I can figure for myself. Mr. Marks wished me in particular to remember him to you. I presume when you get in Nashville you can go to Church again. I see the Mayor seems favorable to our troops. <u>Don't</u> go any farther till you come home

Affect{ionately} Julia

Monroeville March 18 {1862}

Dear William,

I just received your letter written one mile below Mumfordsville and it has been eight days coming. The one that you wrote just before getting there was only three. It does not seem as if there ought to be so much difference. The <u>Lord</u> only knows when you get mine or if you get them at all. This you may rely on that I write one or twice a week. I mailed a letter yesterday to Nashville. I wrote another before that & sent it via Louisville, thinking they would send it on to Bowlingreen. I hope you got it for it was a long one. It does not seem right that I should have to live in such anxiety and it grows worse and worse every day. Mrs. Skinner goes to Nashville tomorrow and will take this, but wether she will find you there or not is uncertain. Zahm's dispatch say'd you were going to start for there last Saturday but if you don't get along any faster than you did in getting to Bowlingreen, you won't get there before next month sometime. You will then be on a direct line of rail road and can come home in a day or two & you told me over & <u>over again</u> that you would come. It is now going on <u>six</u> weeks & as the other

QMs have been home since you have I think that it is your turn next. The children think it is to bad. Betty wrote you a letter which I enclosed in one of mine & Judy has printed one to enclose in this. I will interpret it "Dear Father I want you to come home. I had a nice time Friday night. I had the ear ache while I was writing this letter. I didn't print it very good. We are going to have company to day." She is asleep & I cannot read the rest. She has been sick with her ear & face. Birdie & Fannie are also complaining. The baby has a bad cold & Lucy is sick to night with a heavy cold. Philip {and} Sims with their wives, Louise & Pheby were all here to supper & I had a nice one, a big turkey & chicken pie & we all wished you were here. Dora says "Mother, every night when I say my prayers, I say O Lord take care of my Father while he is gone" certainly He will not turn a deaf ear to such prayers. If I was sure Mrs. S. would find you in Nashville I would fix up a box of nice things but it is so doubtful I don't think it best. Eliza is smart & the baby is a nice one. Tell Will it caused quite a sensation. Every body went to see it. Eliza was sick but a few hours. I have had a bad muddy walk to get your letter & go down every night & send every morning, but am very often disappointed. I do not think but what you write often. I know you do, but there is so much delay in their getting through. It is nearly midnight and I must close.

With much love, Julia

Monroeville March 23 {1862}

Dear William,

It is Sunday and one of the most doleful days I ever lived through. It has snowed for two days incessantly, and the roads are worse than you ever knew them to be in this State. (I will say nothing of Kentucky.) It has snowed one half the time this month and rained the other, and thawed and froze all the time, which is all calculated to make good roads and pleasant weather and happy and contented women {double underlined "women"} and children. Dora said yesterday he should forget he had a Father if you didn't come home pretty soon and all I can say for a few days will not pacify them at all. Perhaps it is not said with as good grace as it was a few weeks ago, for I have reason to feel that it has been a long time since you left home and yet you don't even refer to any time when you might possibly come. You know the object of your taking the situation was that there were three others and it would give you a chance of leaving when the other officers could not. It is six weeks tomorrow since you left and long long weeks they have been. People wonder at my being so cheerful, but my pride and determination have covered up a sad heart many a time. I don't go to church and cry as I have heard of Zahm's wife doing. I am sorry for her but she might better stay at home. I know you have much, very much to contend with but you are constantly moving, changing scenery, and meeting old friends, and are under much excitement so that you could not feel the longings that I do. I hope that you get all my letters. You should have got one directed via Louisville and one to Nashville beside the one I wrote by Mrs. Skinner. One of the many letters you wrote at Bowling Green came through in four days and the other in eight days. There does not seem to be any excuse for it. I wrote you in my last that Lucy had a bad cold. She has been most sick all the week. Yesterday she was taken suddenly spitting blood, which continued part of the day & to day her folks came after her and she has gone home. I think it is uncertain when she comes back or if she does at all, to combine fear with all the other uncomfortable feelings I have. I think I shall not get much rest day or night. I hardly ever go to bed 'till midnight, so that then I shall have to go to sleep. Jo Stearns is in some regiment in Nashville, the one that was in Patrick's store, so Theodore says. I have made an application through Father to

Worcester for an office for you, and God grant you may get it and come home. It seems there are men to be appointed to collect or receive moneys. I think it is this new tax levied. I meant to have saved the papers and sent you the notice, but it got destroyed. At any rate it is worth trying for, for Dewey & Rose of Norwalk were both circulating petitions to get it, but Father wrote directly to Worcester and I am in hopes we may succeed. It is probable the men who ever they are will not take this position before June so Father says. What ever we hear from Mr. W. I will write to you he sent me three papers of flower seeds from the Pattent office this week. The children are well with the exceptions of colds. Judy's ear troubled a long time. I was afraid of a gathering in her head. They have not been to school for a week on account of the walking. I talk to the baby about you a great many times a day but she dont speak of you unless I do, any more as she used to. It is not to be wondered at that she should begin to forget you. I must close & get supper. I wish you were here to eat it with us but there is six hundred miles between us. Birdie just came to me to have me ask you "if Father won't please to write to us when he will come home & say we all want to see him pretty bad." Dora says "tell him it I am a pretty good boy & we all want to see him real bad & we have got a whole pan full of eggs and Major goes off so I don't know what to do with him." Jule says tell him to come home, "Fannie says tell him I want him to come home so bad I most wish I was sick so he would have to". Betty says "tell popy I lady & don't gets any more diury—its all dwide up"

With love, Julia

Monroeville Friday 28 {March 1862}

Dear William,

I am writing in great haste for I have just heard that Mr. Clary was going to Nashville or to follow up the regiment. I suppose it is very doubtful when he will find you. I feel very anxious to know your destination & now William there is one thing you must <u>do</u>. Unless the regiment is disbanded by the first or middle of May you must <u>resign</u> or you will be <u>consigned</u> to your grave with some southern fever. I take <u>this</u> opportunity to say it for I feel more sure of your getting a letter sent in this way. I will try and get a long for a few weeks more, but if you can't get home before that time I want you to come <u>then expecting to stay</u>. You know I said before you left that I would get along just as long and as well as I could but when I said I wanted & needed you at home, then you must resign if you could not get away without. I am constantly anxious & feel that it is wearing on my health & nerves. Josh Waily keeps me as uncomfortable as possible & I am still with out a girl. Lucy left a week ago. I don't know wether she will return or not. She was sick. I wrote two weeks ago by Mrs. Skinner & one before. Matild was here to day. They have not heard from Will since he left Bowlingreen. Does he get their letters? Eliza and baby are well. She is going up to Matilds to stay two weeks in a few days. They are going to have <u>William Theodore's</u> likeness taken as soon as he can sit up & I will send it to Will. I got your letter from Camp Jackson & am expecting another to night. Send some little things to the children for I can hardly hold them any more. They are so impatient to see you. If they can take some things I will send them. Much haste, Julia

Tom Cone has come after this.

Dear William,

This first day of April has been a day of tears to me. I went to Norwalk to see if I could get any satisfaction that would make me feel any better, but was sadly disappointed. I have once or twice at home <u>here</u> heard hard words but never any thing like I had said to me to day by a man I call my Father. I felt very teary and bad when I left here and when I got in Norwalk the people were attending the funerals of the Soldiers, one was Rust in Frank Sawyer's regiment. He was shot through the neck at the Battle of Winchester, and fell dead across his brother's feet. The other was Rogers who put up the stairs for Theodore. He met with a very narrow escape at Donelson, and was soon after taken sick and was in the Hospital at Mound City where his wife found him when he was almost dead. When she went in they told her he died some days before & been sent to Cinnati. She told them she wanted to look through the hospital before she left, and in the fourth story she found her husband. Poor fellow he had just strength enough to throw up both hands when he saw her. She brought home his remains. The places of business were all closed and they were buried with Masonic & Military honors. I stopped in at the store till the procession passed. I told Theodore some of my troubles. You will remember before you went away Father said tow or three times that he had reserved off us all the land that we wanted. Since you left he told me he had let it all to Waily. I asked Waily if he did not reserve me land. He said that he spoke to him about it. I told them both that you wanted just what you had last year. Waily said he wanted me to take what laid next to the bars. I told him it was not good land. He said he knew it. The next thing was that I was to shut the horses up & pay for the calves pasturing so then I told him how much land I had a deed for. He said he knew nothing about it. Father had told him, but he said if that was the case I owned the best of the pasture. I told him his stock could run upon it but I wanted the same privilege. He said he would see Father. After he had seen him Father came up & tried to talk me down. I told him if he had only contracted Sarah McWilliam's land away I had not interfered with it. I was only claiming what I had a deed for. Then the next thing was the hogs. I must fence my land or shut up the pigs or Waily would break the contract. I told him I would see some of them as quick as I had a chance, & would shut the rest up as quick as they would do any harm but Waily wants them shut up now. Then Waily rents Dewitt's part of the house on the hill and puts in old <u>Dave Pooly</u>. Then Waily tells him to put his pig pen right opposite in the front corner of the fence. I saw him making it and went over and told him that when we fenced in that lot that we were to control it & I did not want it there but he could put it where Dewitt's was & it would be just as handy. He said he did not want to harm any body & he would not do any more about it, but this morning while I was down town Waily went & helped him finish it. When I came up it made me about as much as I could stand so I went over (& as I told you) told Theodore my fix. He wanted to know what he could do if he came over. I told him I did not know and <u>I had to give way to my feelings</u>. I dried up my tears & went down. I saw right away Father did not like my coming. He had been over all the day before but did not come near me. I could not keep the tears from my eyes & they all noticed it (I had told many at the stores after he went out from supper (I had to leave the table for my tears). Then I told Mother how I was situated, without any girl, staying alone nights & nobody for neighbors but those miserable drunken wretches that I was trying & had been, to do just the best I could & it certainly was all that I could be expected to do without being harassed to death in every other way. She went out & spoke to Father & he came in & I never heard as <u>cruel</u> talk in the world. He said he did not want me to come there any more & I never came but to make trouble & that you & I had always made him trouble ever since we lived here. He told me I laid him in a lie & done it three or four times before. I told him I had to come for he did not come near me. He said he did not want to come near me for he knew I wanted to make trouble. He said they had got nothing for the land since we had it or only some little things. I told him I did not want that thrown up to me for I would call Mother to witness she had had money. (She said yes.) & it was a poor time to grumble when you was off risking your life to get the means to pay it with & then I got up to go. He then asked me what I wanted him to do. I straightened myself up & told him I did not want him to do anything. After he had talked to me as he had to night & shut the door & come off & <u>he is welcome to all the sleep he gets to night</u>. As for myself I have had to take something for the last ten nights & to night. I feel sick all over. Theodore road up to Matilda's with me. He felt bad to see me feel as I did & that I had the reasons for it. He said he would not care for what he said. I told him if he stood where did he could not help it that I felt under no obligations to Father. I had paid them all off by the hardest. He said he would try & get me the land I wanted & I told him I <u>did not</u> want any now that I would try & get along some way but would not be under any obligations to Father. he said he would come over if he could tomorrow. Hamilton went to him & required all the money that he told me he you owed him then I told T. what you wrote to me. He asked where your books {were}. I told him I thought Benett had them. After I came home to night I went to see him (Benet) he said he would go to A_____ in the morning & look at his store bill & if he had paid any rent that it would be credited & I should tell T. to come to him. Theodore gave Hamilton a round & told him he was no gentleman or he would not take advantage of your being gone for he did not {know} about your business with him. This has been one of the saddest days of my life. I felt William as if you must

<u>come home</u> & now I say so dont put me off any longer than you possibly can.

I got a Thursday paper to night from you & your things from J. Brown. His lungs are in a very bad condition. They say here that he is drawing no pay for he has never been mustered in.

Wednesday morning. I wrote last night 'till I got so sick I could not make another mark. Went to bed got one short nap & was as wild as a crazy person & when it came up before me how far we were apart & that you have never given any encouragement about coming home it made me wild. I feel more & more anxious every day for as the weather grows warmer you are going further south, and it is not your duty to yourself or family to stay longer than you can make arrangements to get away. You ar{e} sworn to me before you are to your country. I am afraid bowel complaint will rage in the regiment. The Surgeon told J. Brown the morning he came away there were four hundred sick with it. I wrote & sent you four shirts & five towels by Clary & Martain & wish I had have known you wanted tea. I had but very few moments to do anything. Eliza got a long letter from Will. She & baby are at Matild's doing well. Mary takes her riding every day. B_____ came & took one wheel off of the big wagon & said Slinker got it of him. The end of the tongue broke off one day while the horses stood hitched. So I am tied hand & foot & I presume if I should try to moove the manure I should get in an awful mess & I dont know what to do. I have just fifty dollars left. I got $3-1/2 worth of oat straw of John Hamilton while the roads were so bad. Theodore says he will let me have some hay. The men came & began the shed, a Mr. Smith & son. I shall have to pay them some. He says he knows you. He wears glasses & seems to be a good man. There is a good deal to be seen to that I am not competent to do. If you were here you could find some sale for the hogs which I dont know any thing about. Foster wrote home he thought the regiment would soon be called into a large battle & every body are anxiously looking forward {to} the result. We had a terrible thunder storm Saturday night. The telegraph office took fire burned the curtains & tore up the ground wires & did much damage along the line. Betty's eyes sparkled when she got your letter. She went straight & put it in her _____{trunk?}. The children are pleased with their candies & gilt kisses. They spend most of their evenings in printing "Father come home" but generally make some mistake so they conclude not to send it. The dime circles are well attended. It is the only place the young folks meet and they really have a good deal of fun. I have been to all of them as a matter of duty & to drowned my loneliness. We must have taken in forty dollars. John Sargent cannot find the last annual report of the schools. He looked through the trunk but did not find it & I looked through all your pockets. Johnny has been very drunk four times, was last Sunday, but generally does very well. I have to pay him about two or three dollars every week. When do you think your next pay will come. Had I better pay Father for the cow? I don't feel as if I wanted to owe him any thing. I have enough wood & oil to last some time. A half barrel of flower & half bag of buckwheat, & some butter. Louisa Bronson has had to moove. If they could not have got a house, Ann would have come to live with me. Betty is real quick. You cant get ahead of her a bit. She always has some plausible excuse for every thing. It is vacation two weeks. Gowdy's sister wants them to go to her. She is going to take a select school. I told her I would write to you about it. They like their teacher & dont wish to change. It is eight weeks next Monday since you left-a long long time. With much love Julia

Libby Beach has a daughter Mr. Slinker wants a settlement with Cos. & his pay. She wishes you to speak to him about it.

Monroeville Thursday 17 {April 1862}

Dear William,

I have just received your long looked for letter* and I tell you I thought if things have got to such a pass, that we could not get a letter, or telegraph, from any of you, you have all better disband or desert, or else the Government had better go to putting up Lunatic Asylums to accommodate those who had been left at home. I believe I took the matter as cool as any one, and looked at it as reasonably, but I did not lie down at night feeling very easy, or comfortable. In the first papers after the battle, the papers mentioned Wood's Division as having got on just as the battle closed, and the Cavalry were pursuing them & then they were not mentioned till last Monday night in the Cincinnati Gazette. I should like to know what your views are by this time about coming home, as you gave me no satisfaction in answer to the letter I wrote you by Clary and I certainly did expect you would say something concerning it at any rate, what you thought you could do. I suppose Sowers will make it convenient to do all the business while he is here and I guess poor Fannie will have to finally telegraph that she is sick. She has threatened to. I wrote you a long letter two weeks ago to day. I hope you have got it, as I do not wish any body else to know the contents. I have not been well since, the affair made me sick. I wish you would let me know if you got it. It was directed to Nashville. To day I have sold six hogs for $2.30 hundred. They come to $18.50. I paid Smith the man who has put up the shed $5.00 he asked for ten but I did not think best to let so much go for the present. I have not got the school money yet. John Sargent asked me to day if you had said any thing about paying Mr. Marks. I told him no. He said you told him to pay McDonald for some oats out of the school money and he did not think Smith would allow so much. I asked him if there was not a balance due you on that wheat. He said he didn't know but there was but he thought you owed him

~ 22 ~

on an old grain account which had run 5 or 6 years. I told him to pay the school money to me and I would pay McD. As for the other I know nothing about it. Darwin, Sarah and the children were down week before last made a short visit. They were here while Darwin went to Sandusky. My sister Louisa has not been near me since you left. She has been through three times. Mr. Bronson left a week ago to go to Pittsburgh Landing with a committee of two others to see to the dead & wounded of Erie County, but I understand when he got to Cincinnati a Mr. Fernal of Sandusky who had a son, Captain in the 72, wished to go so much on his account that Mr. B. let him have the chance and stayd in Cincinnati to look after those who should be brought up there. I sent some tea and handkerchiefs by him. I don't know wether he gave them to Mr. F. or not I hope you will get them some how. I send you two new wrappers without sleeves. Perhaps you will be glad of them. The shirts do not look very nice Lucy did them up she came back after being gone two weeks. Theodore went last week to NY. I don't know how the folks are in Norwalk. I have made the last visit at home for one while. I must close in haste the children are well & send much love Julia

* Since the last letter from William found for inclusion in this section of letters was March 2, the "long looked for letter" Julia speaks of is assumed missing from this collection.

Camp Shiloah Tenn April 26th1862

James Williams Esq
Dear Sir,

With all due respect to you ~~I wish~~ permit me to say. We pass over the bodies of men in this camp many of whom are only half interred that were gentlemen compared to Josh Whaley. and we do not scruple to deal full charges of powder and lead to others like them who are in rebellion against the Government. My motto is: My family. My dear little family first, and my country next. Now <u>so sure as I live</u> and have to travel from here to Monroeville to do it <u>I</u> <u>will</u> <u>put</u> a <u>button</u> <u>hole</u> <u>through</u> <u>his</u> <u>shirt</u> and <u>burn</u> <u>the</u> <u>nests</u> <u>of</u> <u>the</u> <u>drunken</u> <u>rabble</u> that is quartered around them if they continue their petty annoyances with my defenceless family any longer ~~and when I return Whaley will come upon our premises at his peril as well as any stock that may be wandering about my house to my annoyance until I have an opportunity to dispose of~~ & I intend <u>holding</u> <u>the</u> <u>pledge</u> <u>sacred</u> until I have an oportunity of removing them ~~beyond~~ from their now uncomfortable surroundings ~~&I~~ hope in your deal with all of them you will ~~act accordingly~~ be governed by ~~to~~ a timely caution.

You will also ablyg me by placing a statement of any indebtedness you may claim of me in Theodore's hand so I can get it when I return.

It is assumed that this letter, so angrily written by William to his father-in-law, was a draft and probably not sent…and that is why we have it.

Camp Shiloah near Pittsburg Landing Tenn
April 28th, 1862

Friend John
Dear Sir,

Presuming that your inconveniences for writing has prevented you from answering my last or that it might not have reached you I avail myself of another oportunity to draw you into a <u>pow-wow</u> and commence by apologising for the hasty manner I wrote to you from Nashville.

We remained at Nashville twelve days and received an order to March at 6 OC A.M. Mar. 29th Saturday-We were on time. With the prospect of a warm day and we took the advance of Gen. Wood's Division the ballance of which was close upon us. First day Mar. 29th Our Division got under way after the usual amount of confusion. Bear in mind we had always marched alone and had many things to learn particularly Gen Woods ideas of being prompt and expeditious in our movements. The Gen was necessarily engaged in awaiting the move of each Regiment & brigade of his entire command until the middle of the forenoon. Consequently we saw nor heard nothing of him ~~with~~ or his staff & body-guard until that time when many of the Regiment had the pleasure of his acquaintance.

His conversation as he passed from the rear to the front of our Reg. was <u>With mule drivers</u>. Stop pounding that mule or I'll get off and pound you. - See here mister I drive this team and I know my business -- <u>With a Guard of one of the teams</u>. Get out of my way! the guard failed to obey. D--d you get out of my way or I'll cut you down with my sabre. You draw your sabre on me and I'll shoot you. My place is here. I am guarding this team. With ambulance driver. What you doing back here <u>get up to the </u>Reg-- Gen drops in in front of his team and by quietly urging his team he crowds the Gen & some of his staff out of the road. <u>See here</u>

~ 25 ~

<u>mister</u> you had <u>better be careful</u> at first quite angry. but very soon turned around and said -- You done wright. <u>go ahead,</u> G--d it drive over anything that gets in your way until you overtake the Regiment - These with some other incidents occured during the first day and after that we were decidedly favored by him. Some times encamping with him which always tended to keep our men prompt to duty.

Sunday 30th Mar. Day very warm. Our revile sounded at 3 O.C. A.M. Marched 19 miles. More than half of the Infantry gave out and remained by the road side until night where the{y} worked along into camp -- We passed through a fine country.

Monday 31st Mar. Day warm. Revile sounded at 3 O.C. Marched 12 miles. and were compelled to counter march 1 1/2 miles for a camping ground having come upon Gen. Thomas' Division -- Clary & Martin come to camp in the evening -

Tuesday April 1st Day very warm. Marched as usual passing Thomas' Divis. and crossed Duck River on a temporary bridge. The Rail Road & Turnpike Bridge having been destroyed by some <u>famous</u> <u>Southern</u> <u>bridge</u> <u>burners</u> --- Marched 5 miles and encamped 2 1/2 miles south of Columbia. Clary & Martin with us at night --

Wednesday April 2 Day Warm. Marched 17 miles and nothing of particular interest.

Thursday April 3 Day pleasant. ~~Very fine country~~ Passed the residences of Gen Pillow & Capt A J Polk which are very fine plantations and a fine country generally around there ~~ Both places were visited in the evening by our men ~

Friday 4th April Rained hard in the morning. Eight Company men ordered to make a scout about Lawrenceburg under command of Col. Murray, commanded by Gen. Haskill and accompanied by a part of his Brigade - Our boys set about 60 <u>sesech</u> <u>Calvary</u> climbing at double quick out of that place, wounding a Lieutenant and capturing some horses & a quantity of Bacon and took some prisoners and the Lieut.'s sword.

SATURDAY 5 APRIL Day warm. Nothing of interest to day only we were kept back by McCook's Divis. ahead ~~

SUNDAY 6th APRIL Day warm. We passed through Wanesborough about 9 O.C a.m.- Oh <u>Mighty</u> What a county town I am unable to discribe it. I can only say I saw one Tan-Yard and some old houses- Pardon me they had a National Flag flying ~ We moved steadily along until about 10 O.C climbing hills *{inserted above line: "18m Savannah"}* when we began to hear very distant cannonading which within one hour was distinct and very fast and heavy. Moderation and submission was quite oppressive to most of the command but we moved on at our usual pace until about 2 O.C. when orders were received from Savannah for our Division to leave our teams and hasten forward. Accordingly all of them were ordered into a field and the different Brigades & Regiments got in shape when to our disappointment another messenger arrived ordering us to proceed as usual which we did until about 5 O.C. becoming almost nervous and excited by the continued rapid & heavy firing ~ when we were again ordered on double quick to Savanna. Accordingly the teams were again driven out of the road to enable troops to pass and everything got in readiness for moving. Remember we left 8 Cos. of our Reg behind but the remaining parts of command was on hand except those necessary to take charge of about 250 spare horses & the teams when ready to move. My anticipations were very soon lowered. The Gen. ordered that I should remain & take charge of our train and the men left behind and get them into Savanna a distance of 12 {illegible here but probably "miles"} I will merely say I got them in on Tuesday the road being completely blockaded ahead & for a distance, thirty miles from Savanna toward Columbia all which with artilery & teams and all of them wallowing in the mud, the last of which did not reach Savanna for 10 days or more.

The Command reached the River by day light Monday but were kept all harnessed until evening awaiting transportation to

~ 27 ~

Pittsburg 8 miles up the river, but in the evening all was over and on Tuesday they were ordered to scour the country in the direction of Florence to guard the immense train I speak of from any sally from that direction and by degrees matters quieted down & Col Zahm was ~~put~~ made commander of the post until last Friday April 25th when we joined our Divis - at this point - I will now add that the 24th won for themselves <u>very</u> <u>great</u> credit. much of which is written down to the 6th Ohio who do not claim it but honorably place it to the credit of the 24th the 6th being held as reserve - chafing for a chance in - newspapers say that they supported --- Battery regular army batery one of the best in service & which does great execution here & further about their being placed against the Miss. Tigers & Crescent City Guards &C, &C which was the 24th doings instead of the 6th Ohio of the same Brigade -- They captured two guns of the celebrated Washington Battery which worked against the one I mention above which the same Cincinnati writer "Invisable" gives the Gunther Greys Cr{edit} for when they were entirely out of reach of it ~*

Yours in much haste -
Wm. R. Jackson

*It appears that William was defending several companies' actions here and trying to set a story right, one that some anonymous writer, "Invisable," had perhaps sent in to the Cincinnati newspaper. Apparently this letter was, like the one written two days earlier by William, unsent, perhaps a draft for a letter that was later sent. The contents of this letter are corroborated by reports on pp. 93-98, and pp. 834-37, Series I, Vol. 10, Part 1 *The War of the Rebellion: A Compilation Of The Official Records Of The Union And Confederate Armies (O.R.)*; by D.C. Buell's report on pp. 291-96 in the same Series & volume as well as T.J. Wood's report on pp. 376-79.

Monroeville May 4 {1862}

Dear William,

It has been a long time since I have tried to write to you by mail for it seems to me that you would never get my letters in that way. I have expected all the week that Brown would leave but yesterday he had a congestion chill that almost proved fatal to him. Prentice say'd he could not live through another & was trying to break it with large doses of quinine, he still says he means to leave this week. There are a lot of things here for Will and I wish to send you something to eat if he can take them. The baby's picture is here to be sent to Will, his wife & I got letters by Heath. I wish such chances came oftener for we get letters in four days that way. Fannie & Jules have bad colds. Johnny has not been able to work for four days but is better. Dora, Birdie & Betty are well I ask her, what do I call you? "Bettchy change" and what else do I call you! "You own May Ann" she is <u>very hard</u> & sings happy land of Canaan most dreadful crooked, but keeps the tune. She says "my popy do want to see me" but she did not have your picture. We were up to Phillips to a masquerade last Monday. I took Mrs. Earl. Her & I were by far the best dressed. Cambell & a young gentleman from NY were there & you never saw two fellows more taken than they were with us & you never saw a more <u>shocking</u> falling off than there was when we unmasked. They are coming here Tuesday evening, I wish you could be here. I tell you we are doing all we can to be cheerful & keep up. I had to go to Prentice last week. My back had sore spots along the bone & my head was so bad I could not do much. He said I had over taxed my nerves, he gave me powders and a wash for my back. You see I condense my letter, I thought when I got this paper it would write all my letters to you. This is the last sheet. I shall cut it into & use the other half to send Brown & I am in hopes by that time you will be home. We have cold winds, & a late spring. Morton is about the

~ 29 ~

same. It is thought Center cannot get well. Fish brought him home.

Have you got the last letter I directed to Nashville? Do try & find it. There was two sheets of this paper, it was written the first of April. I have not got the school money yet. I have payd Smith $10 and owe him $15 more. I also let him have two pigs $3.25, I have $15 left. You must do as you think best about sending me more, I want you to keep plenty yourself. Theodore sent me shingles & lumber enough to finish the shed, he said not pay him till I got more money. Josh Whaly acts like another man since he came over & talked to him. He took the land that you ploughed last year which was five acres by measuring & three which joins it end ways back of the fence *{here Julia drew the shape of this piece of land}*. The slips in the Church were sold last Monday. There had been some sold when I went in. Dan Williams bid a very good one off for $25 so the next time I run up to 25 & Ed Prentice bid against me & finally set around to see which he would like & chose my seat, they all said it was to bad. I said to Lil Williams I would set there, or on the bench by the stove, I never would buy or rent any other slip for Prentice did not want that seat. So I left the Church. Mind I did not have any words I only explained why I wanted one. But I tell you the men all took it up. Roby said "all you have to do is to go & set there". Brown saw Prentice & the next day Prentice sent word to me I could have the seat - Martain said he would give Ed $50 for the seat, but I guess among all my friends he would have a good time getting it, if he was not meaner than the <u>Devil</u> he would not try to head us off even to a seat in church & I told Bennet & Ike _____ so. Bond & Hillyer have mooved to Norwalk. We hear nothing of the other battle since taking New Orleans we hear the rebels have left Corinth. Hoping to see you soon I will close with much love from all the children & myself.

Affectionately, Julia

Camp in the Woods 4 miles from
Monteray or where Mr. Warner left us
May 11th 1862 "Sunday"

Dear Julia,

Here we are anxiously waiting for a decisive battle at Corinth 9 miles distant from our camp. There is some kind of a skirmish every day. Our line was all changed yesterday and we now confidently expect a general battle to commence tomorrow. Monday, Silas was in a brush yesterday when he heard the music of bullets very plainly.

Our Regiment has two companies out all of the time which are relieved every morning. In the brush Silas was in Maj Foster {and} Maj Paramore were both there and a line came from Headquarters that some of them acted badly in retreating and the matter is to be investigated and the impression in camp is that Maj. Foster is the responsible party. Capt. Flannagan was there and acted with much bravery and some military skill.

The main army is five miles in advance of us & we have a pleasant camp and got permission to remain here instead of moving up in line.

I don't hear from you from some cause or other. Do you write to me. The majority of the entire army wants to face homeward and I am bound to make a break as soon as I can see a possible chance.

We get Cincinnati papers in 3 days and get them quite regular but the many comforts of home we cannot get so readily ~ I have never seen the Pkg sent by Mr. Bronson. I hope my babies will get their letters and answer them soon. Kiss all of them & many to yourself.

I am going to the River to day a distance of 12 miles to get some clothing for the Regiment ~ I shall stay all night on board of a boat ~   Your affect{ionate} Husband
                                          Wm. R. Jackson

~ 31 ~

In Camp in the Woods
Six Miles of Corinth ~ Miss
Friday May 17th 1862

Dear Wife Julia,

We advanced to day and took our position with the army but immediately in rear of the main body of Buells Army. All the Cavalry of his Army Corps is encamped with us.

Every part of the Army was under arms today and from every appearance a general engagement seems to be expected. There has been about fifty reports of Artilery upon our right this P.M. 6 O.C which may indicate an engagement to-morrow. Our Army advances very steadily but cautiously and maintain the ground they take. Fosdick & myself & nigger Sam have just completed pitching our tent and arranging to live as comfortable as camp will permit. Our ten{t} at this time is alone and upon a side hill facing the East with beautiful scenery in the valley below. He {'Fosdick' written above the line} occupies the right hand side with his cot and me the left and my box with a Desk I picked up the middle and rear of the tent. We have the sides all up which gives a fine circulating air. Sam and our saddle & traps occupy our servants' tents on our right. Maj. Paramore and a Dr. Dunn from Ill. are located about two rods above and close to the road. Most all of the rest of the Regiment is on the other side of the road. The top of our Desk is ornamented for the present with five loaded pistols and two canteens, Towels, brushes, candlesticks, &C.

This will probibly be our home until we lick them at Corinth. Every company was ordered to be under arms at 6 O.C this A.M. and was kept so until 2 O.C ~ All saddled and bridled and ready for the fight~

Your very thankful letter of May 4th came to hand last night which is all I have heard from you since Sowers arrived and it was a perfect stimulant to me to hear from you and the children.

I am exceedingly glad to hear of Mrs. Earl's return on your account notwithstanding. I may have reason to fear the impression you & her may make in some of your flirtations. If you fail to make an impression with the N.Y. or some of your neighbors, come down this way and I will guarantee your perfect success~

Many here would prefer a Masquerade Ball to a Cannon Ball or a Musket Ball. I suppose some of my friends miss me at these gatherings. I this moment hear much cheering in a Regiment near us. I hope it is good news from the direction of Corinth or Richmond. We have a Telegraph only 8 miles from us direct to Louisville & Cin~ so we hear all of the important War news as soon as you do-

Well the news has reached our camp that they have surrendered at Corinth. We don't take the bait so I'll go on with my letter. Let me hear how you maneuvered with your party and who you invited and what they talked about. Our refined talk is about the Butnub Chaps meaning as you know the Southerners who all wear butnub briches. Will has a chance now to show himself. Gaylord has been unwell several days and Will is the only one to command the company. I will say here that Jno Brown has not arrived here yet.

I suppose your modest demand for money is granted by this time. How did all the children talk about their letters & money & how did Lilly act. Tell her that I say that you must all stop calling her Betty. Was the old boy rather sentimental & Birdie pleased all over and the girls ready to commence at once to answer their letters. I have only seen two or three little boys or girls for some time then I gave some crackers and a couple of 5 cent pieces they look so poor. The children all that I have seen in this southern climate look puny & white ~

Peaches here are as large as the ball of my thumb and there bids fair to be an abundance of bl{ac}kberries, plumbs & huckleberries.

I have scarcely seen a peach orchard but what the Army has completely destroyed by tying horses to the trees~

Don't trouble any more about the school money. John has a bill in my hands of 14.40¢ against Sower to collect. We expect to be paid again in a few day{s} or as soon as we are ready for the paymaster. I let young Morton have $20 to get home with. Give no credit to the evacuation or surrender story. I must close.

Kiss all the babies.

Your affect{ionate} Hus{band}
Wm R. Jackson

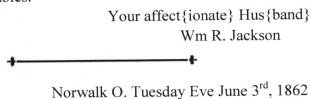

Norwalk O. Tuesday Eve June 3rd, 1862

Dear Sister,

Your letters of 24th & 25th ult. to Mrs. Kellogg now received by her today. Father being over to Monroeville brought the principal interest to us and afterwards Mrs. K. came over with the letters-Eliza Goodnow also rec'd a few lines from Geo Probert in relation to William's sickness. The tidings of his sickness has of course occasioned a good deal of anxiety to Eliza and Matilda - the latter being quite out of health is as usual inclined to put the worst face upon everything and this has made E. more nervous than she perhaps otherwise would be and she wishes me to write to you ~ She came down to the store this afternoon & wished me to telegraph to you to have Wm return with you &c but I satisfied her that there were other ways likely to prove more beneficial*that was abandoned ~ As you wrote Mrs. K. in your letter of the 25th that Wm Jackson was quite unwell and you intended making application for a furlough for him that he might come home. Eliza found that Will might be left there sick and suffer for want of proper care - but I assured her that it was quite improbable that you would come away leaving him sick and that if Will was sick enough to obtain a certificate from the physician and not too sick to travel his now wishes and feelings would induce him to come home with you.

You wrote Mrs. K. that you would remain awhile longer in Camp unless your family required your attention at home. The children are all well but I understand all are not well at Belleville though as I did not see Caroline I do not know exactly who is sick nor how sick-but I suppose she will write you herself and give all the particulars. If she should desire you to come home sooner than you otherwise would if Will is still sick I hope he may be able to obtain a furlough and come with you. If this diarrhea should continue upon him he will of course be unfit for duty and would recuperate much sooner at home than there. I hope you will keep them advised by writing as often as you can for you know how nervous Matilda is in such cases and it takes so long to get a letter from there that she will keep constantly imagining the worst. I cannot see the benefit of having men remain in camp sick-totally unfit for duty when by coming home they might so much sooner be able to go again into service with renewed health and energy and should suppose upon a physicians certificate the commanding Gen would readily grant the leave of absence But I must confess my ignorance of Army discipline~

The weather for the past week has been rainy and quite unpleasant though vegetation is very forward.

Richard Goodnow sailed for England last Saturday in the "City of Baltimore" in company with Will Gardner. They expect to be absent about three months visiting the Great Exhibition at London traveling through England and Scotland visiting Paris and perhaps some other cities on the continent. I fitted him out in good order and he carries sufficient letters to insure him a safe conduct through his journey ~ Mary G. has been quite under the weather for some days past but is now better. Eliza's baby is now very well. At our home all are in usual health. We are looking for Louise up this week.

Hoping that this may find all in better health and that you may all return in safety soon. I remain

Truly yours
Theodore Williams

Mrs. Julia B. Jackson
Pittsburgh Landing

Photo taken from the Commerative Biographical Record of the Counties of Huron and Lorain, Ohio available at www.archive.org.

Cincinnati July 5 1862

Wm R Jackson Esq
Monroeville O
Dear Sir,

Yours of 2nd inst addressed to my cousin Moore Fosdick came yesterday and I took it out to his residence, Glendale, 15 miles from the city last evening. I write at his request and enclose $23.40 amt. loaned him by you for which kindness he returns many thanks - he feels quite mortified that he should have so neglected it. The excuse however is a good one & I can trust you will over look the ommission. Poor Moore has a hard time - he is still confined to his bed & is quite feeble - has had a severe attack of Billious fever & now is suffering from Pleurisy.

It affords us both pleasure to hear you are improving. Many kind regards to your lady -

Reg. Aqm {Regimental Assistant Quartermaster}
Chas R Fosdick

Monroeville July Saturday 12th {1862}

Dear William,

Your "chief of staff" arrived here this morning with the Ladies. You know I am no judge of horses, but I can see they have very fine limbs. I dont know where I shall find pasture for it is very short. There has been so little rain but I will get around and see what I can do. Jim will return this evening so as to spend one day at home. He has talked a "blue streak" and so have I. He thinks you will be at home soon and I am sure I hope so for it seems a long time since you were here. You know it snowed hard the day you came. There is a pleasure party going from here to Detroit soon if you were here we would go. Theodore is going to begin to build in a week or two. Mrs. Calligan is going

~ 37 ~

East Monday. Mrs. Cotton will keep house for her. I dont see anything of Hellen or Mary. I saw Jose Clary last Sunday she had many inquiries to make about you. I think she thinks much of both of us. She gave me a pressing invitation to come and spend the day but dear me I dont get any chance. I pitted and can'd a bushel of cherries and half a bushel of currants this week. I have had a young girl through the week. Cant you come home to stay a little while or make arrangements to take some of us back with you. Jim says he is going to give you fits for not letting him know how much money you gave him. He says you said "here Jim here is four hundred dollars put it in your boot" but when he got to Cincinnati he had to open it to get some more to pay his expenses and there was a good deal more. He took $20 out. I dont know how much you gave him, I just gave Jim $5.00 so he should not get short. Must close for the cars have come.

Love Julia

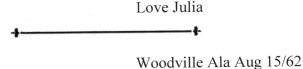

Woodville Ala Aug 15/62

Dear Julia,

I sent a letter to you by Lieut H. Terry. Capt. Wooster has been staying with us a day or two. He will return home in a few days.

The first thing after breakfast Probert, Wooster, Capt. D____, Lieut Tall, myself and Eight private{s} went out three miles from camp to get apples, peaches and green corn. The only peaches we get are clingstones.

It is the roughest country you ever saw in these mountains. It is almost impossible for even a footman to climb them they are so rocky. Our breakfast was fried pork and hard bread with coffee. Our dinner was pork, hard bread and boiled corn & supper about the same with the exception of some bread we make. After dinner three women appeared in camp at the

Col{onel's} quarters wanting to trade with the Regiment. Such specimens of humanity you never saw. They came ten miles with two dozen of eggs, one peck of potatoes, one peck of apples, one galon of cider, 1 half galon of picked cucumbers, beets & peaches, to exchange with us for salt, coffee & sugar.

Zahm called upon me to trade with them. They came to the tent and took seats and the first word spoken by them was <u>Have any</u> of you <u>men any chawing</u> tobacco. Kimble the clerk in our tent gave each a chew. One of them said that is the best <u>chaw</u> of tobacco I have had in six months. They live in the mountains at a place called the Sinks near the <u>buck</u> <u>snort</u> <u>grocery</u> <u>ten</u> miles from here. They sat here and chewed and spit and got their salt &C delt out to them at the rate of 30¢ per pound - One of them remarked that the tobacco was the <u>bustinest</u> best tobacco she ever <u>chawed</u>. Their dresses were fastened with thorns -

Our battalion of the Regiment started on a scout on Monday and came upon a company of Bushwhacking Gurillas amounting to about 125 and made a decent upon a desent upon them {sic} and they took to the mountains leaving eighteen horses to our men all saddled and bridled. The Captains, Cap Gurley's with the rest. The{y} wounded only one man.

The appearance and the movements of the men are quite different from what it was when you saw them. They are cheerful, fat, and lively. Young McEwen is as fleshy and heavy as Angel or Jno Jillich. Charly Bennett is larger than his father. I think I am fleshyer than when I left home. About chewing tobacco I have not seen a woman here but what chews tobacco and the two I spoke of asked for tobacco and filled their old pipes before they got on their horses or as they called them <u>Mars</u> meaning mares.

The conclusion is that the Bushwhackers have had enough of the 3rd Cavalry. Col Murray has forfeited his respect with the men very much since Zahm left the Regiment all of which I will explain - be somewhat guarded in your praise of him. Geo. P. is down upon him - as well as many others.[10] About the 18th Geo. P. and myself will know what we are to do. Tell the girls to be good and Dora to be smart and know where his clothes are when he gets up mornings & kiss pussy real hard for me.

Your affect{ionate} husband
Wm. R. Jackson

Woodville Ala Aug 23rd 1862

Dear Julia,

I am remaining with the regiment at this date every day expecting that an order will reach us ordering our discharge. I accompanied Companies A & D on a scout to the River which proved to be one of the most succesful the regiment has ever made. We brought in six prisoners $960 in money, 100 sesesh letters on their way into Tenn, 21 mules, 16 Head of Cattle & any quantity of Negroes. One of the prisoners was a captain.[11] We had a rare time reading the letters. Sower, Center, & McLelland have not reached the regiment yet, we heard of them at Bowlingreen ten days ago.

I am fearful that this letter will not reach home much before I shall, owing to a break in our line of communication. I have not heard anything from home since I left. I want to get home about the 1st Sept. if possible. I should like to see all of you. Remember me to the children.

Your affect{ionate} Husband
Wm R. Jackson

Chapter 1 Notes

1. *The War of the Rebellion: A Compilation Of The Official Records Of The Union And Confederate Armies* (O.R) Washington: Government Printing Office, 1880; Series I, Vol. 10, Part 2 Correspondence, p. 76.

2. For more on Grant and his victories at Ft. Henry and Ft. Donelson, see Reeder, Colonel Red, *The Northern Generals;* New York: Duell, Sloan and Pearce, 1964. Also, Shelby Foote's, *The Civil War, A Narrative Fort Sumter to Perryville;* New York: Random House, 1958, pp. 194-209. Also see www.civilwar.org/battlefields (accessed November 2014).

3. For more on Shiloh, see Foote, *The Civil War A Narrative*, pp. 340-48 and 350-51; Bruce Catton's *This Hallowed Ground The Story of the Union Side of the Civil War;* Garden City, NY: Doubleday and Company, Inc., 1956, pp. 109-20, and www.civilwar.org/battlefields/Shiloh & www.nps.gov/resources.

4. Population of Monroeville - From *The History of the Firelands*, p. 52: The 1860 census shows Ridgefield Township with 1128 people and Monroeville Village with 1257 residents.

5. About letters printed in Civil War era newspapers see: www.bgsu.edu/library/cac/nworesources/civilwar.html. This Bowling Green State University site has a collection of letters that were printed in the various Ohio newspapers.

6. *O.R., Series I-Volume 10-Part Two Correspondence, etc.* Special Field Orders No. 31 from General Halleck to J.C. Kelton, assistant-adjutant general, p. 139, part VI.

7. Catton, *This Hallowed Ground*, p. 74. Robertson, James I., Jr., *Soldiers Blue and Gray*; Columbia, South Carolina: University of South Carolina Press, 1988, pp. 122-44.

8. Dyer, Frederick H., *A Compendium of the War of the Rebellion;* Cedar Rapids, Iowa: 1908, p. 119, lists Wm. R. Jackson as resigning as "Supernumerary."

9. Reid, p. 769. Also www.bgsu.edu/colleges/library/cac/cwar (Northwest Ohio in the Civil War-3rd Ohio Vol. Cavalry) Center for Archival Collections.

10. From *This Hallowed Ground,* p. 74: apparently a Lieutenant Colonel (Douglas A. Murray), in charge of the regiment while the Colonel (Lewis Zahm) was away, was quite a bit stricter; this caused a mutiny, of sorts, among the men who wrote up petitions and letters to those at home, who in turn wrote letters against the unpopular Lt. Col. It was William T. Sherman who made the final decision to send the missing colonel home and retain the unpopular lieutenant colonel. See also, reports from Lt. Col D.A. Murray to Col. J.B. Fry, Chief of staff of the Army of the Ohio in *O.R., Series I, Vol. 16, Part I Reports* and Major Paramore's report on pp. 38-42 in Thomas Croft's, *History of the Service of The Third Ohio Veteran Volunteer Cavalry*; Toledo, Ohio, 1910 (available online at www.archive.org, accessed November 2014).

11. According to a report from Major Paramore sent to Colonel Lewis Zahm, recorded in the *O.R.(Series I-Volume 16,* pp. 870-71*)* August 19-20, 1862-"Scout from Woodville to Guntersville, Ala. and vicinity, report of Maj. James W. Paramore, Third Ohio Cavalry: the Captain was Capt. J.B. Turney, Co. K, First Tennessee." The number of mules and head of cattle listed in the O.R. was slightly different than the number William mentions; however, most of the other details were in agreement with what William wrote. Much about this capture as well as other parts of the letter are included in the section about the Third O.V.C. in Reid's book, p. 764.

Chapter Two

Outfitting the Seventh
Mid-September through December 1862

"Recruiting was very lively, and the Companies were all filled by the first week in September, and the Regiment was then organized as follows: Colonel, Israel Garrard; Lieut. Colonel, George G. Minor; Majors, Wm. L. Raney, ____Norton, and James McIntire; Adjutant, T.F. Allen; Q.M. W.M.R. Jackson; C. S., John McColgin; Surgeon, Isaac Train; Asst. Surgeons --- Tullis and _____Barrett..."[1]

R. C. Rankin

Due to the abbreviated way William signed his name - "Wm" or "Wm R." - he was occasionally referred to as "W.M.R." Jackson.[2] After mustering out of the Third and a brief furlough at home, he re-enlisted on September 15, 1862, with the Seventh Ohio Volunteer Cavalry, again as Quartermaster (QM or Q.M.) and began "fitting out the 7th O.V.C." as he wrote Julia the next day, September 16, 1862. This was one day before The Battle of Antietam or what has become known as "the single bloodiest day" in our nation's military history. By most accounts, the Battle of Antietam Creek, near Sharpsburg, Maryland saw as many as 23,000 men fallen. Although casualties from the Union armies were about 1000 more than the Confederates', this battle was seen as the "victory" that President Lincoln was waiting for before introducing the now famous Emancipation Proclamation. The preliminary proclamation was issued only five days later and made public only seven days after Antietam; however, it would not be formally issued until January 1, 1863.[3]

There are only two letters in this section, both from William, and ironically, in his first letter from the Seventh O.V.C., he writes about declining the offer to become Quartermaster and how he is waiting for "a position that will suit me better than that of Quarter Master." There are no other letters from Julia or William for the remainder of 1862. It seems probable that the family was all together at Christmas, which, even before the war, was a time of "sobriety and somberness" where families went to church together on Christmas day and then most likely had large family dinners afterwards with small gifts exchanged. Thomas Nast, the German immigrant who was an artist and writer with Harper's Weekly at that time, was asked to draw something to go along with Clement C. Moore's 1821 poem 'The Night Before Christmas.' His illustration depicted the pot-bellied, jovial character we know today but Nast also depicted Santa as a Union man![4] Whether William went home or his family came to be with him, by the tone of William's letters it seems he would have made every effort to be with his family any chance he could.

Cincinnati Sept 16th 1862

   Dear Wife,

   I am buisily engage{d} equiping and taking charge generly in fitting out the 7th O.V.C. at Camp Clay which is about 5 miles from the city.[5] I remain there during the day and return in the Evening. Col McDowell insisted very strongly last evening that I should take the position of Quarter Master and I declined and gave him my reasons but still he urged me to remain with him and help him get his Regt. into the field. As near as I can learn the line of operation for it is be along the Ohio border.[6]

   McDowell is one of the moving spirits in all the military here and I shall endeavor to place him under sufficient obligations in addition to try to induce him to help me to a position that will suit me better than that of Quarter Master.

With regard to the money hold on to it until I can come home. Pay Webb $10 -- Pay Murphy 10 and Nathan for Trunk. R. Martin $10 -- if it becomes necessary. You had probably better square up with W. Prentiss deducting the $9 --

I came away and left my summer coat & pants. Send them & some shirts in a trunk or carpet sack by Express ~

Care Adams Express Cin

Yours Truly
Wm. R. Jackson

I saw Caligan this morning -- he is well

Cincinnati Oct. 22nd/62
"Wednesday"

Dear Wife,

Yours of Sunday Evening* has just come to hand. It grieves me to hear of you being so lonely and having no help but is a relief to learn that the children are better. I sent them some pictoral papers yesterday which may amuse them for a short time. Notwithstanding I am in the bustle and confusion of the city I never had time hang so heavily I expected Co. G.[7] at home last evening and he has not arrived. I am anxious to get to Ripley as soon as I can I will look about as soon as I get there and come to some conclusion about our future operations. I spent the evening Sunday at Sam {Saul?} Sargents and met D Steele and his daughter there. She is very pretty. Mrs. Steele about the same. I see two or three companies of the 3rd Cavalry and Maj. Sidele were taken prisoners in K.Y. since and released on parole[8].

Don't confine the children too close during this pleasant weather in a warm room let them have the fresh air in the middle of the day. Kiss all of them for me and tell those that are well to be kind and help you and I will remember them when I come home again.

Your affect{ionate} husband
Wm. R. Jackson

P.S. You have not said how your _____ ague has been disposed of my health has been very good for two or three days I never was so much troubled with stomach, until I had a violent bowel complaint for one day since then I have felt very well and my apetite is natural.

You had better ask Jno Sargent to buy you some wood.

*no letter from Julia, dated "Sunday Eve" or Sunday 19th - (that would fit in this time period) was found in this collection.

During the years of the American Civil War, artist Thomas Nast was drawing Santa Claus wearing a blue coat with white stars over red & white striped britches.

For more information go to http://dburgin.tripod.com/cw_xmas/cwarchristmas.html

Chapter Two Notes

1. Rankin, R.C.; History of the Seventh Ohio Volunteer Cavalry; Memphis, Tennessee: General Books, LLC, 2010, p. 2.

2. Most likely because Rankin and other primary sources list William as "W.M.R." the website www.itd.nps.gov/cwss also lists William R. as "W.M.R. Jackson."

3. For more on Antietam and the Preliminary Emancipation Proclamation see: Catton, Bruce, *This Hallowed Ground,* pp. 157-58 and 166-69; Sandburg, Carl, *Abraham Lincoln, War Years, Vol. 3.* New York: Harcourt, Brace and Company, Inc., 1939, pp. 549-55 and pp. 577-90; and Foote's, *The Civil War A Narrative,* pp. 685-702. Also see: http://www.nps.gov/anti/historyculture/freedom.htm.

4. Clement C. Moore's poem, written in 1822, was originally entitled, '*A Visit from St. Nicholas,*' and was later changed to '*Twas the Night Before Christmas.* ' Two websites that describe in detail how Christmas might have been with the soldiers as well as on the home front are: www.americancivilwar.50megs.com & www.civilwar.org/education/history/on-the homefront/culture/Christmas (accessed November 2014).

5. Camp Clay was located outside Cincinnati, Ohio.

6. The Seventh O.V.C. earned its nickname "The River Regiment" because most of its companies were comprised of men from Southwest Ohio counties that bordered the Ohio River.

7. Colonel Israel Garrard (see Persons of Interest Appendix).

8. For Major Charles B. Seidel's report about this incident, see the O.R., Series I, Vol. 16, Part I Reports, pp. 1146-48.

Chapter Three

Hoping something will turn up this spring to bring this thing to a close.

January-July 1863

"That on the first day of January, in the year of our Lord one thousand eight hundred and sixty-three, all persons held as slaves within any State or designated part of a State, the people whereof shall then be in rebellion against the United States, shall be then, thenceforward, and forever free..." [1]

Abraham Lincoln

Nothing in either Julia's or William's hand gives us a clue as to how they might have reacted to the famous Emancipation Proclamation, officially issued on January 1, 1863. By some accounts, both the South and the North felt unprepared for the "revolution" that might occur as the proclamation became official. Many feared violent uprisings by Negroes on plantations all over the south as they were granted their freedom, at least on paper. There were reportedly very few instances of violence but several accounts tell of large, public celebrations by Negroes and known abolitionists.[2] However, William and Julia seemed to have other concerns as the war began to look like it would march into its third year.

Union Major General William S. Rosecrans, who had taken over command from Buell in October, 1862, was dealing with an army that was greatly diminished in numbers due to increased illness and injuries of its men as well as many who were deserters or absent without leave. By the end of 1862, it was clear that Rosecrans was well liked by the enlisted men who had given him the affectionate nickname, "Old Rosey." Rosecrans was said to be personally brave and possessed moral courage, but also thought to be obstinate and this apparently worried Lincoln at times. In spite of his shortcomings, Rosecrans was granted permission by War Secretary Stanton to get rid of officers who were guilty of "pillage, drunkenness and misbehavior in the presence of the enemy."[3]   As the New Year approached, he and his Army of the Cumberland of roughly 44,000, moved away from Nashville, toward Murfreesboro, Tennessee. This must have pleased Lincoln as he had apparently been urging Rosecrans to leave Nashville for several weeks. At the same time, Confederate General Braxton Bragg was moving his Army of Tennessee, about 37,000 strong, toward the same area. The opposing armies would meet on the eve of the New Year and begin this ferocious battle at Stones River, one in which several surviving soldiers described the bloody field littered with so many dead horses and bodies of men wearing blue or gray as "a slaughter pen."[4]

While the volunteers in the Third Ohio Cavalry were fighting in or recovering from this horrific battle in Middle Tennessee, William was continuing to assume more responsibilities with the Seventh O.V.C., which seemed ever wary of the movements and whereabouts of John Hunt Morgan. A Confederate officer known for consistently going against the orders of his own commanding officers, Morgan had already displayed his tactics in raids into Kentucky, including his famous "Christmas raid" into Elizabethtown. Meanwhile, much was being written about Union General Samuel P. Carter's successful December raid into East Tennessee, such as this from the *New York Times* on Jan. 8, 1863: "We are inclined to think this expedition of Gen. Carter will prove the most extensive, well ordered and successful achievment {sic} of the kind that the war has produced. Even the Richmond Examiner says that *'the raid is certainly a most daring one, and argues an audacity in the enemy (the Unionists) which they were not supposed to possess'.*"[5]

The full extent of the damages in either middle or northeast Tennessee probably was not yet known by either Julia or

William when they wrote their earliest letters of 1863. Julia's letters in this section are the saddest of all the letters, as she tells William about the deaths of several friends, killed in various battles or dead from disease. In Julia's first letter of 1863, she tells the details she knows about the Battle at Stones River: "...the 101st Col. Stem is killed, Lieut. Col. badly wounded, 125 of the regiment killed and missing, there was only 400 able to do duty when they first went into battle."[6] In her letter dated February 5, she shows her fortitude when describing how she deals with goods not delivered, and then later uses biblical references as she expresses her grief for the families of those whose loved ones will never return. She tells William details of all the funerals she attends and seems especially saddened by the death of their friend Silas. Julia sends William the (June 1) letter from "Sile's" father with the tragic details of his son's accidental death, "...the first of our ten children we have been called to follow to the grave." This letter from Amos Gould is one of eleven written by others to either Julia or William in the first six months of 1863.

Julia rejoices at news of the "possession of Richmond" (May 10), news that every Union man and woman hoped to hear, which unfortunately, proved to be a false report. As with today's news reports, telegraph reports of the 1860s were not always accurate, as is obvious from an article from *The Norwalk Experiment* entitled, "False Telegraph Report." Dated May 14, 1863, this article said, in part, that "the reported capture of Richmond, which was spread all over the country last Saturday evening, was a most heartless 'sell'; and the wonder is that the authorities at Washington, knowing as they no doubt did, the utter falsity of the report, should allow it run through the next day uncontradicted." Julia continues to tell William of the trials she faces, including an incident with Fannie and her schoolteacher that she expounds on in half of her January letters.

William's letters in this section are filled with the latest on his increasing responsibilities with the Seventh O.V.C. and in almost all he continues to ask how Julia and the children are. As in previous letters, William describes the countryside and the events he thinks would interest Julia, such as the "man who bleated it out for Jeff Davis" and how the men of his battalion handled this particular Confederate sympathizer (January 8). He reminds Julia of the immensity of the tasks he is charged with as in his letter of June 6, where he tells how he is "...controlling about 350 to 400 teams and from 2000 to 2500 horses & mules that have been turned in by the Army south of Stanford." Julia and he are often sending packages back and forth, either by mail or another person with the largest "package" being a mare sent by William to Monroeville. Later, "Bendigo," the Negro mentioned in William's of February 9, is given the task of riding a horse, Prince, home to Ohio. When "Ben" finally arrives in Monroeville, he seems to be hired as a farm hand and stays to help Julia. William also tells of another of Carter's raids into East Tennessee, one in which he (William) took part. He writes (May 6) of General Burnside's imminent arrival at Lexington and tells Julia "it looks to me as if there was to be a move in the direction of Knoxville."

Ambrose E. Burnside, of Indiana, reluctantly accepted Lincoln's offer to command the Army of the Potomac, formerly under McClellan's command. "Dear Burn," as McClellan often addressed his friend in letters, had earned his first star at First Bull Run. Later, however, he drew a great deal of criticism for mistakes made at Marye's Heights near Fredericksburg, Virginia (as well as previous engagements). In his book, *Never Call Retreat*, Bruce Catton seems to come to Burnside's defense, saying that "his army was being systematically and ruinously demoralized, not by its losses at Fredericksburg, but by the leaders who tried to capitalize on those losses." By January, 1863, Burnside was replaced by General Hooker, upon

Burnside's self-imposed withdrawal from his latest appointment. However, within two months, Lincoln gave Burnside command of the Department of the Ohio.[7] His new headquarters would be in Cincinnati along the Ohio River just north of the slave state of Kentucky. Since both southern Ohio and most of Kentucky were known to have strong anti-war sentiment, Burnside issued his Special Order Number 38 on April 13, 1863. Designed to stop support of the Confederacy, not just within the army he commanded but within the public as well, this order went so far as to threaten death for those who ignored it. This order was subsequently criticized, as was his controversial arrest of the well-known Peace Democrat, Clement Vallandigham. Vallandigham escaped death when President Lincoln intervened and exiled this renowned "Copperhead" to the Confederate states.[8]

In some of his letters William continued to appear hopeful that the war would end soon; however the war seemed to be showing no signs "...that something may turn up this spring to bring it to a close..." (March 27). The regiments did not average 300 men when Sherman wrote to Grant in June. Sherman's letter said, in part, that two Major Generals were attempting to get more men into their regiments "...that a draft is to be made & that 100,000 men are to be assigned to the old regiments & 200,000 to be organized as new troops."[9] It certainly appeared that more than the weather was heating up as spring melted into summer.

Ripley O Jany 3rd 1863

Dear Wife,

The Battalion started yesterday. I leave to day and leave my business all settled in Ripley ready to pay. I got myself very comfortably fixed before the train started. I got a very good blanket of Mrs. Wile for $3.00 ~ so you need not send one. Send my Holsters & Breast Collar if I fail to mention it when I again write. How did you get along going home? I started the mare in good condition the next day after you left at noon. Let me know how she arrived as soon as you can. I left a quantity of gunny sacks Boxes, bbls, &C with Capt. Tally to dispose of for me.

Yours in haste
Wm

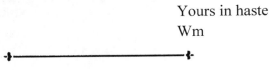

Monroeville Sunday {January} 4th {1863}

Dear William,

You would like to know I suppose how we got home and also how Kitty got along, &C, &C. Ourselves we arrived at 10 OC the next morning after we left you but the horse was not ship{p}ed till Thursday & got to Clyde Friday. I sent Mr. Corwin up Wednesday & he stayed till she came. I gave him money to pay his expenses, as you told me to. When the horse came she had no blanket, or halter, nothing but a <u>chunk</u> of a rope, hardly enough to tie her with, & the freight <u>not paid</u> so of course he could not bring her. The agent said she was to be reship{p}ed to Monroeville & there would be no car till Monday so he came home but left her in care of Tom Manahan. He said he knew you well & said he would pay the freight on her & bring Corwin down in a wagon & let him lead her, but the weather & roads were so bad that he thought it best for the horse to stable her for the two days & he would see that she was put on the cars all right. There were a good many men standing by & all admired her. It will lower my purse some to pay all the expenses connected with getting her home. John Brown thinks I can get Homer Clary to keep her. He has the ...{page torn here} there and has plenty of straw & keeps the yard covered knee deep with it. I told him to speak to him & let him know. I went to Sandusky New Years & took them a nice turkey. Found Judy looking very well. She declared <u>stoutly</u> she was not coming home this winter. Fannie will go down next week. Louisa made arrangements with the teacher about her. There are a great many of the little girls of the place that go to the school. Louisa had some company for them in the evening & nice entertainment for them. Sophia came to see me & I returned her call. She lives very nicely. Her husband is in Toledo. Cornelia is in Cincinnati. The old lady is failing very fast. I paid five dollars towards Judy's board & had to get her some things. I found everything looking well, four of the nicest hogs fatted that we ever had. I have not settled with Caroline or her Father yet. The cows were turned into the field the day I got home.

George Probert & Anna Nickels were here yesterday. He leaves for the 3rd Cavalry (to fill the Adjt's place he has resigned & is at home) his appointment & commission were sent to him before he knew anything about it. He seems please{d}. He thinks it fortunate for your regiment that Skinner resigned. He says when Skinner came from Virginia he came to him to know where he could sell gold. He had $250 to sell & also treasury notes & that he had been conniving with Army commanders & had to resign.

I have been almost sick with cold on my lungs & the baby also. I was afraid of croup with her last night. Dora seemed to have chill & fever Friday. Fannie is better for the last three days. Theodore has just returned. Mary[10] has been sick & they did not expect to bring the baby home alive but they have all got home. He will begin to know some of the anxiety of married life. There is bad news from the 101st. Col Stem is killed, Lieut. Col badly wounded, 125 in the regiment killed & missing. There was only 400 able to do duty when they first went into battle.[11] Calligan is safely at home. I have not seen him. I think you must have had a tedious march. The weather has been so bad. I thought I should have got a letter from you last night but did not. Write some explanation about the mare. I will pay the charges & Dane said I could collect it again if it had been paid by you. I will keep Caroline here for the present so if I should hear from you that I could come to you I should have no trouble in leaving. Betty woke up this morning & crawled over me expecting to have a romp with you. "where sis papa gone" she looked disappointed enough. Mr. Bronson had to ask a blessing the second time because the young lady had not got her seat.

Julia

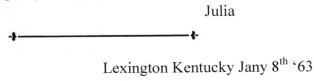

Lexington Kentucky Jany 8th '63

Dear Wife,

We had a severe snow storm here last night. I saw a sleigh or two out today in the City.

It surpasses any country I ever saw between Maysville and Lexington with the exception of a few miles near the celebrated Blue Lick Springs. The inhabitants don't seem to appreciate the quality of their farms. You can see their enterprise in stock growing as you pass their farms and see their splendid herds of cattle, sheep, and mules.

I was disappointed in the appearance of the City of Lexington there is but little taste displayed in the buildings with the exception of a few very fine mansions. The plantation buildings and yards around the city are generally large and some of them very fine mansions and the farms large and well cultivated, with very long ranges of stone fence.

We enjoyed two or three very pleasant days during our march and about as many uncomfortable and wet. In passing through one place last Sunday, one fellow bl{e}ated out for Jeff Davis and before he had time to close his mouth Lieut. Smith of Co. H. drew a revolver upon him and told him not to move a step or he would shoot him. Capt. Eells went to the head of the column and reported the case to the Col. and asked permission to shoot him but the Col. ordered some of them to give him a good pounding. Upon which Theo Allen returned and gave him two black eyes and then administered the Oath of Allegiance[12] to him and made him take it much to the <u>division</u> of those of the Battalion that were crowded around with their Revolvers drawn. The Buildings at the Blue Lick spring are burned they were upon a large scale the owner was a violent sesech and it is the general belief that some of the union troops set them on fire. The water that is sold and so celebrated in almost every city in the country is a general compound of stricken Eggs, sulphur, lime and salt ~

It is my belief that we will remain here or in this vicinity for a month or two and probibly longer, and I must confess I am well pleased with the idea. I have no other grounds for my belief than that Gen. Granger says he will concentrate all the cavalry and form a Cavalry Brigade here or near here.

I am anxious to hear how the mare reached home.

Kiss Pussy and remember me to all the children and to as many friends as enquire after me.

Your affect{ionate} Husb{and}
Wm. R. Jackson

—⸱————————————⸱—

Letter written in pencil and not legible in places

Monroeville Tuesday 13th {January 1863}

Dear William,

I received your letter last night it found us about as you left us. Julia is complaining of her side again to day, the weather is cold and dreary and blue. Father called yesterday to get those papers for Richard to put a stamp on and I gave them to him. No doubt my friends all feel very comfortable in thinking I am staying here to take care of things but they will not get a chance to congratulate me on it unless they come here to do it.

Billy has got entirely over his lameness and seems to feel well. Barny has been fixing the cow yard so that he can let the hogs into it and shut up the one to fat. Pork is 18¢ at the market. I have very little to write about for I have seen nothing or nobody.

Mr. Clock told me they had heard from Hellen and that she was enjoying herself, no doubt she is.

I had a letter from Darwin and Sarah last night they are all well. There is a Mite society at Mrs. Minors to night it is very doubtful about any of the familys going.

Last Thursday was a bitter cold day the children went to school as usual. Because Fannie was five minutes too late she was not allowed to go near the stove even at recess till just before school was out. The teacher told her she could go just two minutes. It was so cold here at home with big fires in three stoves that I could hardly do my bedrooms work. She came home crying with teeth ache and seemed to have suffered so with the cold. I felt very indignant but she went in the afternoon and had just such unreasonable treatment. There were two broken panes of glass close by her seat. The next morning I wrote a note to the teacher saying "Unless Fannie could become more comfortable I should be under the necessity of taking her out as she had tooth ache or earache most of the time and I was not willing she should suffer so with the cold". After reading it she came and said Fannie was you cold yesterday she said yes, she stood a minute and turned on her heel and said "well I can't help it". I saw John Sargent in the evening and told him what had passed and if she could not help it I wished he would tell me who to go to that would help it. He went into the school the next morning before Fannie got there and told her what Fannie had told me and after he went out and Fannie came in she stop{p}ed her and said Fannie do you know you told your mother a lie *{last page smeared badly...}* and then asked the scholars if they heard her say so the little girls and rough boys said she didn't and all the large girls and Frank Smith said she did say so. That afternoon she asked to be excused for her music lesson but she said she could not be excused without a written excuse. It has been some time since I have been under the control of a <u>district school teacher</u> and it had been under stood all quarter that she would come home so of course I didn't write any, and she did not get home till nearly dark so this afternoon I took her out. I would take her out but she is the only girl and {page badly smeared and on fold here}... the only boy in the school. I dont think I feel amiable enough to bear much from any body. It is nearly mail time.

With love Julia

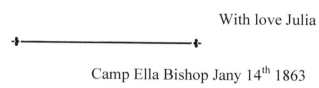

Camp Ella Bishop Jany 14th 1863

Dear Wife,

Yours just this moment came to hand. The 1st letter has not come to hand yet it is probibly in the office here and will turn up. The freight was not paid upon the mare and $14 was not much out of the way inasmuch as she was car{ri}ed from Clyde to Monroeville. I am very glad you have so good a place for her as Homer Clary's. Let her remain there for the winter if he will keep her. The Blanket was a very old one that she started with so it is no great loss.

How did she please Darwin and others? About the coat I am unable to call to mind the coat. Sell it low enough and dont bother about price. You must bear in mind Julia that I have a great deal upon my mind just at this time in getting my a/c up in good shape and it only adds to the burden to have you write so despondingly. You must be aware that we are yet unsettled for the winter and when we seem to be settled permanently for 6 or 8 weeks, I will try and act as far as possible for our comfort and pleasure.

McClean made out his a/c all satisfactory ~ It seems some times as if I could not carry in my head the amount of business I have to think of but thanks to the great I Am there seems to be a prospect of seeing the end of the great burden of it before many weeks ~

I will send you some money should you need it ~ I felt very gloomy for a day or two about Henry Terry's death as well as anxious about E{d}Beach.

The troops were all reviewed by Maj. Gen. Wright yesterday ~ It was a fine display ~

Your affect{ionate} Husb{and}
Wm. R. Jackson

Monroeville Thursday 15th {January 1863}

Dear William,

It has been snowing a little all day but not enough to make sleighing. I expect the roads are very good. Dora has a fine time with his sled. He starts from the top of the opposite hill which is a glase of ice and comes clear accross the bridge. He is a very good boy. Fannie's school trouble did not end with my last letter. John Sargent very imprudently went into the school the next day after I spoke to him and repeated all that I said to him (and I guess with some little alterations) that did not make the matter any better) and just as he went out Fannie came in for morning School. Miss Montgomery met her at the door and said "did you know you told your mother a lie" and seemed very angry (I think I told that part to you). I went to the office to put your letter in and then went to Mrs. Minors to put my mite in, and the teacher was there. I went into the hall after the collection to get my things and John came rushing Miss Montgomery out there and introduced us and, evidently to have her talk the thing over with me but just at that juncture Lill came and asked her to go and play and she went. Then Sargent said I want you to talk this matter over with Miss M. I said I don't want "to talk with her if she talks to me as she does to Fannie" and then told him how she met her and what she said. I said <u>lie</u> was a word I would not allow in my family, but (mind she had gone) while we were talking she passed through the hall again but did not stop so he had the talking to do. He got a good deal excited. She had denied everything to him, said Fannie had never handed her a note, she had never read one from me. That Fannie has always been to the stove and stay'd just as long as she wanted to and made out that she had told several up and down stories. He thought if she had I ought to know it and if the teacher was in the fault they ought to know it. But I could see plainly that he sided with the teacher. He then said when Fannie told me that the doors were ordered to be locked that it was not so. There had never been such an order made only to keep them locked through prayer time. I thought he said more than was necessary and took a very wrong time and place to do it in Minors hall. Several persons had come to listen to what we were talking about. I left just as soon as he stop{p}ed. I came up with Harriet Williams and I was crying so I told her my trouble. She said she thought Miss M. was a queer girl any how. Well I came home with the heaviest heart I ever had. I told Fannie and she was so astonished why Mother I gave her the note she said. I told her to think it all over for I did not want the teacher blamed but I wanted the truth known. I never closed my eyes till day light and I dont think I ever passed as dreadful a night. After breakfast the next morning I told her to go to school and tell Miss M. that I thought they were both to blame and <u>stick</u> to what she thought she had said. So at recess she went to her and told her that she did not want to make her mother any more trouble than she had to have and that I thought they were both to blame. But the <u>Lady</u> flew again and said she was not to blame at all, and she didnt see that it was any thing for me to go to Mr. Sargent about, and still through the blame all on Fannie so Fannie went out and came on home and told me I was sorry she...

For in the afternoon I told her to go back and be a good girl. I did not see any other way for her to show her innocence. So she went back and after school the teacher told her she wished to see her "now Fannie" she said "this has been all a misunderstanding. Tell your mother I beg her pardon and am sorry I have done anything to make her feel so bad for I saw she felt bad last night. I suppose I lade her note away some where but let it all go and dont say any thing more about it and I wont". The child came home with a light heart and I thanked the Lord that she was thought a truthful girl again. At night when the roll was called for the credits the Teacher said as she looked at Fannie "there is a girl that I always mark 10 for she has been the only one that has not whispered". I got no letter last night but one the night before. Julia felt better yesterday but not as well to day. I hope to get some money soon.

Affectionately Julia

Monroeville Sunday 18 {January 1863}

Dear William,

It is a lovely day but very snowy under foot. I have been to church this afternoon. Mr. Marks had a very good sermon teaching upon Hillyers and Henry's death{s}. Oh I have felt so sorry about it. I cannot get over Henry's death. I was in hopes he might come home so that you and I might show him such attention and respect as he <u>deserved</u> and wanted and of assuring him that we felt satisfied with the way he had filled {the} position you had been "influential" in getting for him, but that pleasure has been denied us as well as many others who have

~ 64 ~

looked for the return of friends and oh! The wives and Fatherless children that have nothing to look forward to but the lifeless remains of those they loved best being brought back to them and their graves to be their only comfort.

William I feel as the child did in Fanny Ferns book "if I only had a good place to cry" where I could cry as long as I could, and as hard as I could as if I might get rid of some of my sorrow, but I have felt just so full of tears ever since I left you and if I write to you about it, you must not blame me for "out of the abundance of the heart the mouth speaketh". Moses Wooster had been sick before the battle & telegraphed to his wife to come and bring his two little girls. She asked her friends and his about going and as a matter of course they discouraged her. After waiting a day and a half she concluded to go any way, but when she got to Louisville she found she was just that much to{o} late, she could not get a pass & had to come back. He walked seven miles expecting to meet her at the cars and he wrote back "there was no wife for me". I should think it would haunt her as long as she lived and they must blame themselves for not helping her to go. I should have got just such encouragement last spring <u>if I had asked advice</u> but thanks to <u>no one</u> I went and <u>we</u> and <u>they</u> know the result. Fannie got home yesterday. She seems quite well. I asked Betty last night when I took her to get her to sleep where her papa was. She shook her head but said nothing. I asked her again. She said "she didn't want to tell". I asked her why she said "cause I to tied". I will send you a box I think Tuesday. I would send you some fruit canned but am afraid it would freeze. I hope I shall see you soon and hope you will write very often till you do come.

Yours with affection Julia

Monroeville Sunday Eve 18th {January 1863}

Dear William,

I have written you three letters before this but waited untill I got one from you before I wrote the first one. It has been gloomy and dismal for the last three days and thawing very fast. The roads were getting quite good and it seems such a pity to have them break up again. I wrote to the Dr.* last week to send me a hog from N. Haven where they butchered but they had got through and packed all their pork. Elizabeth wrote to me that he had engaged one for me. I shall have to pay $12 to $15.00 a hundred I suppose but I had got thoroughly tired of running to the market, and none of the rest have any judgement about getting meat. Did you leave a bill unpaid there? I went to pay them what I owed them and they said it was a good deal more than I expected. I understood you to say you paid for the tongues. They sell pork for 18¢ and butter is 40¢. Barny fix{ed} the cow yard and let all the hogs into it but the one sow and she is fatting nicely but it will be several weeks before she is fit to kill. I should think two or three hogs might be fatted on the waste corn around the forage shed, and killed and barreled and sent up. I dont know as it would do but I know I used to see a good deal wasted where the cars were unloaded. My apples have not come yet. I sent Barny to see about them. Simmons said he thought they would be in this week. The concert went off Friday evening. I did not go for I did not feel like it. I believe they took in $50 but there were some expenses to be paid out of that. I went down that night to put the letter in for you respecting the sheep for I did not feel like taking the responsibility without your knowing it. I signed my name on them for you. Dick said it was necessary. I hope I did right but I suppose we have a paper that holds them for the sheep if any thing goes wrong. I had the worst walk and the wettest pair of feet you ever saw. I forgot the mail did not leave till noon. I dont know how the mail train connects or how long it takes my letters to go through. I should think you could be very comfortable at Beaufords and dont see why you are not contented and happy.

You are not pressed with business and your meals are always ready, and a comfortable room to go to at night.

I dont see why you are not content. You are so much better situated than you have been many times. Jule is about as usual. The rest of the children are well. I had the pleasure of telling Sargent that the teacher that I thought <u>he was inclined to side with</u>, come down when she got over her spunk, and made him feel a little <u>green</u> about bringing her out in the hall for her to talk the thing over to me and as soon as she was introduced to turn on her heel and leave <u>him</u> to do the talking. "Now" I said "I stood there to be talked too and why didn't she talk". "Well I know—well" and that was all he could say. I told him there was one thing certain the child had been kept dreadfully uncomfortable there, and it was the teachers place to speak about the glass being out of the windows, and not mine and if he had been through with what I have for the last four months with the girls, he would not want them exposed unnecessarily. I did not mince the matter a bit, for I felt very indignant. He said, she said Fan was the best scholar she had, and had been the least trouble. I aint afraid but what she will come out at the top of the heap somewhere. Poor Judy I am sorry to have her get behind her, but she gets along faster with music. One reason she has all her time to practice. I want to get Florence a cloak for Christmas. I don't know what it will cost but she has nothing for cold weather. I will make the money go as far as I can, but you know I had been without for two weeks nearly and had debts to pay.

Barny has gone to Baptist prayer meeting. He would like to hear from his girls and know if Maddison Campbell has been to see them

With much love Julia

*Referring to Dr. Abijah Beach, married to William's sister, Elizabeth.

Monroeville Monday 19 {January 1863}

Dear William,

I wrote you yesterday & have not much to writ{e} about to day.

I had to pre pay the express charges. I don't think I can get along unless you send me some more money unless you are coming home very soon. I send you all the papers in the envelope just as you left them with the addition of your commission. I have tried all over town to get you a pair of mittens & drawers but could not get such as I wanted. I hope you will enjoy the head cheese souse & sausage. The fruit is pears & strawberries, five pairs of socks & four towels, breast straps & holsters. I hope you will get it all safe & let me know as soon as you get it. The snow is going off and it is cloudy and gloomy. I hope to get a letter to night.

With love Julia

Monroeville Thursday 22 {January 1863}

Dear William,

I have just written to Birdie & Judy to come home. I had thought of going to Bellville but the weather and walking are very bad and I am not well enough to under take the trip. I felt that it is an unnecessary expense to keep Jule in Sandusky at $2.00 per week while I am staying here. If I could get rid of the old man I would try to get along with Caroline and her child. It makes unbounded confusion but I have got to worry my way through some way or other. I don't think there has been one pleasant day since I came home and that was New Years Day. A storm began here the same day it did with you. It rained two days since the snow still lay heavy on the ground & the worst walking & roads you ever saw. You ask me to write you the news about town but I know none & think there is none. Darwin was here in the evening & of course did not see the mare. George Clary is the only one that has expressed himself respecting her. He said she was the finest animal he had seen for years. The others have said nothing perhaps there is a feeling of jealousy upper most. Scouton said he would keep her till after this storm & then send her to Clary. I am almost out of corn fodder. Shall I buy straw or hay? I saw John Brahm about flour. He said he would bring me some but he has disappointed me so much that I expect to have trouble. I hope you have got the box I sent you last Tuesday & are enjoying the contents. Let me know if you got it - I sent your papers in it. I write often & hope you get all my letters. Did you get the first one I wrote you about Jule in it? I have not heard from Birdie since I came home. I wrote to Bellville to send her up Saturday if she wanted to come so they will all be here by the time <u>you</u> get home. I must close and take my letter to the office. It will be an awful walk.   Affectionately Julia

Headquarters 7th O.V. Cavalry
Camp Ella Bishop Jany 25th 63

Dear Wife,

Your nice box of traps come to hand all in good order yesterday and the Col Adj. McColgin & myself enjoyed a good supper of part of the contents. The weather is very mild to day. We had a mounted dress parade this P.M. and just as it was dismissed Gen. Leslie Combs one of the prominent men of K.Y. made his appearance and requested the Col. to reassemble them, as he wanted to see them and speak to them. It was accordingly done and he made them a fine speech. He said to day was the anniversary of a battle he was in {in} 1812 50 years ago in which Col. Garrad's grandfather commanded as Brigade Maj., &C, &C concluding with a fine and patriotic speech ~

You seemed this time rather indefinite about my coming home when I said as soon as my business would admit of it. I am very busily engaged making up a 4 months report which {is} my first and only business until it is completed and then an effort for home. Maj. McDowell is here and said he would arrange with Gen. Granger for a leave of absence for me as soon as I wanted it. He and his clerk is here to pay off our Regiment in a day or two.

They are so strict here that they only permit one officer and one private to pass out of the Regiment in one day but McColgin & myself have a pass at will but mine is used very little ~ Lexington does not interest me very much. It is not as fine a city as Nashville.

You had better buy a ton of good timothy hay instead of straw or stalks and if necessary get about 1000G of bran for the cows - and have it occasionly fed to Billy and be sure to have Billy well salted. I am as foolish as ever about my horses. Prince and Dave are there when I ride the sorrel horse, Joe. I think him the horse for comfort. I wish I had Prince at home.

I certainly believe I command more respect in our Regiment than any Maj in it. In and about my tent I am treated by all men with due civility. Why don't you say or write something about the 3rd Ohio. I have not seen a word about it since the terrible battle at Murfreesboro.

Have the girls go to school and tell all of them to be good children. I am troubled as usual with dyspepsia but don't give up to it. ~ <u>Kiss</u> <u>betty</u> tell her I want to see her.

Your affect{ionate} Husb{and}
Wm

Headquarters 7th O.V. Cavalry
Camp Ella Bishop Jany 27th 63

Dear Wife,

Matters remain about as much as usual in and about Lexington with the exception that Gen. Granger has been ordered to Nashville and Gen Gilmore is now in Command here.

The weather for twelve hours has been Excedingly disagreeable with rain snow and mud. I have not had my breakfast yet but when I do I expect to enjoy some of the sausage you sent to me. We have no difficulty in getting good marketing.

Our pay rolls are being made out to pay our Regiment to the 31st Dec. For fear you may be in want of some money I enclose you $10 and will send you more after pay day ~

I have nothing to write that can interest so I'll close and go to breakfast.

Remember me to my friends and the children.

Your Affect{ionate} Husb{and},
Wm

————————————————————

Monroeville Feb 5th Thursday
{letter written in pencil}

Dear William,

I was very much gratified in hearing from you last night & in learning that you were comfortably situated. I do hope you will be permited to stay where you now are for some time. The last ten days have been a worrying time for me. The roads continued so bad, so long I did not know what I should do, so many outs - out of flour, out of hay, out of wood, and no prospect of getting either. The hay I had engaged but the storm came in so bad the man could not haul it. John Boehm has disappointed me two weeks after promising me repeatedly. I had sent money to the

~ 71 ~

mill for Bran, thinking to hurry them up in sending it, but after waiting four days last Friday morning in all that storm I put on my things and started thinking to make a splinter fly somewhere. I went to the mill & asked the man if he didn't think it was too bad for a woman to turn out after waiting as long as I had & paying him before hand. He said it was <u>sure</u>. He said I should have it in a half hour then I told him to put in a half sack of flour & paid him $1.77 & before I got home the flour & bran were there. So much I did do last Monday. John Sargent sent me a load of hay, not very good but better than none. As to wood, I am out. Old Corwin has gone to meeting up to Clyde. Tuesday I went into the woods & picked up enough to do with a day. It was the coldest day this winter. I left word with Ike Smith to send me up some but it dont come. I have tried in every direction. The roads are now frozen & it has snowed all day. May be it will come from some where. Every one else is in the same fix. Theodore says when neighbors meet on the street instead of asking how their families are, they ask how is your wood pile. I went to John Roby but he would not let me have any from the Brewery. Caroline is doing the chores. Darwin was here last week & spent the evening. He advised me to get all the cotton goods I would want for some time as they were going so fast….

I have got some prints at Theodore's for $2__ & I got some bleached muslin at Green's. I should have got more but did not have the money to pay him for what I did get but told him I should have it in two weeks. You wrote me you were going to be paid in a day or two, but in your last letter you said nothing about it. Did they fail to pay you as you expected? One dollar goes just as far as a half dollar used to. Wood is $3.00 per cord, flour $8.00 & every thing in proportion. Some times I feel as if I would like to break up housekeeping. The children are all at home & going to school. Betty says "Mama you will wite to Papa & tell him to come home won't you, won't you & take her to church-won't you mama". She sat a long time & cried & the tears ran.

Last evening the remains of Hillyer & Wooster came home. Their funerals were Saturday. Hillyers in the morning at our church & Woosters in the afternoon at the Episcopal in Norwalk. I think all the Lawyers in Norwalk were here from Father down to Tim Strong. There was a train sent over at noon for them. I regarded your feelings as well as my own and went over. Theodore was over & was to act as pall bearer for Wooster. I had cried my eyes most out in the morning & it seemed as if it would almost kill me in the afternoon. Oh that poor woman & those two dear little girls. William Jackson, if he could have raised up from his cold burial case & seen their agony wouldn't he have felt that they had the first claim to his life & the country next? He loved his family & now what desolation. Merciful God the grief that I saw & felt that day & it was only a drop in the ocean of misery this dreadful war has brought upon our people. The fatherless children & the widows would all the gold of Ophir have repaid for one hour of their grief at what was their husband's fame to one hour of their heart's anguish. Two beautiful wreaths of white flowers and evergreen were laid on his coffin & his over coat & sword across it was all. He was very natural the night they got him home and it was all she had to comfort her. His trunk was burned with a part of the train by the rebels. She thinks there was a letter in it for her as he left no message for her. He had been so low for days before the battle he lost so much blood was why he kept natural. Hillyer could not be seen. His leg was broken Wednesday & not set till Friday. He was shot through both. Directly after he was wounded he took his little book from his pocket and wrote "Dear Maria I am wounded & lying on the cold ground". He was taken to the same room with Stem & Wooster. He thought he was going to get well till a few minutes before he died when the Dr. told him he must die soon. He said it was hard to die so far away from home & friends but he died happy & in defense of his country. He took his keys & wallet from his pocket & his rings from his finger. Everything was taken good care of & the same man that took good care of him brought him home. For four days & nights he laid on the bear floor. Matild really thinks their affliction worse than hers. Caroline has three brothers in the 19 Michigan & they have been in camp near Danville for some time. She would be glad to have you try to see them. They are in Company K, Mat, John, & Dwight. Zahm has received the discharge he applied for last fall. That is his resignation has been accepted. He is at home. Doan was here yesterday from the East. They look for Henry's remains the last of next week. Can't you come home? When Bennet & Jim Hillyer got to Nashville they found Zahm & he sent them to Murfreesborough with the same escort that came in with him. He gave them cavalry horses & clothes.

Affectionately Julia

Westchester Feb 5th 1863

My Dear Aunt,

I suppose you have heard before this of the death of mother & Elizabeth which were both sudden at the last. We knew cousin Liz could not live a great while but the Doctors thought she would live until June but she passed away very rapidly and I do wish you could of been with her and seen her it was perfectly beautifull to see her so peacefully resigned and she died very easy. Mother was over on Saturday to see her corpse and came home in the afternoon and on Sunday morning when I went down she looked so well and we breakfasted together and she looked as bright as I have seen her in a year and after Breakfast she went up stairs and put on a new dress I carried down to her and came in to know how she looked and was in very good spirits. She walked down to dinner alone and after sitting down to the table she was taken with paralysis and we took her up stairs and rub{b}ed her and she came to so as to speak to us and we thought the worst was over but in a few moments she had a very hard convulsion which lasted about three quarters of an hour. She then rallied for a few moments and had another convulsion which lasted about two hours then she became perfectly quiet but insensible and breathed very easy and seemed very comfortable untill she breathed her last which was half past nine. Friend Mary M_____ and John Thomas, Cousin Amelia & Maria Clara, Father and myself were with her when she died. Amelia was over to Brooklyn & Sarah was so sick that she could not leave her bed. We buried Liz on Monday and while we was up to Westchester with the Funeral Sarah was confined poor soul. We felt very anxious but she got along very nicely. She has a nice boy and is getting along very nicely. Mother was buried the next day. It was almost too much for us to go through with but our Heavenly Father gives us strength when we need it. Amelia has not been out of her bed since Mother was buried. The Doctor felt very anxious about her on Monday but she is better know. Beck was down yesterday and found her quite comfortable but very weak. I fear she will not be long behind her mother & sister. Richard's wife had a daughter last Thursday and is getting along nicely. You can imagine dear Aunt what a trying time we have had all round but it is all done right. He that doeth it does all things well. I do wish you would write to us. It seems as tho we hear very little from you but I hope now we will hear and see one another soon. With much love to all members of your family I remain affectionately your nephew

Thos B Bowne

Harrodsburg KY. Feby 9th 1863

Dear Wife,

We arrived here in good shape yesterday "Sunday" after a short march.

I am ~~again~~ quite comfortably settled again in town occupying one of Gov. Mag{offin} office buildings for an office and store room. The camp is distant about 1/2 mile. I have no arrangement for board yet but expect to have no trouble in getting a comfortable place. I have all of my staff around me Smith, Spears, Jim Cain, John & *Bendigo* an Alabama Negro who was with the 3rd Ohio at Woodville Ala. He is a pure specimen of a negro as I ever saw. He was with our Bat{tallion} of that Regiment that was taken at Lexington by Morgan last fall.

The majority of the inhabitants here are sesesh but throughout the county the union sentiment predominate.

I wish I had some news to write you or something that would interest you. Did you ever get the Fine Comb I sent you from Lexington also the 10$ - I sent you 10$ in my last letter from Danville, making 20$ ~

The Michigan Regiment that Caroline's Bro{thers} belonged too left for Nashville at the time Gen Granger left Lexington. That was about ten days before we got to Danville.

I am very much obliged to you for your long letters, and I would repay you with the same had I anything to write about.

I am glad to hear that the girls are going to school and hope they will all be good children. I think of all of you very often.

Very affectionately

Wm

Dear William,

I received two letters from you last evening one from Danville with $10 enclosed and one from Harrodsburgh. I hope you will be fortunate enough to find a good boarding place again. I feel bad to hear every little while that you are going farther on. As long as the regiment stays in Kentucky I will try to get along but <u>will</u> <u>not</u> consent to your going into Tennessee. I have never felt that it was your duty or mine to have you go into the army again. It is only the one <u>consideration</u> & I do feel that with the promises you have had from influential friends that you ought to get a permanent situation and I should not fail to remind them of their promises if I was in your place. You have been with the 7{th} almost six months and have filled your place as few could and to the entire satisfaction of the Col. and I think he is under more obligation than you are. Who offered you the Post at Danville? And you have never told me who your Majors were. Paramore has the vote of the Regiment for Col. The thing has been laid before the Gov and I suppose he will get it. Zahm's idea in resigning was to be promoted to Brig. General he thought Worcester would work the thing through for him (so Ike Smith told me). I rather think he is a good deal disappointed. She will have to stop her howling. I spoke to Hellen about the confab at Hubbles. She said they did strike fire there for a while, but she could not tell me how the conversation began but she said she liked you & she was determined to take your part. I shall probably give Mrs. Clary a swipe that will cause her to say something back <u>if she dare</u>.

Yesterday we paid the last tribute of honor and respect to Henry's remains, the funeral was conducted in Masonic styles (which as far as their forms went, were very disgusting to me). Mr. Marks preached the sermon which I think was much better than Hillyers and at the close he had a long address to the

~ 77 ~

Masons which occupied altogether to{o} much time and I think nobody cared to hear it! I had sent for Mr. Bronson to come up and I think the family felt pleased that he did come after the Masons had made their parade after the sermon. Mr. Marks said that he was pleased to say that his friend Mr. Bronson would make a few remarks & I think they pleased the congregation more than all that had been said or done. I saw Mr. Weed in the evening & he enquired if Mr. B had gone home & he said he was so pleased with what he said he felt as if he wanted to take him by the hand. I went to the depot Monday morning to meet the remains. The family came up & Mrs. Bennet she called me {to} one side & said she hoped I would be at their house as much as I could while his body was there. I went down with them & in the afternoon Calligan & I went down & got Mr._____ & we had the case taken out of the box. I took linen sheats down & made wreaths of evergreen to lay on the case it was a nice one and when we got it fixed it looked as if the poor fellow had friends. He was kept till Wednesday Some looked at him but said they would not have known him. I did not see him. I went from the house with the friends & when we got into the church (it was at the Baptist on account of it being the largest) there had not been seats enough reserved. Finally the relatives were seated & there was no seat for me. There was others behind me. I stood till I saw they were not making any arrangements to get seats for any body so I started & went over to Roby's office & asked Rural for a chair. He offered to carry it for me but I told him I could not put him to the trouble so I took it myself & when I got into the hall of the church the men looked dashed. Wilson offered to carry it up the aisle. I told him I would carry it my self. I went on through the crowd and the next Albright tried to take it. I told him <u>no</u> I would take it myself so I took it up near the pulpit & had a comfortable seat. I think a good many saw it & some felt a little shamed and I felt under no obligations. I thought how you would have bit your lips. Smith was the only one that closed their store. I do certainly think it is the most heartless unfeeling place I ever was in. H____brought me half cord of wood & said he would bring me as much more $3.00 a cord. Old Corwin* crawled back this morning. He has been gone two weeks to meeting and left us in these storms to do the best we could. Caroline has had a most uncomfortable time doing chores & getting wood cut. I finally heard of an Irish man & went & hunted him up. He came & cut the half cord of wood yesterday. I feel as if you ought to come home & stay long enough to get wood contracted for & flour & such things that cause me so much anxiety. Boehm has not been near me with flour. I will not ask any one any more to interest themselves in my behalf. Lillian was sitting in the kitchen to day & I was talking with Caroline. She says "Carrie, Carrie, I was in de woods & Santa Claus come & took me to papa, & papa do me mama, & mama do me some dinner & I was a little baby" I guess it was original with herself I don't think she ever heard it. The children are all at home with colds a real Tyler grip. Sunday night I thought Jule would have croup, Monday & Tuesday nights I thought Betty would certainly have it. I was awake most all of both nights gave her oil twice & croup syrup she is better. Last night Florence was taken the same way. I have given her the same remedys to day. Fannie's has been dreadful in her head & on her lungs & Dora is afflicted in the same way. I have a bad cold from being so much exposed nights. The children were very much interested in their school & I was very sorry as well as they to have to keep them out. Birdie fell at the school house & cut her badly just above her eye brow. It has nearly healed & I think will leave no scar. Betty is sitting on my lap. She says papa had better come home & see his sick little Betsy Jane. She spoke in the same three of four times in the night. They all think you write about it but don't come home. I don't say much about it to them any more. It is dark & I must close with love Julia

*Caroline's father (Samuel) Corwin.

Harrodsburg K.Y. Feb 13th 1863

Dear Wife,

Yours come to hand. The boys are all getting their pay to day and I expect to get mine this evening but probably not in time to make up a package to send to you. I think I shall send you about 50$ in small change.

I shall be able to make an effort to get home in the course of ten days or two weeks. I am fearful you do not consider the importance and the immense amount of labor there is about making up my reports but I have the satisfaction of thinking they will be better than an average & there will be a candle box full of them.

I could have been post quartermaster at Danville but I have no desire for a place of that kind. There is responsibility and no pay for it and no certainty of remaining any more than I now have. We have every civility extended to us by the citizens here and are strongly pressed to come and dine take tea &c. But my time is too much employed to avail myself of their civility. I had an elderly gentleman the <u>son</u> of the <u>renowned</u> <u>Joe Davis</u> of K.Y. invite me very cordially to ride out and dine with him. If I bring Prince home you may calculate that he will always be mine so long as I can own him or I will give him to <u>Dora</u>. He is one of the pleasantest dispositioned horse{s} I ever saw.

If Mrs. Clary is so much troubled about my debts let her have her husband pay 20$ for me.

I will write you again Monday. The mail leaves here very early in the morning by stage.

Love the children for me
Your affect{ionate}
Wm

Ripley, O. 21st Feby 1863

Lt. Wm R. Jackson
Dear Sir:

In my letter yesterday I omit{t}ed the date and time also number of rations to enable you to make out certificates at least it may be necessary for you to be in posses{s}ion of this information and I do not wish to put you to the trouble of making an examination of the adjts. {*adjutants'*} books unless you desire so to do.

Commenced 5th Oct. ending 17th Nov.
Number of rations 203.30

Very respectfully
Alex Jolly

My a/cts for subsisting (recruits) previous to 5th has been paid

Monroeville Friday 6th {March 1863}

Dear William,

I suppose you are anxious to hear from Ben & the horse and so am I. They have not got along yet and I should think it was high time. Your trunk came Tuesday evening and a letter from Mr. Spear but he said nothing about them. I hope the nigger has not been to{o} smart for <u>you</u> and gone off with Prince. Dora claims him if he ever gets here. I never have said any thing to Theodore about him. I got two letters from you last night & one the night before. I have not written for the last week. I thought it was so uncertain about it getting to you. Your last letter of the 3rd* came in two days, before that they had been five & six days getting here. When I read to the children that you were homesick I must say you got very little sympathy for they all clapped their hands and jumped & said "<u>goody, goody</u> now he'll come home he's homesick, he's homesick". I looked for a letter in your trunk but could not find any, other things were all safe. Where did the watch come from? Had I better get a piece of fine unbleached muslin. I have none. It is $7.00 here & quoted at that in NY. It would <u>only</u> come to $15. I have some nice bleached for shirts that I got some time ago for 30¢. I have spent a good deal of the money you sent me but it has all been for necessary articles that have since advanced in price. Write to me what to do with the rest if you are not coming soon. It is just where you put it. The little box is at Roby's yet. It is pleasant but the worst roads you can imagine. Did you have trouble about selling the sacks left at Ripley? I read a letter in your trunk from Capt. Jolly respecting them. I asked Betty what I should write to you. She said wite to Papa that his little Betsy Jane had a cold a little while ago and I want him to come home & take me to <u>church</u>. Darwin thinks she is the most ready and apt in her answers of any child he ever saw. She comes now & says tell Papa to come help his own Mary Ann. The children are coming from school. Judy has not been to day on account of her cough. Mrs. Ward, Lill & Mary Williams & myself walked over to McDonalds yesterday & had a very pleasant visit. They all want to see you at Phillips. Louise Campbell writes that she cannot get a yard of shirting less than 50¢ in Orange or NY. I went with Mrs. Ares last week & spent the day at Dans. Maria seems quite cheerful. They have got their house fixed very nice. Mr. Bronson has immortalized himself here in what he said at Henry's funeral, so many have spoken to me about it. There will be a convocation of ministers here next Thursday. There will be eight or ten in town. Mr. Bronson is to preach one of the sermons. There will be three. I will write as soon as Ben gets along & if you should hear any thing about him let me know for I feel very anxious.

With much love Julia

*This letter from William was not in the collection.

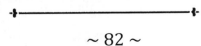

Monroeville Sunday 8th *{thought to be March 1863}*

Dear William,

This half sheet of paper will have to make the return trip to Dixie, as I found myself this Sunday morning without any thing to write upon, & the only alternative was to tear off this unfilled part of one of your letters.

I began to feel very anxious about Prince & Ben but think perhaps they have returned to you, as the excitement died out so suddenly. If they should get along, I will write immediately. Caroline is talking of leaving next month she wants to see to her own house & making her garden. She has done all the chores for the last six weeks & has been very faithful to me, but I have had a great deal of confusion to bear on account of her child. If you come home remember them with some little present. I wish you would get Dora a cap in Cincinnati & Birdie a nice doll. The girls have nice ones & she has none. They have all coughed dreadfully for the last week & yesterday there were spots in Julia's throat showing symptoms of Diptheria. I went to Prentice & got medicine & to day he has been up to see her. He said I must watch her closely & left Pidoplaline[3] which I shall avoid giving if possible. She says it is five months & a half since she has seen you, & thinks you have lately added one month more on your report. It used to be four, & now it is a five month report. The Methodist church has lately been sold to the Romanist where they now hold forth. The Methodists have bought the Baker place where John Brown is & he is going up on the camp farm. He told me that his brother had bought it for forty five dollars an acre. Ruth is clear down again & has no wish to get up. I think the weather has something to do with it. There has been two snow storms within three days & no one pretends to get out with a team. Lillian says she is always going to be my little Betsy Jane & she don't want Papa to buy any more own little May Anns "&

if Papa do I will go & be a horse" & when she gets angry she always threatens that she will "die & go up to heaben & then you wont have any more poor little Betsy Janes". I have not been up to Hellen's since I came home & see but little of her. Her husband is now Col. stepping over Murry and Foster which I think will show up to the Norwalk folks the estimation in which their man was held in the Regiment. You have never written me who your Majors were & has Minor got well. Ask him if he gets any chicken gizzards? Hellen & Mary Martain came for me to go to make Mrs. F_____ a visit but I had a bad sick headache & had to decline. I called there once, she lives very nicely & I guess rings in with the Norwalk Episcopalians, you know she is way wise. I was in the Drug Store last night & George Clary came clear accross the room to enquire after you & said he wanted to see you very much & enquired all about you. Perhaps he has heard there is some feeling between his wife & me. Everyone enquires after you & I suppose the reason your letters are not answered people have all been looking for you to come home, for I had told them that you had written that you were coming soon. I should like to have kind of a housewarming when that long looked for time does come. My Columbus paper has stop{p}ed coming & I do not get any news. I suppose the pay has men out but I will wait & let you fix it. The dime circle meets here next Tuesday night & they promise a full house. The children are growing fast & I think they are learning fast but they have had all sorts of walking & weather to contend with. Theodore is talking of going to New York soon. Their baby is getting real pretty. I saw her at the store. They have not been over this winter. The old horse is lame. I was in hopes of getting a letter last night but did not get it. Makes Sunday a little shorter. You wrote me a real good love letter* but I would rather have it verbaly.   With Affection Julia

*This "love letter" wasn't found in this collection of letters.

Harrodsburg K.Y. Mar 8th 1863 "Sunday Even"

My Dear Wife,

I have be{en} expecting Speer and Smith for a week past and have also {been} expecting to hear from you but have not since they left here or since the horse could have had an oportunity to have arrived at home.

I am quite out of patience about their remaining so long at Cincinnati. I expect them certain tomorrow.

I shall make an effort to get home before I complete my papers inasmch as they have delayed me so long.

The Col{onel's} Bro is here from Minnesota making him a visit.

Yours in haste. The mail closes soon. Kiss betty and remember me to the children.

Your affect{ionate}
Wm

Lexington Mar 27th 1863 "Friday"

My Dear Julia,

We have the appearance of a pleasant day which every one in camp will enjoy even to our horses and mules & niggers.

The Regiment is down on the Kentucky River and it is reported here that our forces are across the river and are occupying Danville again. I said to you in my last* that we had a mule team and ambulance captured but they have turned up after driving 84 miles in two days in circuitous route to get around the rebels.

It is much pleasanter here than it was last winter because there are but few troops here and we have not so much trouble in procuring Forage & wood and we have a clean sody piece of ground for a camp & close to town.

I received your letter yesterday and Smith got one from Ben and they were pleased to hear from him and I hope he will appreciate our kindness and be a good boy and try and make a man of himself ~

War matters do not look quite so warm as they did a day or two since. The guards in the City picked up a Rebel Maj last night in town and found 4000$ confederate money upon his person.

They are constructing a fine <u>forte</u> on the west side of town as much as to say you come to Lexington and compel us to go into it and we will shell and burn the town, and leave the ashes for you.

I wish I had some news to write that would interest you more than war news ~

I saw some very nice rings for children yesterday when I was in town and maybe I will purchase 3 of them, and send them to them as soon as they learn to write.

Gen Burnside has not arrive{d} here yet but is expected hourly when the inhabitants expect some change in the Military about here.

I would enjoy your company very much such a day as to day very much and I hope something may turn up this Spring to bring it to a close so we can be together. I look upon my visit home as one of the pleasantest weeks of my life and am in hopes we can enjoy many more such soon.

L_____ <u>them</u> <u>little</u> <u>gal</u> <u>for</u> <u>me</u> & kiss the children & one <u>huge</u> <u>embrace</u> to yourself.

Your affect
Wm

*This letter was not found.

Lexington K.Y. Mar 29 "Sunday"

My Dear,

I am here yet. We were disappointed in getting horses the other night and I remain here until they are to be had. The teams went as ordered to the Kentucky river yesterday morning all but a few men left here to lead horses. I shall probibly be here a day or two yet waiting for the purchase of horses.

Some of the old troops of Bur{n}side has arrived here and more are coming so I think the rebels will be sorely disappointed about coming into Kentucky this summer.

Say to the young man that I saw a saddle to suit him which I will buy if he will try and learn to read & spell & be a good boy, which I know he will.

{Letter ends here.}

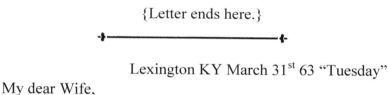

Lexington KY March 31st 63 "Tuesday"

My dear Wife,

Yours come to hand making great complaint about my saying that I choose to remain in the service or something else,*   It is us{e}less to explain to you the desire I have for this war to come to a close and this pleasure of being with my family but when you consider that my greatest aim I have is the comfort of my family in {the} future, and the folly of fretting while I am in a measure compelled to remain or ask for a resignation to be accepted which my pride would restrain me from doing as long as I have my health ~

You have money enough in the Box. You will find some 100$ bills, use one if necessary and have Ben look around for hay for you. I have Deposited in the Northern Bank of KY about a thousand Dollars and I am in hopes of increasing the pile some more. I simply think you do me injustice in finding fault with me. Let the bridge remain as it is and if you require it get Jim Hamilton or Saul Clock to pasture the cows or horses rather than have any anxiety about it.

Let me know whether you <u>receive</u> this <u>letter</u>. I saw about 400 negroes at work on the Fort yesterday. I have been in camp all of the time until they moved from here. Since then have been at the Hotel.

I shall probibly remain here a day or two yet.

Kiss Pussy & spank Julia for abusing her so bad -

Your Affect{ionate}

Wm

* William is probably referring to Julia's of "Thursday 12."

Monroeville April 3rd Friday {1863}

Dear William,

I received three letters last evening one written the 30* one the 31st and one the 1 of April* which came through quicker than any I have ever got and it seems as if they might all get through as soon. One of them was the one that you wished me to let you know whether you I rec'd it. You are mistaken when you think I am fault finding for I am not but I am to{o} <u>jealous</u> of all of your love and good feeling to have you say you are better satisfied in the army than out of it for it certainly keeps you from our family. Now I know all the <u>IFS</u> and <u>buts,</u> all the <u>advantages,</u> and <u>considerations,</u> and I feel that we have been separated two, or nearly two, years of the best of our lives, and some days it seems as if I could not live and be separated any longer, and {it} was just one of <u>those</u> <u>days</u> that I got your letter, and it made me feel very bad, for I think the term of the war is all very uncertain, although things look brighter, and it will certainly be necessary to keep the army mooving a long time yet. I am very glad you had the pleasure of meeting Gen. B and when you come home again, you can tell me all about what he said, and what you said. I suppose you will go back to Danville and Harrodsburg that is the regiment seem{s} to be mooving in that direction. I was sorry to have you leave Lexington and go farther from home. I feel anxious to know what Burnside is going to do and hope you will write very often for I have no other means of knowing. I dont see any papers. Will Brown met me on the street last night when I was going to the PO. He said I ought to have brought a wheel barrow to take up my mail. I went accross to Bennetts to see about some hay and said to him I had just got three letters from you. He streched himself and said "I golly he must like to write better than I do." Wednesday you know was the first of April, well Ben declared he would not be fooled but he had a great deal of fun fooling the children and tried Caroline but he could not fool her. He tried to think up something to fool me with but could not so I thought I could help the girls. I folded a sheet of paper and had Caroline write on it April fool and put it in an envelope, then I took a postage stamp off of one of your letters with the Lexington stamp on it and put it on & got Caroline to direct it. I went to the office that evening and got two letters from you, and this one for him brought home & gave it to him, he looked at it a good while, but when he saw it post marked Lexington and he was expecting one from Emma Moore, so he finally opened it. He stood with his back toward me. Pretty soon I saw his shoulders begin to jerk & then I saw his mouth begin to open away behind his ears & then a yak, yak, succeeded, then convulsions. We had an addition to our family this morning. Peggy has twelve smart pigs and we are looking for another lot soon. Ben wants to know whether you will bring his violin or if I shall get one here. Tell him you will get him one. Betty says the horse you call Pussy is hers. I think you will have quite a stud of horses.

A few nights ago I was invited to a surprise party at Homer Clary's by Mrs. Cone. There was seventeen went over in a four horse waggon. Mrs. Hamilton & husband, Mrs. Fish, Taylor, Hellen Scouton, Walt Smith's wife & cousin Margot, Mary Ann Morrison, Mrs. Dwight, Thalay Hathaway & brother, Mrs. George Clary & C. _____. Mr. Hildreth of Sandusky addresses the Union club. I wish you were here to go with me. I feel your absence more and more every day. Yours affectionately, Julia

I saw Darwin a few moments this morning at the cars. He came for Jimy. Frank Goodnow took dinner here. I gave him fritters and honey and wished you were here to have some.

Yours affectionately,

Julia

*Letters dated Mar. 27, 29, 31st but no letters dated "30th" or "April 1" from William were found.

+———————————+

Lexington, KY Apr 5 {1863} Sunday Morning

My Dear Wife,

I am remaining at the Phoenix Hotel yet but shall take to my tent as soon as the regiment comes here on Tuesday. I visited Ashland again yesterday. It is a lovely spot but everything about it looks dilapidated and is going to ruin since the ungrateful son and unprincipled wretch deserted it and joined the rebel army to fight against a government his father loved so much.

His monument stands in full view of the sacred spot about one mile and 1/2 distant and on a tablet within the valt you find inscribed this pure patriotic and unselfish sentiment -

I can with unshaken confidence appeal to the divine arbiter for the truth of this declaration, that I have been influenced by no impure purpose, no personal motive, have sought no personal aggrandizement, but that in all my public acts I have had a sole and single eye and a warm and devoted heart directed and dedicated to what in my best judgment I believe to be the true interests of my country.

Enclosed is a sprig of evergreen from Ashland -

I have no news to write. I would like to be at home to day. Kiss all of them

Your affect {ionate}
Wm

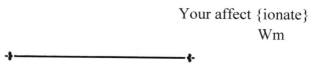

Monroeville Apr 12th 1863

Dear Friend,

I presume you are anxious to hear from the children. They are all well. Lillian calls me mother. She got provoked at her Uncle Bronson yesterday because he told her that that dirty child had not washed herself yet. He told he did not get provoked when she told him that - she said he was not a little girl. that pleased Mr. Bronson very much. I think it was smart. she wanted me to tell you to bring her a Doll.

Your Brother was over yesterday and measured off the land for you. it is just the other side of the piece you had last year. he said Mr. Whaley wants to put small grain in the piece you had. I asked him how soon he expected to go East. He said he did not know for he was waiting for to see if goods where not going to be cheaper. I gave him the sample.

Col. Paramore came home last evening. He is going to deliver a speech at the Hall Tuesday evening. I am going to try and go. Caroline went Friday evening. The Dime Society is postponed until Thursday evening. Birdie and I went to church this afternoon. The girls did not want to go. It rained this morning so that we did not go out. We had a very hard thunder storm last evening unusualy so for this time of year.

I hope you are having a plesant visit. I am geting along nicely with the children. They are very good. Dora is one of the best boy{s} ever was. I told him I would tell you so he wants you to bring him a boat. Ben and Caroline have not had any more trouble. Charlie was not here all day yesterday.

All the children send their love to you and there Father. Much love from me.

Yours in haste
Cordelia

P.S. since writing my letter Ben come in and wished me to tell Mr. Jackson that instead of geting him a violin he would rather have a Coat-

(Letterhead)
Head Quarters Third Division,
Army of Kentucky

May 6th 1863

My Dear Wife,

I arrived here last evening and shall possibly return to Monticello KY in a day or two.

Capt. Van Ness said to me again last night that he was agoing to have me ordered to report to him for duty. I asked him where he was agoing to put me and he said at the hardest spot he could find and then qualified it by saying at the place where there was the most to be done.

I{t} looks to me as if there was to be a move in the direction of Knoxville. We have full possession to within about 85 miles now.

I was with Carter last Friday and we chased about 2500 Rebels 9 miles and killed about 20 and there was only one of our force killed. The bugler of Co. L was shot just as they entered town.[13]

It is a destitute looking place at Monticello and even the secesh were glad to see us drive them out - I find that riding agrees with me for I have done some hard riding for a few days past -

I am satisfied that I am agoing to remain in this state, but would be better satisfied to have the thing closed up this spring -

I shall not possibly hear from you for a day or two or until I get back to the regiment -

Remember me to my friends and kiss every baby for me.

There is a Hop as you will see by the enclosed at the Phoenix tonight but I shall not attend inasmuch as I have no good Dry Goods here -

Your affect {ionate} husband
Wm R. Jackson

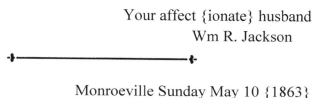

Monroeville Sunday May 10 {1863}

Dear William,

The day has been a fine one. I crawled over to Church this afternoon. The Church was full all day. Mr. Weed has gone East and the <u>Pisterians</u>* all seem to patronize our Church and I think quite as willing to be friendly as we. I took a pill of quinine Friday and had no chill yesterday but am so debilitated I can hardly keep around. I think I shall have to get something to strengthen me. I do wish you could get settled, I dont know as there is anything you can do to hurry up matters but if there is I wish you would do it. Your last letter was from Wednesday till Saturday getting here. I should like to have gone to the dance with you for I am afraid I shall forget how. Will the camp move to Monticello. I don't like to think of your going any farther and I hope if you change positions you will be so situated that I and a part of the children at least, can be with you this winter, if the war does not close up so as you can come home. There is most

Glorious news and it seems to be confirmed this morning by a dispatch from Rucker to John Gardner that our troops have possession of Richmond and God Grant that it is so. I told Calligan that I would give thanks all day and dance all night if I only had a chance (I dont mean to night) and if it is so there is Glory enough for the gallant men who have done it and oh how I would like to have been where I could have heard their cheers when they took the Confederate Capitol. Louisa is making kind of a general visit. She came over with Father and called at Phillips Friday then she came on here, and he went and got the carriage and drove to the big gate and waited for her. I have got so I care nothing about the way he acts, but the family will probably have a chance to see it one way or the other. The ... {writing smeared here} trees are all in full blossom and what there is left of the Peach trees. I hope you have got the box and have made your Sunday dinner on a part of it. How do you get along with your papers? I think you must be about through by this time. I am so in hopes then you will get a furlough to stay with us awhile. Ben ploughed Caroline's garden yesterday so I think she will have to go next week and I don't know what I am to do. I had a good Irish girl engaged but as a matter of course was cheated out of her. I am looking all the while for one but the fates seem against me. Louisa is going up to Toledo this week. Calligan said he heard every man there was drunk this morning that they celebrated all night. Old Corwin just came up and said they were having a time in Cleveland. I tell you I wouldn't blame any boy, man, woman, or child, for having a regular good time. I feel as if I wanted to take Dora's "Old Flag" and go on the top of the house and stand and hold it till the time of rejoicing was over and I shall certainly illuminate the house if they celebrate here. Come home and help me do and if they have a time in Lexington send for me and I will come on my head if I cant any other way.

Has Hall got back yet and how are all your staff? How did the orderly of Co. K find his family? The Children have all gone to

Sundy School Betty with the rest. She does want to see her Papa real bad.

Theodore went to NY Friday. Write often.

With much love Julia

*No doubt Julia was using one of the children's word for Presbyterians.

Camp Near Somerset K.Y.

My <u>Birth Day</u> May 14th 1863

My Dear Wife Julia,

Your short letter come to hand this evening saying that you was sick. I am sorry and can only say I am in hopes you will get over the chills soon. I judge from your letter that you had not heard that we like <u>Hooker</u> had recrossed the river again not because we were compelled to by the power of the enemy but for the want of supplies- We are remaining quietly in camp 6 miles from the river and have our pickets on the river and along it for 70 or 80 miles ~

Gen. Carter is in command of all the forces in and about here. He can concentrate 30,000 men in 36 hours. The enemy is reported in strong force on the other side of the river but I have the audacity to believe that we could drive them away from their position on double quick if we were prepared to cross the river again.

It is almost equal to Hamburg and Corinth about here on the living, there is nothing to buy that is eatable, no hotels and generaly a country almost as poor as Corinth.

We are enjoying the danties you sent me. How often I wish that I could be at home to enjoy some good meals with you and the children. I want to see them very much and I would give you the kiss you spoke of were I within reach. I expect to sell another

Horse in a day or two for 130$ then I have another to sell at 100$~ and then I must buy myself another.

I telegraphed to Van Ness to day that I was ready to report to him at any time now and I anticipate that he may send me to Stanford. I assure you {I} have no desire to go any farther than I am toward Tennessee. Your orderly has returned. Some of them remarked that they wished you could stay about Headquarters to urge their claims for a leave of absence.

Mrs. Garrard told him to say to you that she envied you your stay with the Regiment.

My staff is generly well and my Chief of Staff Cain has not drank a drop of liquor since I put him in jail at Harrodsburg last winter and is generaly a good {man}-

I am taking about 3 drinks a day of 11 year old Burbon Whiskey and I think it agrees with me and as long as it does I shall try and get it to use.

Remember me to all our friends and write often and tell any and all of them to write to me. You probably understand what I mean about getting a 1000$ of the money deposited with Theodore to use in speculating. Say to him what I want it for. There are government Claims in abundance that can be purchased at a profit through this State. Dont send it until I am within reach of it. If Henry Bronson wants to take a trip down here let him come. About a week at this time would satisfy him.
~ Kiss my pet child and all the rest

Your affect{ionate} husb{and}
Wm R. Jackson

Send Father $10 more money

Monroeville Thursday 21st {May 1863}

William dear William,

I have just heard of the death of our good friend Sile. I cried my eyes almost out when I heard of it. I dont know any of the particulars. Doan sent up word by Ben and I saw Nickels and Anna in Cleveland yesterday and they told me they understood his remains were brought home last Monday. They also said his Father had heard from him only a few days before he got the dispatch that he was dead and the letter said he was well so the conclusion is that he was killed in scouting. I shall write to the old gentleman to find out all they know. I felt very much gratified to hear his remains had been sent to his old home and feel as if I would like to make a yearly pilgrimage to his grave and oh if he has only joined Charley* in Heaven. How glad he was to welcome him there and how complete their happiness must be where all is peace. The only two outside of our own family** that I felt an interest in have laid down their lives for their country and there is no death more honorable but how bad I feel to know that it is so, that I can no longer think or look for their return. There are many little kindnesses that will ever be fresh in my memory and I shall always remember Sile as one of our best friends. Do you remember the ball which he made Dora when he was in camp here and the morning he came up to say good bye. I gave him money to fill his canteen with molasses. You know we have the picture that he had taken for Charlie of himself. It is very much faded but I think we can have it copied. I will write you all about it when I learn the particulars. I went to Cleveland yesterday for half fare. There was a mass Union meeting. I went to get some things. I got me a pretty plain hat and a black silk sacque and parasol and one for each of the girls. I will write again tomorrow. It is so dark I cannot see.

With much love Julia

*Julia is referring to their first born son, Charles Benjamin.

**The other person outside of the family to which Julia refers is most likely Henry Terry.

Monroeville Friday 22nd {May 1863}

Dear William,

I wrote you yesterday and told you I would write again to day. It has been a most confusing day. Caroline has been washing and this afternoon all the schools have been in the woods & they have kept up a constant run to the house for a drink. I have been in search of a girl this afternoon & as a <u>matter of course</u> did not find one. Caroline starts this evening to Michigan to visit her mother in company with her brother, Dwight, the only one left out of the three. The two others died in the spring of sickness.* She will be back next week but not to stay. I don't know what I am to do for I am so miserable. I am troubled almost all the time with pain and weakness accross me. I had to stop at John Roby's and ask for a glass of ale before I felt as if I could get home this afternoon. Oh I do so hope you will get to Stanford or some place where you will be comfortably & permanently settled and then may be you can arrange to have your family with you. I feel to{o} blue and unwell to live alone. Ben has done quite well since I gave him the last scolding. I suppose there never was a worse scrape than the one he was coaxed into and I think it was <u>abominable</u> that such men as Calligan and John Bennet should countenance such things. We don't expect any thing better of Doan & Prentice. I tried to treat Doan civily when he first came back but "the dog has returned to his vomit again" and he is as bad if not worse than ever. Ben came in Monday noon and said he felt bad. He could not sleep the night before and I knew how bad he had been and he was ashamed to be where I was for he knew I was a nice woman. I had told him what to do and how to do and if he had only minded what I said he would have kept out of such trouble. He said Mr. Spears' folks had told him just what I had and he had been such a fool not to remember it. He did not want to see any of my folks for they would know it and they were all such good people. He said people in town did not speak to him as they used to. I told him that was his guilty conscience. He knew he had done wrong and felt as if every body else did. He said that night he started to come home and got part way and they called him back that there was as many as fifteen white men in it and if he had done what he saw some of them do, he would just want to die. He never saw the like he almost cried. I told him I was glad he felt bad and if he was sure he would behave himself I would try to help him out of it when any one spoke of it. Would Camp do well to come down to the regiment with a lot of hats. He wanted me to ask you. Charlie S. will go with the mare next week. Can't you come home soon? It is nearly nine weeks since you left & you thought you might be home much sooner. Write often. It takes your letters so long to get here.

Affectionately Julia

*Julia is referring to Caroline's other two brothers, Mat and John; see Persons Of Interest appendix for more on the Corwin brothers.

Somerset KY May 26th

Dear Jackson,

What number of mules shall I expect in April and May -"lost and died"? I have had to abandon our reports for the time being to assist in arranging the "ordinance" and to that end you can greatly aid me by calling on Lt. Ridenour Ordenance officer and procuring a receipt for ordinance turned over by Lt. Rich last December and also one for Ordenance turned over by Miner in April. Rich sent the former back to be corrected and Miners Receipt has been mislaid or lost.

I shall finish your papers by Saturday without fail. We did not feel much like work yesterday. Your departure had rather a gloomy affect on the Q. M. Department and we passed the afternoon in bathing, sleeping, lounging and moping like a brood of chickens without a parent's wing to shelter them from the storm. The only consolation we had was to sit on the cots with our pipes and discuss the happy hours we had passed in your employ. George returned to his smoking to drown sorrow and then started to town to drink some ale, returned sober, went to bed and slept till morning. Mac feels about as lonesome as ourselves.

There has nothing new occurred since you left. The Col. called Hall and myself into his tent to drink some of your whiskey and the Col. Proposed a toast to your health which was heartily drunk.

Write to me as soon as possible and oblige.

Your sincere friend,
C. T. Smith

P.S. Dont send your reports away until an error is corrected. The hundred blouses were receipted for by Norton and entered on the abstract and carried thru to date on Camp Garrison.

Belleville May 27th 1863

Dear Julia,

Father received your letter with the ten dollars. It could not have come any more acceptably for he was trying to raise money enough that day to go to Mansfield and pay his tax. It seem{ed} providential coming just at that time for it just helped him out of his trouble. He did not want to keep it for the purpose you wrote it was for, but after considerable talk on my part and Elizabeth's we persuaded him you and William would rather he would have it than not.

There has nothing been said to Mother about geting it or the letter as she is very weak and feeble. Dr. and Elizabeth* thought she would only worry about William and she had better not know about it. We are afraid Mother will not live through the spring. She is failing very fast.

Kitty is about the same. I suppose Mother wrote you she had a sore on her back. It has proved to be a lumbar abcess. It will probably run as long as she lives. It makes a great deal of trouble.

I was over to Mrs. Colley's yesterday. She is very low. I think she cannot last but a few days.

I am going up to Mansfield in about two weeks to sew for Jule** for a while and if I think I dare afford it, we will come up to Monroeville and visit. Julia want{ed} to go the last time I was there but I could not then for want of time. Since I was at your house a year ago I have made thirty one (31) shirts. What do you think of that? And that is not all the sewing I have done by a great sight. I could not tell you how many dresses. I have spent but little idle time. I am making myself two dresses one Elizabeth gave me. Ettie is in Mansfield taking music lesson{s} is getting along very rapidly her teacher says.

Give my love to all the children. I dreamed of Dora the other night. I thought he and Betsy Jane was here and were having a nice time.

You ought to let some of them come down. I wish you would drop in some day. We looked for you all last winter.

Accept my thanks for my present. It came like Father's just in the right time.

Excuse haste
Caroline

* Dr. and Elizabeth are William's sister and husband, Dr. Abijah Beach.
**Jule or Julia that Caroline refers to is her (and William's) sister.

Lexington May 27{1863}

My Dear Wife,

I have just arrived here from Somerset a distance of 80 miles over the dirtiest road I ever saw.

I received an order to report to the Chief Quartermaster at Lexington for duty- I don't know what it will be yet.

The mail comes in a very few moments so I will close and write again to morrow when I may know what {I} am agoing to do.

Your affect
Wm

Lexington Friday May 29 {1863}

Dear Julia,

I shall go to Nicholasville tomorrow or next day where I shall establish an office and commence operations. I am agoing to get 80 teams here to morrow, and send them on the road. I am flatered that I can make a nice comfortable business of it as soon as I can get my trains regulated. And as soon as I have that accomplished I expect to get an oportunity to run home a few days.

Captain Van Ness seems disposed to let me manage the whole thing as I think best - They have a police passing along the different roads whose business it is to arrest every Wagon Master who permits a teamster misuse or maltreat them or disobey instructions that they are to be governed by.

I am trying to get Smith with me, & should like Henry Bronson if he has any fear of the draft. I have some money I can spare you say about as much as I gave you when you returned from here - I am in hopes pay day is near at hand - I wish you would or could make some arrangement to have the two girls go to Sandusky and attend school I am so anxious to have them come out a little and have them far enough advanced to take music lessons -

I made another pretty good operation in horses to day ~

I want you to keep your eye well on Ben and the horses not to have him misuse them in any way. They are impressing all of the negroes about here to work driving teams and diging

We are having the 1st rain for many days. Corn is very backward all through the state -

I didn't expect to hear from you for a day or two because you have probibly sent my letters to Somerset. Direct them now to Nicholasville to Wm. R. Jackson A.A.Q.Master <u>No.</u> 7th <u>O.V.C.</u>

I seem to have some friends in this place and all of my staff looked sorry enough when I left there and expressed themselves so the Adjt General at Somerset tried hard to prevent having me detached to come here but I out generaled him -

What has Scouton done with the sorrel mare.

Remember me to every body that seems to care for me. Kiss all my babies and a bunch to my <u>big gal</u>.

Your affect{ionate},
Wm

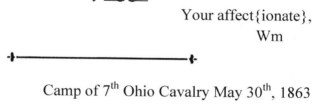

Camp of 7th Ohio Cavalry May 30th, 1863

Dear Jackson,

Turner (wagon master) is now out of a place by the reduction of the train. He does not wish to return to his Company E, and has asked to me to allow him to be detailed as Wagon Master in the post train in the employment of the Division Quarter Master. It occurred to me that you might want him. If you do you had better have the detail made.

Lt. Carr spoke to me as you requested him to do about Smith. I will be very glad to accommodate you when the business of the regiment is got into a condition that he can be spared. Whether he can be spared at all or not is a question that you are able to form an opinion about better than any one else.

I would be glad to hear from you about your present position, and what particular department you have charge of, how you like it so.

Very truly your friend
Israel Garrard

Lt. W.R. Jackson 7th O.V.C.
Q.M. Dept Lexington KY.

Let me know how to address you. Carr says that you are Captain and A.Q.M. Let me hear from you about the horse question as soon as possible.

Monroeville Ohio May 31st 1863

Wm. R. Jackson
Dear Sir,

Father wished me to answer your telegram, which was received last eve.

He directed me to say that he was so situated that he is unable to accept your kind offer for which he is very much obliged.

We have moved upon the farm and he has 8 or 10 men at work on the farm and house. The latter was very much out of repair and it required his whole attention to tend to it.

We are well, having very fine weather, rather dry until a day or two since when we have had several nice showers.

Old Sqr. Crippen died this P.M. and John Neill is very bad off he is hardly expected to recover his sickness is inflammatory Rheum.

Capt. Colver is here. He was severely hurt at Louisville, KY by the kick of a horse, had his jaw broke in two places.

Arthur Franklin was wounded in the late battle at Fredericksburg taken prisoner and has since died.

Capt. McClellan is at home.*

Capt. Scouton has been very low some time but is gaining now.

Daniel Clary died some time since.

Well I guess that this {is} enough to digest for one time.

Good eve.

Yours with Respect,
Will J. Brown

*Mr. Brown is probably talking about a local man, Thomas McClelland, rather than Gen. George B. McClellan.

Sullivan June 1st/63

Mrs. Jackson
Dear Madam,

I will answer your letter and inform you of the particulars of the sad accident that ended Silas' life. I will take an extract from Lieut. {Isbell's?} letter "On the morning of the 12th of May we were ordered out to drill-the drill was target practice. Everything went off in good order and all fired their carbines three or four times after we went closer to the target to fire off our revolvers where it came to the Sergeant's turn he went around again and taking aim his cap missed fire. He got into his place with ranks and while there with the rest of the men he made the remark "my revolver did not go off this time. I must put a new cap on to be ready to try again." While so doing he held his revolver with the muzzle towards his face turning the cylinder around to find the tube to put the cap on. His horse shook his head causing the cock to slip from his fingers and fall on the tube. The ball went in between his eyes entering the brain causing death instantly. It had been the wish of the Sergeant if he should die or get killed while in the army he hoped his body would be sent home therefore we complied with his wishes. At the time he was shot Lt. Newman was on his left he tried to hold him on his horse and before he fell his last and only words were "O God" and in ten seconds he expired. We gave a history of the deceased soldier's life to a historian from the date of his enlistment to the day of his death. He was a good and faithful soldier and we cannot speak too highly of him. Had he lived {he} would undoubtedly have been promoted (ere long). He was loved and respected by all who knew him." I have now given you the particulars in the Lieutenant's own words. His death was a hard blow to us all, especially to his Mother and I in our old age. We had hoped he would have been spared to return to us but God has {ink smeared here-*ordered or ordained*} it otherwise and therefore we will endeavor not to repine. He was the first of our ten children we have been called to follow to the grave. His body was expressed on the 13th and sended here on the 18th. He was buried on the afternoon of the 19th at two o'clock. He was buried with military honors. He lies sleeping in my orchard - a beautiful place where my family will be interred. There was between 5 and 6 hundred people at his funeral. The text was in the 4th chapter of James 14th verse. "Too what is your life" It is a great consolation to have his remains brought home and have a decent burial. I would be very happy to have you visit us. I would be happy to hear from you often.

I remain yours truly,
Amos Gould

This letter was badly smeared in places. Written across the top of page three as a postscript: Silas had a long disk knife that your little Charley gave him. It is in my possession now. He prized it highly.

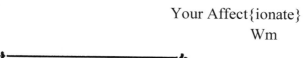

Lexington June 2nd/63

My dear Wife,

I received your letter of the 22nd May also one enclosing the sketch of Jno Morgan. I am anxious to learn what was the matter with Silas whose death I morn very much.

I shall go to Nicholasville to day and expect to remain there.

I telegraphed to Jno Brown asking him to come and help me just to act as Master of Transportation and look after things but have not heard from him.

I turned out 75 teams from here yesterday and shall send 25 more to day - There was one Maj. General and 5 Brigadeers here yesterday and it was not a very good day for officers either -

Hickman Bridge is to be the general headquarters instead of Cint.

Did you receive my letter enclosing a certificate of entry for 160 acres of land that I sent you from Somerset?

Kiss <u>pet</u> <u>child</u> and say to Fannie that I got her letter and was very glad to hear she was attending school - Remember me to all of the children & all my friends & an effectionate embrace for yourself ~

Your Affect{ionate}
Wm

Lexington June 6th/63

My dear Julia,

You may be somewhat surprised when I inform you that I am ordered to Stanford to relieve the Post Q Master there. It is almost or quite equal to the Post in this place. They have given me a great deal more than I can possibly attend to but I shall go in and try and come out O.K. I will have to receive and issue all the supplies for almost the entire army left in K.Y. besides controlling about 350 to 400 teams and from 2000 to 2500 horses & mules that have been turned in by the Army south of Stanford - I got a detail to day for Smith Ross & Cain and as it now is I shall be compelled to keep six or 8 clerks at least. Captain Van Ness said to me to day that if I would get a letter from the Col he would recommend my promotion to a regular A.Q.M. Maj Mcdowell is here paying off our troops. What would you think of sending the girls to Mansfield to school and to take music lessons there and board with Julia*. Have you ever received the warrant for the land 157 3/4 acres. I think H____ will return here.

Burnsides Army Corps is leaving here as we supposed for Vixburgh

Your Affect{ionate}
Wm

*William is probably referring to his sister, Julia, who lived in Mansfield.

Somerset KY Sunday a.m. June 7th 1863

Friend Jackson,

I send you by Jim Kain the reports of March, April and May, complete except your signature. I waited a few days to hear from you in reference to the disposal of mules and concluded to take the responsibility and expend them as I deemed necessary.

I presume you had ere this received my letter in reference to the (100) Blouses, they were not erased from Norton's requisition and therefore copied in abstract M and no. 51, Clothing, Camp Garrison in the Dec. Report, and following to Feby. included. March, April, and May are "correct".

There is nothing new in this vicinity. We are surrounded by stagnation a prison in any civilized country would be preferable to this. Hall is keeping matters as straight as he knows how. The principal labour falls on the subscriber.

Lt. Carr brought a message to the Col. from you in reference to me but I have heard nothing in reference to it, except a remark from Allen who informed me that I had better remain here as something better might turn up. I imagine the something so far in perspective will never approach. "while the grass grows" the horse starved" {*sic*}

I shall be pleased to hear from you if time is not too precious with you.

Truly your friend,
C. T. Smith

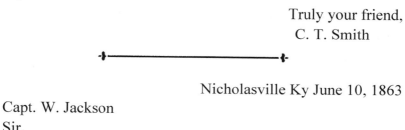

Nicholasville Ky June 10, 1863

Capt. W. Jackson
Sir,

The enclosed line in my behalf from Capt. H_____ I hoped to have delivered to you in person.

I have had the pleasure of seeing you in Ripley & have to thank you for the very great kindness extended to my wife & sick son in April last.

If you can find an opening for me in this department a line from you to the care of Capt. H_____ A.Q.M. will reach me.

I am Respectfully
W. Johnston

Cincinnati O June 11, 1863

Capt. Jackson, A.Q.M.
Nicholasville, Ky
Dear Sir,

I left at your office a letter of Introduction from Capt F. W. H_____ of this city.

Up to this first of this month I have been Inspector of Troops to his Department & am now thrown out of business owing to the fact that the forage department has been taken out of the hands of Capt H_____ & given to a Capt. McClung.

I visited your office to see if you could give me a situation or help me to one either in your office or in Lexington. I sold out my business in Ripley soon after the commencement of the war & this is not the time to commence anew.

If you can secure me a situation in your office or in some other you will confer a verry great favour.

My son has sufficiently recovered to join his Regiment at Somerset & is now pretty well.

With the hope of hearing from you on this subject soon

I am your obl{iging} ser{van}t.

W. Johnston

Care Capt. F.W _____ A.Q.M. Cin ~

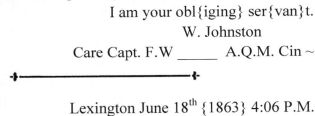

Lexington June 18th {1863} 4:06 P.M.

My Dear Wife,

I am about leaving for Stanford to return the property received by Capt. Earnest. I requested to be relieved of either 200 trains I have or of the post and it was my choice to leave the Post and be with the trains. I only have to organize a regular train of wagons from Hickman or Kentucky river to Stanford and haul forage only. As soon as I get the thing running I will have but little to do myself and by that means be in and around headquarters which will enable me to know and be known there.

Everything is to be move...{letter torn here}...Lexington & Nicholasville ....Stanford to Kentucky River...that is to be the main Depot for every thing hereafter.

You remember it is 6 miles south of Nicholasville. Direct my mail until you hear from me again to Nicholasville. I shall be at Stanford only a day or two -

Your Affect{ionate}

Wm

This letter was torn in places making it difficult to read.

Monroeville Sunday 21st {June 1863}

Dear William,

I sit down again as usual this afternoon to write in the midst of confusion and feeling very blue and much discontented at our present way of living. It has been four weeks since I have had help. I have had to be on my feet almost constantly ~~on my feet~~ whether I was sick or well, and I do feel as if I could not stand it any longer. I dont want you to think that I want you to leave your situation but I do think you ought to come home as soon as you can possibly leave and make some different arrangements for me. You will probably find employment in KY for some time to come and that will be profitable, and there is no chance here. So I feel as if all the stock on the place might be sold off say one cow and all the hogs and it would cost no more to send Ben to where you are with the two horses than it will to buy hay & corn for them till fall here and then they can winter there for nothing. That would dispose of every thing but one cow and Major. I think I could get old Mrs. Hollis to come & stay in the kitchen to see that the place was not injured, and I think you could get board for us, I mean all of the children. Two rooms would do. I know it would be expensive but if you only laid up fifty dollars a month it would be better than you could do here and I could be relieved of the care, anxiety and work that I have had so long and we could be together. There has more than one told me lately that they could see it was wearing on me and I know it too. I wish you would try and see what you could do. If the Hotel is possible, I would rather go there than a private house on many accounts, but you must act as you think best about that. The children need you and your government, advice and council, for you must know it has been a great charge on me the entire control of the five as well as the management of every thing else. Perhaps you will think that I write a good deal in ernest but I tell you I feel so and have been feeling in the same way for many weeks and have only been waiting for you to get settled to write it too you.

The Rebels are about as near us as you. they have come into Pennsylvania. I hope our army will bag them before they can get back. You ask about Ben's scrape I think I wrote to you about it in one of my letters. It was soon after I came from Lexington. There was an awful creature came to the red grocery and a lot of white men got Ben and Banty's nigger after her. They were out till nearly day light and then came and laid in the barn and had her in the woods between here and the R Road nearly all day Sunday. I did not know where he was but the next day gave him an awful scolding & he was saucy but I settled him. I had told him to be in by ten o'clock and he did not come at all. In about a week after I heard of the scrape I did give him one lathing to & he told me all about it. I think the men were more to blame than he was. I dont want him any longer than I can help. I dont like him. He has no manners and thinks he can speak to me as if I was his equal. Zahm's nigger was here again to dinner and Ben said "give me some milk or something to drink". I said If you please. He said "I did not say so to him nor the children did not". I told him it was not my place to & I had never had any one to work for me that spoke so disrespectfully. Zahm's man told him it was not right. But that is just the principle he goes on. Judy has just come to me to have me ask you if you wont be home by the fourth of July. We shall all look for you then. Birdie says she thinks you might come. Fannie wants you to answer her letters. I told Betty that I was going to the Office to put in a letter for papa. She said "tell him I want him to come home and kiss his pet kittens for I've waited long enough." She got out of patience the other day and stamped her foot and said "Mama I wish to the Lord that you would give me a needle". You dont write to me as often as you need to. One of your letters was written on the 11th and the next on the 17th.* I wish you would write every day. There was a little boy mashed all to pieces Friday on the rail road by the crossing by the name Jr Brady. There is a school picnic this week. They go to Huron. The children dont want to go & I am glad. The Drs. think Mary Chapin can live but little while. Think <u>hard</u> of what I have written and answer very soon.

Your lonesome old girl Julia

*Neither of these letters from William was in the collection.

Lexington June 22nd/63 Monday 6 O.C. <u>AM</u>

My dear Wife,

I have just returned from Stanford and have turned over the stuff there to Capt Earnest the person from whom I received it -

I now have 350 teams to supply Gen Carter's Army with forage and my headquarters are now at Nicholasville but will be at the River as soon as arrangements can be made there. Capt Simpson seemed to regret my leaving Stanford but I cannot say that I did - It has been quite cool here nights and mornings for a day or two past. I shall return to Nicholasville to day again. I am here to get money to pay some teamsters who are very much in kneed of their pay.

The troops about Somerset are most of them starting on an expedition believed to be toward Tenn -

Remember me to my nice little family & kiss all of them

Your Affect{ionate}Wm

Chapter Three Notes

1.   "…and the Executive Government of the United States, including the military and naval authority thereof, will recognize and maintain the freedom of such persons, and will do no act or acts to repress such persons, or any of them, in any efforts they may make for their actual freedom." (From the Emancipation Proclamation)

2. Sandburg, Carl, *Abraham Lincoln*, Ch. 34, pp. 8-28.

3. Catton, *Never Call Retreat, the Centennial History of the Civil War.* Garden City, NY: Doubleday and Company, Inc., 1965, p. 38.

4. Ibid., pp. 35-47. Also, for more about the "Slaughter Pen" or The Battle of Stones River, see www.civilwar.org/battlefields (accessed October 2014).

5. Carter's raid into East Tennessee: see Rankin (pp 4-7) and *"Carter's Raid and Its Results,"* ww.nytimes.com/1863/01/08/news (accessed October 2014).

6.   About the Battle of Stones River (Murfreesboro, Tennessee): there were several articles in at least three issues of the weekly *Norwalk Experiment* (January 22, February 5 and 13, 1863) about the deaths of Col. Leander Stem, Lt. Col. Moses F. Wooster and 1st Lt. Asa R. Hillyer, of the 101st Ohio Volunteer Infantry (O.V.I.). Also, Henry Terry of the 24th O.V.I., listed as Lt. Col. in one article and as Major in another, was among those reported killed.

7. For more about Burnside's appointments (and disappointments), see: www.history.com/topics/american-civil-

war/ambrose-everett-burnside (accessed October 2014) and Reeder, *The Northern Generals*, pp. 68-70 and 174-75.

8. For more on Vallandigham and Burnside's Order #38, see: Catton, *Never Call Retreat, pp. 171-75.* Also *www.ohiohistorycentral.org*/w/General_Order_No._38 (accessed October 2014).

9. Sherman's letter (June 2, 1863) to Grant*: O.R. Series III, Vol. 3 Union Correspondence, etc.* pp. 386-88.

10. Julia was probably referring to her sister-in-law, Mary Goodnow, Theodore's wife.

11. See note six above.

12. The Oath of Allegiance to which William was referring was a document signed by persons during and after the war to show their allegiance to the Union. See *Glossary* for more information.

13. About Carter's April 30 (or May 1)1863 raid, William wrote "one of the 7th O.V.C. was killed;" Carter's dispatch mentioned in the *O.R., Series I, Vol. 23, Ch. 35,* p. 304, said "no loss on our side, except one man supposed to be captured."

Chapter Four

Camp Nelson and Fear Filled Times on the Home Front
July - September 1863

"...wish that I could feel that I should be with you before many days."
Julia Jackson, August 9, 1863

The small town of Gettysburg, Pennsylvania was waking up to a day that would change their town and the history of this war forever at the time William wrote the first letter in this chapter, after his breakfast "July 1st 6 ½ o'clock." General Lee's Confederate troops and Federal troops commanded by General George Gordon Meade were about to converge in southeast Pennsylvania and begin the three days of fighting that have become the most famous of all the crucial battles of the War of the Rebellion. The name Gettysburg, "the turning point of the war," and the "bloodiest three days of fighting" are words that even non-scholars of the Civil War know about this particular well-known town-turned-battlefield, now a National Military Park. William was just settling into his new job at Camp Nelson, a newly built Army depot in southeastern Kentucky, but he let Julia know he is aware of the news in other states: "I am greatly in hopes that they will get Lee snarled up in Pa." The war had crossed over into "Yankee" territory and those in surrounding Northern states were showing concern.

In the same letter of July 1, William describes the setting at his new assignment at Camp Nelson and writes, "this Camp is a mammoth affair." He tells of his "managing a pretty big affair" (as Acting Assistant Quartermaster or A.A.Q.M.) and also of his spot "among the Cedars." In subsequent letters from Camp Nelson, William mentions the victories in Pennsylvania "which if well followed up must break the back bone of the rebellion" and also of "the fall of Vixburg" where Grant had been relentless in purging the Mississippi Valley of any rebel presence.

From where William sat in Camp Nelson, however, a more immediate concern continued to be from the ever elusive "Jno Morgan," who William mentions in several letters. William writes Julia in the first letter of this section, "I would not be surprised that we were stired up here in Kentucky before many weeks but I hope not." Later, in his letter of July 5, he writes that "Morgan is at Lebanon..." (Kentucky).

Kentucky, the state that tried to stay neutral but was reported to be mainly Union in sentiment, was just a stepping stone for Morgan and "about 3500 men" as they worked their way north; William also included a map of "the situation at Lebinin" in this letter.[1] General Braxton Bragg had sent Morgan into Kentucky but specifically ordered him *not to cross the Ohio River*. Rankin's history of the Seventh O.V.C states, "great credit is due to the colored people for the information they gave" that was instrumental in helping the Seventh O.V.C. capture Morgan and many of his men. Fewer than 400 of Morgan's rebels made it back to the Confederacy, most of his troops, including Morgan's own brother-in-law, Basil Duke, having been captured and imprisoned in Ohio penitentiaries. Although much has been written of this most famous of Morgan's raids, there are conflicting stories as to what benefits, if any, the Confederacy received as a result of his venture into Northern states.[2]

William's descriptions of Camp Nelson, named after Major General William Nelson, were accurate; covering 4000 acres it *was* a "mammoth affair!" Located between the Kentucky River and Hickman Creek, it had approximately 300 buildings and included anything associated with a quartermaster depot, recruitment center, and hospital. This very important supply depot for the Federal armies in Kentucky and eastern Tennessee also housed The Adams Express Post Office[3] from which William and others sent their letters home. This large "camp" also housed a bakery that was reported to have baked 10,000 rations of bread per day. The defense of this garrison was essential; the supplies and the quartermasters that managed them were a critical part of the support for several of the offensive campaigns such as Burnside's 1863 "Knoxville campaign" and Burbridge and Stoneman's Southwest Virginia Campaigns of 1864.

Located about thirty miles southeast of Lexington and only six miles from Nicholasville, Camp Nelson is probably best known as being the largest recruitment and training center for African-American troops or "colored troops" (United States Colored Troops or U.S.C.T.) in Kentucky and the third largest center of its kind in the U.S. As more and more Negro men attempted to join the eight new Negro regiments forming at Camp Nelson, so too did their families, along with other runaways, try to find sanctuary there. This camp/depot was also a refuge for Southern Appalachian poor whites that had nowhere to go after their homes were ravaged by the war that had come to their small farms. Unfortunately, many of those families, black and white, who sought refuge at Camp Nelson, were "removed" when the Camp found itself overwhelmed with the number of people and unable to feed or house them all. Sadly, many of these refugees died as they tried to make it to Nicholasville or Lexington during the severe winter of 1864.[4]

There is only one letter in this chapter written by someone other than Julia or William. William's sister, Sarah, in her brief letter to Julia, mentions another sister, Elizabeth, who "has returned from the East" and "was in the midst of the riot." Sarah may have been referring to the three days of rioting in New York City. An organized crowd, reacting violently to Lincoln's newly enacted "Conscription" or "Enrollment" Act, began in New York City attacking first the Superintendent of Police and eventually working their way through the city. Estimates of anywhere from one and one half million to five million dollars in property damages (depending on the source) were incurred and an unknown number of people, mainly of African descent, were dead. Some weeks later, at least 10,000 troops from the Army of the Potomac were sent to restore order there. Other cities such as Boston and Baltimore also saw violence after the Enrollment Act became official; however, New York City suffered the most in property damage and in numbers of people injured or killed. The draft continued to be controversial all over the North but according to several sources, Ohio exceeded the number of recruits requested and reportedly contributed closer to 330,000 men who served for various terms during the Civil War.[5]

There are only five letters from Julia in this section and she only briefly mentions any fear about Morgan and his move into the North. Her main concerns remain with the children, one of whom is sick for days, and having enough food for them. With the exception of one letter, all of Julia's in this chapter are written in August and all speak of new fears for their safety. From strangers who "very much frightened" the children to "the same miserable set in town," she exclaims that she "would as leave be within sight of the rebels, and feel that I had some one to protect me, yes rather." She continues to implore William to send for them and in each letter writes in this vein "…I have never felt so timid and really afraid as I do now." (August 9)

In three of his letters in this chapter, William again mentions General Burnside, "the Ninth Army corps," and "preparing for east Tennessee." Burnside was at Camp Nelson for less than a week, but William seemed impressed with him and on August 14 wrote, "every thing is on the move here day and night preparing for a move upon Knoxville." William writes home often in July and seems to especially love to tell of his horses or those in his charge!

Apparently after helping to supply the troops for the invasion upon East Tennessee, William made a brief visit home and then does "conclude some arrangement" to have Julia and the family with him as there are no other letters for the remainder of 1863. In the last letter of 1863, the angriest yet from Julia, she writes mainly about an incident with Ben. It appears that Ben was possibly a runaway slave, one of many who'd sought sanctuary with a Union regiment. After this letter dated "Sunday 27," Ben is never mentioned again and without his last name, it is almost impossible to learn what happened to him after Julia and the children left for Kentucky.

———————————————

Camp Nelson KY July 1st {1863}

My dear Wife,

I got my breakfast at the river and saddled the finest and best riding mare in Kentucky and am here at headquarters at 6 1/2 O Clock. My responsibility <u>seems</u> so great because I am in charge of the post during the absence of Cap Morris being the ranking Q Master here. It does not increase my labors materially only that I have to assume the <u>dignifyed</u> a <u>little</u> <u>more</u>. This camp is a mammoth affair. They have constructed buildings and warehouses enough to make a good sized village & there is an innumerable amount of workman troops and teams and teamsters and Negroes ~

I have all of my little ranch at the river 1 1/2 miles from here. My tent is pleasantly situated about 100 feet above the river and on this side directly oposite of the cliff you admired so much on the other side at the end of the bridge ~ I am getting my teams in good working order so that I can accomplish the duty assigned to me promptly and with very little confusion. I send out 100 teams per day and keep 10,000 horses and mules supplied with forage. If they will only let me alone and continue at that duty I can eventually make it very easy ~

My friends at home may look upon it as managing a pretty big affair being the only head and front of the whole thing say 400 teamsters, 325 teams or 1600 head of mules, 50 horses and a blacksmith's sadlers & wagon shop ~ but I seem to have complete control of the men and have but little trouble with them. I keep Jim with me and I have 14 very good wagon-masters & their assistants. I stay in my tent nights and take my meals at a house at the other end of the bridge. <u>They live</u> <u>tolerable</u> for K.Y. but their sleeping did not suit me as well. I prefer the old bed and the pleasant spot I have among the Cedars.

I would not be surprised that we were stired up here in Kentucky before many weeks but I hope not. I am greatly in hopes that they will get Lee <u>snarled</u> <u>up</u> in Pa and that some good may result from his adventure on our side ~ We only have about 12,000 to 15,000 men in this part of KY a force that I fear is not sufficient to hold KY beyond a contingency ~

If Gen Mead fails in accomplishing something against Lee Lincoln's administration is <u>gone</u> <u>up</u> sure owing to the disaffection in the north ~ and the clamor to reinstate Gen. McClelan ~~

I am inclined to look upon the move of the Democrats not so much as an opposition to the war as a decided opposition to the administration and to his manner of conducting the war, a part of which may be justafiable but rather <u>imprudent</u> at the present <u>crisis</u>.

I see Frank LeBland is one of the committee to wait upon Lincoln asking the release of Valandingham~

Remember me to all my friends & kiss my pet children for me and a hundred for my loving wife.

Your affect{ionate}
Wm

My health remains very good

Camp Nelson 11.O.C. PM
Sunday July 5th 1863

My dear Wife,

Some excitement here to night. Morgan is at Lebanon with about 3500 men and report{s} say Wolford {with} the 7th & 2nd Ohio are in behind them and commenced fighting with them at day light this morning and the 8th Mich & 9th Mich & a full batery of artilery advanced from Danville this a.m. and reach{ed} Lebanon by 10 O.C. this a.m. and the 44 & 45 Ohio & 112 Ill{inois} Mounted infantry will reach them in the night to night & possibly conclude the fight by bag{g}ing Morgan and his party.

The situation of Lebinon is as marked out

The{y} brought ten prisoners her{e} just now from Somerset of Morgan's men.

It is time I went to bed so good night.

Your affect{ionate},

Wm

(The first page of the original letter is included on the next page)

~ 123 ~

Camp Nelson 11.06 PM

My dear Wife
Sunday July 5th 1863

Some excitements hue to night.

Morgan is at Lebanon with about 3600 men and report say Wolford the 7th & 2d Ohio are in behind them and commenced fighting with them at daylight this morning and the 8th Mich & 9th Mich & a full batery of artilery advanced from Danville this AM and reach Lebanon by 10.6 this AM and the 44 & 45 Ohio & 112 Ill Mounted infantry will reach them in the night to night & posibly conclude the fight by buying Morgan and his party.

The situation of Lebanon is as marked out

The brought ten prisoners hue just now from Somerset of Morgans men

Camp Nelson Ky. July 6th 1863
9 O.C. Monday Evening

My dear Wife Julia,

There is one of the usual scares on through out the State. Morgan was at Lebanon yesterday and our men fought with {him} but we have no particulars as to his movements. All last nigh{t} and all day to day the road has been completely lined with teams men and woman in buggies men and negroes on horse back, men and boys driving mules, horse and cattle all going north and every thing in Lexington in the shape of Govt. property covering this horse & mules driven & teams in every possible shape.

I believe about the last enstallment is on the way here and here. I assure you this is at this time a busy and important camp. We mustered the Employees of the camp this evening. Capt. Morris mustered about 600, Capt Pratt 200, & myself about 300 all ragged and dirty & all teamsters. They meet again in the morning and get arms ~

I remarked to you that I had a pleasant office. I am becoming a good deal identified with Gen Burnside's Head Quarters' men which I trust will eventually make it agreeable for me. I will give you a little history how matters are situated here. Gen Hartsuff command{s} the 23rd Army Corps in the field & he has chief QrMaster who controlls all of the QrMasters in the Corps and Captain Hall controlls this Depot and reports directly to Gen. Burnside making him Chief Q{uarter}M{aster} at the post. Then there is Capt. Morris of the Gen staff who has charge of all of the transportation and I have 350 teams assigned to me which I am to use and keep forage supplied for the troops in front, and I assist Capt Morris. Capt. Pratt has charge of the building and constructing about the camp with QrMasters Stores, Camp & Garrison.

I am in a large house with {a} hall in the center and Capt Hall occupies one room below Capt Morris the other myself one room above and Col Stockton of Michigan Commander of the post the other.

I have no desire to dive head and ears into a big QrMasters business. Latshaw & Noble are non est & Lexington too this is the point and the only military point in Kentucky.

I received your letter this P.M. of the 21st from Stanford in which you speak of boarding - I am as anxious as you to consumate some thing but as the saying is <u>I can't see it yet</u> as matters are at this time about here.

Now comes the surprise I started Jim Cain for M{onroe}ville with two mares and a yearling colt and a pkg containing money he does not know the amount.

I want a pasture to turn them into and a good one found while Jim is there. The largest mare is one of the best saddle animals I ever saw and very kind to ride and easily managed with a curb bit. the only unpleasant thing is that she is very nervous & timid but not ugly. The other is not so pleasant but is easily managed. The other is as fine a blooded colt as can be bred in any country - I can only say one thing I have got the reputation in the Regt. and when I am known as pretty sharp on horses & I can say I have made money in every horse I have handled I have made something. I should not have sent the mare home but I concluded the rebels might just as well get a govt horse as my own. I should like to have Darwin take the colt and I will arrange so we can both get some good stock. If he takes any particular fancy to the small bay mare I will let him have her. I would not object to sending Prince to Father* to use & keep for me - You may be surprised when I say I have another mare her{e} - I will keep her and sell her if I can before I come home I have been offered 200$ a great many times for the big mare size & was offered 150$ for the small one but to day no sale. If I was at liberty now I could buy horses at my own price about here - while the scare is on they are not valued very high -

I send you the pedigree of the young mare to show to Darwin if you see him - I want you to keep it carefully - It will be latin to you but he will understand it. I sold Eells my horse Joe for 150$ then bought him of{f} him for 110 and got all of his horse rigging and then sold him in ten minutes for 110 again keeping the rig{g}ing. As soon as this matter settles I shall come home. I gave Jim means to get him around -

Your affect{ionate}
Wm

*William is probably speaking of his own father, Benjamin, who lived in Bellville, Ohio.

Camp Nelson Ky. July 7th 1863

My Dear Wife Julia,

Thursday evening 10 O.C. and I am ready to retire on one of the inn bed steads such as you saw at Stanford.

The excitement has almost subsided and in a day or two you will hear of the refugees returning to their home. We learned of the fall of Vixburg to day and any amount of Good news from Mead.

Jim left Lexington this morning for Monroeville. There is nothing left at Lexington belonging to the Army and this is probibly the busyest place in Kentucky. I sent my teams on the road for Stanford again to day -

Kiss my pet children and just guess how I would like to be with you.

Your affect{ionate}
Wm

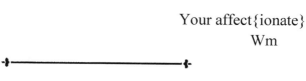

Camp Nelson July 8th 1863
Wednesday Evening

My dear Wife Julia,

There seems to be no news to write so cheering as our perview of Victories which sum{m}ed up amounts to nearly 60,000 killed wounded and prisoners which if well followed up must break the back bone of the rebellion[6] ~

You chastise me severely for not answering some of your letters now my dear it is quite impossible for me to do it until I receive your letters which owing to my moving about has necessarily delayed them from coming to here. I am now as perminently settled as it is possible for a military man to be I am at a camp that is perminently located as much as Camp Chase[7] and I see nothing to prevent me from remaining here some time. I expect to be at home soon and then I can answer all of your questions more fully. I imagine you would feel rather uneasy to be here with 5 children and Every day expecting to see the raged and lousy secesh rushing in upon you. So leave the matter there until I see you.

Your affect{ionate}
Wm

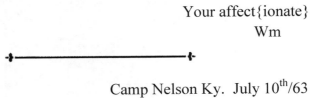

Camp Nelson Ky. July 10th/63

My dear Wife,

I expected to have taken a french[8] for home to day but Capt. Hall & Capt. Morris requested that I should wait a few days owing to the press and unsettled state of affairs here and then Capt Hall the chief QMaster said he would give me a furlough.

Capt. Morris also told me that they were arranging to send me to take charge of the post at Nicholasville just the place I would like on the RR and but a moderate amount of business. They don't like the man that is there. Capt. Hall, chief QrMaster, is becoming quite easy and affable with me.

I expect Chas Smith here this morning. If I go to Nicholasville and matters settle down in KY I will make an effort to have you with me.

A scare again last night expecting a raid from some of Morgan's men.

Your affect{ionate} Wm

Camp Nelson Ky. July 15th {1863}

My dear Wife,

I have an order or rather arranged with Captain Morris to go to Nicholasville and take the post there. and if it is possible before taking it I will make a running visit home and see my pet family. I talked with the Captain this evening and if I can arrange to keep McFadin there a few days he says I can beat for home.

I imagine that I can influence the Captain in my behalf so much so that I can remain there.

Well I suppose you are expecting Jno Morgan up in the vicinity of Monroeville as I understand he is beyond Cint. I am afraid Jno has stired up a mares nest by crossing the Ohio.

No person here knows where the 2nd & 7th Ohio, 1st & 11th Ky & 8 & 9 Mich Cavalry is they left Lebanon Ky in pursuit of him & have not returned yet. We suppose they are some place on the Ohio River.

Kiss the children & several for yourself.

Your affect{ionate}
Wm

Monroeville Sunday Aug. 2 {1863}

Dear William,

I wrote to you a week ago to day* and have not written since for I hardly know where to direct to, and have been very busy. I was much disappointed in not hearing from you last night. I have only received one letter from you since you left beside the note you sent from Cincinnati. I went to Toledo Monday morning and came back Tuesday evening. I took the three youngest children with me. I found them all well and very nicely fixed in their house all new papered and carpeted and a large addition behind. Julia has been real sick for four days so that the Dr. has called every day. It was an attack of dysentery with a good deal of fever she seems very much debilitated and dreadfully nervous. I had the two Mrs. Cone{s} here to tea yesterday they sent me word they were coming and between all I am about used up I ache all over. I think yesterday and to day have been as warm as any weather I ever knew. Thursday afternoon there was a very hard storm here the big lightning struck the old building where Harkness kept his high wines and in an instant it was all in flames it also consumed all of Vancise buildings. Harkness' loss was estimated at $4000. The man has brought me six cords of wood for which I paid him. Mr. Callan brought me a load of hay and Katys last opperation was the afternoon he brought it to take a lighted candle up stairs in the hay to hunt for a chicken. Now how much can I trust such a girl?

The lace you got me was very pretty but more expensive than I expected. The dress goods makes up quite pretty it was so wide that I made out to get a dress out. 'Delia finished it last night. She will go home to morrow. I am sorry to have her go. I do not like to stay here nights alone and am anxiously waiting to hear something from you. Betty came in with three large sunflowers while {we} were at tea last evening. I said Oh Betty who gave you the nice flowers she said "Miss-Miss-Miss guess and then you'll know". You understand she could not remember the name. It was Mrs. Hollis. Mrs. Cone said "did you ever see any thing like that". She sat at the table the other day spelling 'X. M. W. Y. t. cow'. Aint that good spelling she asked. I think five more awkward letters could not be put together. do write me something soon.

With much love Julia

Judy says write to Father I want him to resign and come home.

*No letter from Julia, dated Sunday, July 26, was found in the collection.

Nicholasville K.Y. Aug 3rd 1863

My dear Wife,

I am comparratively speaking settled at this place and very pleasantly situated for service in the Army. As soon as I see what the probible situation and disposition of the 9th Army Corps which is expected back in this state is I may be able to conclude as to how perminately I am situated here and shall then conclude some arrangement for having you and two or three of the children here.

The Rebels made a dash into Stanford last Friday and cleaned out all of the stores there and made all of our folks skedadle. they also had possession of Lancaster nine miles this side and captured two trains of 25 wagons each that I had just turned over to Morris.

Our forces pursued to the Cumberland River and took over 400 {men?}. I furnished transportation from here yesterday for

260 of <u>Scots</u> <u>Louisiana</u> <u>Cavalry</u>[9] captured by our forces near Stanford.

Ask Zahm if he has any knowledge of Scotts Cavalry. There was his Lt. Col amongst them and several Captains and Lieuts. I only ask that I will be permitted to remain here and I think I can do my duty quite comfortably.

The 7th has not returned from Ohio yet. I had a long conversation with Wolford on his return and he gave me full particulars of the chase after Morgan and speaks in the highest terms of the 7th ~

Remember me to the children.

Your affect{ionate}
Wm

—————✦————————————————✦—————

Monroeville Wednesday afternoon
{assumed to be Aug. 5, 1863}

Dear William,

Ed Fish called last evening to let me know that he had received a letter from you and intended to go to Kentucky to night. I only wish I was going with him & hope I shall have an invitation soon. The children were very much frightened last evening while I was gone to the Post Office. Kate went out to milk with Dora and Betty in the cow yard. As she got up and turned to come in there was a dreadful ragged, wretched looking fellow spoke to her. He had his pants unbuttoned and he <u>wet</u> her dress & then run after her to the gate. Dora & Betty ran screaming to the house. I came home with Birdie and found the doors all locked & all of them frightened most to death. On my way home I heard that Squires' house was entered the night before and robbed of their silver. So with it all I took Fannie and started for some one to stay with us. I cast around but could think of no one but one of the Corwins. I went to Angel's & found that Chub's wife & child were sick.

Then I went to Caroline's. Her father was abed & asleep & she sick, but after hearing my story he got up & came over, & said he would come again to night. I have hardly slept one night since you left. I would as leave be within sight of the rebels, and feel that I had some one to protect me, yes rather. I wrote to Julia yesterday about taking the girls and requested an answer immediately so that I might know what arrangements to make. Mrs. Hollis says she would not stay here one night for half the place is worth. Tell me what I had better do. Miss Mason, a dress maker a friend of Mrs. McDonald said last night that she would stay in the house. I think she is a nice girl. I have just $30 left, & out of that I must pay for a sack of flour, & the buggy files and shoe the children all around, beside living out of it till you send for me, & shall have their fare to pay. So I think you will have to send me what you think I will need to pay my traveling expenses. When you write your letters come through in two days. I would send you some eatables, but you say you have a good boarding place, & you took all of your clothes with you. I hope you enjoyed your fruit, & cake. Paramore called to see me yesterday. He is expecting to hear from the President this week. He asked me to go to the Isolands {Islands north of Monroeville in Lake Erie} and Put in Bay. A party were going, but of course I could not leave home & the children. I have had to stay here very close all summer. I must close, eat my supper, and take this to the depot. hoping to see you soon.

I remain affectionately yours Julia

Dear William,

The children have just started for Sunday school, even so
Betty, and I am all alone. I feel very blue and lonesome and am
anxiously looking forward to the time when you will send for
me. I have been sewing very hard all the week trying to get
childrens clothes made and organized, so I can go when you do
send. Julia has got quite well again but was real sick and
miserable for ten days. Delia came home last Monday. I kept
her as long as she could stay so that I should have somebody to
stay with me nights. I have never felt so timid and <u>realy</u> <u>afraid</u> as
I do now, and I think every night when I go into bed I will not
stay so another night, and yet I don't know of any body that I
could get to stay with me. Friday night I stay'd all alone with the
children. Kate went to town and did not come back 'til the next
morning. I did not go to bed till twelve and was frightened and
wakeful all night. I don't think it is right for me to have to stay
so alone. It seems to make it very uncertain when you will send
for me, waiting for the army to return from the south, and what
has there to do with your keeping the situation you have. The
man brought seven cords of wood and would have brought more
but I did not feel as if I ought to spare the money and told {him}
I would let him know when I wanted more. I can get Corwin to
cut it just by <u>dribs</u>. It has been extremely warm here for the last
two weeks and showers almost every day. there is not a potato
left in the garden, and Whaly is fretting at me about the little pigs
destroying his. I wish they were all sold. I am glad you are
comfortably situated and have less to do than you have had, and
hope when I see you again, you will feel and act more like
yourself. I saw Mr. Stewart last night he wished me to be sure
and remember him to you. He did not know that you had been
home and regretted not having seen you. Calligan has gone East
after his wife. Cyrus Cook takes his place in the office. I think

Morgan and Duke must feel somewhat mortified at having their heads shaved and wearing the Penitentiary stripes. You know that is where they have sent them. Now I think they ought to be made to make arms for the Union Army. Harrison Terry came back last night I have not seen him to speak with him. Paramore has returned. I heard that his case was refered to Rosecrans, and if he did not reinstate him the President would. I hope it is so. I should have written oftener but was afraid you would not get my letters while there was so much commotion in K.Y. Shall I send to John Brown's and get your saddle? Will has promised often enough to bring it home but does not do it. Betty says "tell Papa to kiss his pet children and mama". The weather is so warm they are all very irritable. I hope to get another letter from you tomorrow night, and wish that I could feel that I should be with you before many days.

Affectionately Julia

Cleveland Aug 9th

My dear Julia,

The little box came all right and I intended to look for the things as soon as I could find a breathing spell. It is pesky hot. Am sorry to learn that you are not all well. Do not get sick this hot weather as the bed would prove an uncomfortable companion just now. I am going to Belleville this week. Elizabeth has returned from the East. Was in the midst of the riot and I have no doubt is full of remarkable incidents and glad to get home. I expect Etta to return with me. I was sorry that I forgot my box of roots and yerbs. Caroline will think I did not appreciate them. It is Monday and I must close for dinner will be non ext {*non existent*}.

Love your sister,
Sarah R. Jackson*

I had a small party the week after I came home.

* Sarah Jackson is William's sister, as is Elizabeth mentioned above.

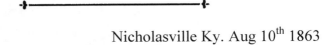

Nicholasville Ky. Aug 10th 1863

My dear Wife,

I am most of the time actively employed at my duties here but nevertheless I have a pleasant post comparatively speaking with the general employment in the Army.

It has been excedingly warm for a day or two past and I have one luxury a plenty of clean clothes. I have a good wash-woman and her prices are not so ruinous as I have usually been compelled to pay.

We hear nothing more about any raid but our men are actively engaged in preparing for East Tennessee. I expect the 7th O.V.C. through here to day from Cint. Geo Ross has been spending some days with me and would be glad to remain.

Has Ed Fish said anything about coming here. I offered him $60 & rations. Morris goes into the field and Capt Noble takes his place. So I expect I can get Smith & Spear.

McDowell has promised me to make an effort through Capt Dickinson Cint to have me remain here as permenantly as possible. There is a prospect of the government taking full possession of this Rail Road they are making this issue through me as the receiving QrMaster here to make them comply with certain requirements or refuse to certify to them freight a/c.

Remember me to all my friends & kiss pussy that little girl & all the others for me & one to the <u>big</u> girl although I hope she is no bigger than she was when I left.

Your affect{ionate}
Wm

Nicholasville Aug 12th 1863

My dear Wife,

We had a fine rain yesterday evening and we are enjoying a pleasant morning. The 1st enstalment of the 9th Army Corps returned yesterday morning and the rest are expected every day. Gen Burnside was here last evening and I sent his bagage down to him this morning and kept his horse for him the evening before.

If the Ninth Army Corps gets back and I am continued here I shall then look upon my position here as some what permanent - but I am some afraid that some QM of the Corps may be looking after this place. I wait and see what I'll see.

The 86 Ohio was coming in all last night. My room is directly opposite of the Depot and near the track and they disturbed my repose.

I must close. I am call{ed} away on business at the cars -

Your affect{ionate}

Wm

Nicholasville Aug 14th 1863

My dear Wife,

Every thing is on the move here day and night preparing for a move upon Knoxville. I assure you I have my share of the machine to keep moving. All of the supplies of Forage, horses, Subsistence, Ambulances, Arms, horse equipment & medical stores &c, &c. all have to pass through my hands at the post here and I can only say that I am well satisfied with the way I have managed things thus far.

I have the whole programm of the movement. They go in 4 colums one by Cumberland Gap, Big Creek Gap ~ Albany, and Pound Gap ~ Gen Burnside goes by the Cumberland Gap ~ The Army will be 50 to 60,000 strong composed of the 9th & 13th & 23rd Army Corps.

Fish arrived here last evening. as soon as there is not so much crowd and confusion on this rail road and the army gets out of the way, I will send for you if I remain here or the prospect is that I remain.

The Col stayed with me night before last and wishes to be remembered to you. he said he wanted to send me four of his Photographs of different kinds that he had taken in Cin~ ~

When he left in the morning when he left {sic} he said in his moderate way, Jackson I am sorry you and I cannot be together more than we are now. I was in hopes of hearing that Paramore had been reinstated. Remember me to the children.

Your affect{ionate}
Wm

Monroeville Sunday {Aug.} 16th

Dear William,

I wrote to you the middle of last week by Fish and suppose he got through to you all safe. Some of your letters have encouraged me to think you could find a place for me and then again letter after letter comes and there is nothing said about it, it keeps me feeling very unsettled, and yet I am fully determined not to stay here as I have done.

You may think me very unreasonable in saying & feeling so, but it is certainly no more so than to expect I am going to stay here alone, and live as I have lived for the last two years. I have got Old Corwin to stay here nights since our fright and must be under eternal obligations for the favor. There is the same miserable looking set in town yet and I have always felt afraid of them.

We had a hard rain here to day and have had thunder storms almost every day for two weeks. The children have gone to Sunday School. I cant write for I feel bad, and in no mood to write. Perhaps I shall get a letter from you tomorrow night that will make me feel better.

With love Julia

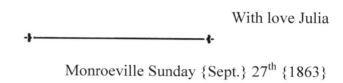

Monroeville Sunday {Sept.} 27th {1863}

Dear William,

I of course have very little to write about as soon after your leaveing. I have just been provoked dreadfully by that wretched nigger Ben, he came up to the gate and sent Lillian in to call me out, I went on to the stoop and the most insultingly he talked to me he said he heard I said he ~~"took"~~ stole, I told him I said he took a horse cover and sirsingle and sold it. He said they belonged to him, Jim Kane gave them to him. I told him fine gave him the sirsingle and handed me the cover. He told me I had better keep my mouth shut up he would tell how I wanted him to steal nails of Whaley (there were two that laid in the brook and I thought they came down stream and told him so, and told him to bring them up and put them on the cow pen) Delia sat by the window and heard him. I know if you had been here you would have shot him and the only thing that would serve him right would be if possible to let his master know where he was.

I know I could stand and see him whipped good. I asked him why he didn't come and ask you if the cover belonged to you. He said he knew if he saw you you would scold him and he knew he wasn't going to take it. I wish you had never sent him up here. I think he is a desperate, ugly fellow, and I wish he was dead.

~ 139 ~

I hope you got through all safe and are well and that I shall hear from you very soon. I dont feel or cannot realize that you have been home, Several came to me at the depot where they saw you get on the cars to know if you were going back so soon. Cone sent the next morning and sent the mare. I have tried in several directions to get hay but have not succeeded yet it seems a difficult thing. I went to Norwalk yesterday to do the errand you wished me to. I asked Betty last night where you was she said you had gone way down <u>Souf</u> and the <u>webbles</u> had shot you. The children all felt bad to have you leave.

Affectionately Julia

Chapter Four Notes

1. William's report of 3500 men was exaggerated; most accounts say Morgan had about 2000 men with him on this particular raid into Ohio and Indiana.

2. Rankin, page 9. For more on Morgan's 1863 raid into southern Indiana and Ohio see: Ramage, James A., *Rebel Raider: The Life of General John Hunt Morgan*; Lexington, KY: University of Kentucky Press, c. 1986 and Horowitz, Lester, *The Longest Raid of the Civil War Little-Known & Untold Stories of Morgan's Raid into Kentucky, Indiana & Ohio*; Cincinnati, Ohio: Farmcourt Publishing,1998. Also: www.ohiohistorycentral.org/w/John_H._Morgan (accessed October 2014).

3. For more on Adam's Express Company visit www.adamsexpress.com (accessed October 2014).

4. For more detailed information about Camp Nelson see: Sears, Richard D., *Camp Nelson, Kentucky, A Civil War History*; Lexington, KY: University Press of Kentucky, 2002, as it is filled with facts, letters, official records, and diary entries from various soldiers and officers. Also, www.campnelson.org (accessed October 2014) OR visit the Camp Nelson Heritage Park, in person. Not far from Interstate 75 in Jessamine County, KY, it is a park that any Civil War or history buff would enjoy visiting.

5. For more on the Northern Draft see: Sandburg's *Abraham Lincoln, War Years II*, pp. 359-77; www.etymonline.com/ (accessed October 2014). Also: www.ohiohistorycentral.org/w/Conscription_Act (accessed October 2014).

6. William was referring to Union victories at Gettysburg and Vicksburg, in which Union losses were far fewer than Confederate losses. While the total number of casualties at Gettysburg alone was somewhere around 51,000, there were an estimated 31,000 Confederate casualties in *each* of the major conflicts with Gettysburg lasting three days and Vicksburg's siege lasting almost seven weeks.

7. Camp Chase, named after former Governor of Ohio and Lincoln's Secretary of the Treasury, was a military staging, training and prison camp in Columbus, Ohio, during the American Civil War. All that remains of the camp today is a Confederate cemetery containing 2,260 graves.

8. William's of July 10, 1863 -See glossary for this term (french) not used in this manner today.

9. William is probably referring to the First Louisiana Cavalry Regiment organized in September, 1861 by Louisiana native, Colonel John Sims Scott. This regiment was known as one of the most heavily endowed, money wise, as many of the troopers were sons of planters or their relatives. They participated in more than 75 engagements during the 2½ years between November 1861 and April 1864.

Chapter Five

"Home Is No Home Without You"
July through December 1864

"The year is ended. Good bye 1863, and may God grant that success attend our labors for our country in the year so soon to open." [1]

Elisha Hunt Rhodes

No doubt, officers and enlisted men alike, those in blue and those in gray, were praying similar prayers as 1863 drew to a close. Certainly those in the south whose homes had been ravaged by the war prayed for the end of this conflict; those who waited in the Northern states for their soldiers to return were just as fervently seeking Divine intervention to bring this war to an end! In the North, that end could come only if the southern states would agree to pledge their allegiance to the Union from which they had seceded. For the South, victory would depend on maintaining their independence. In their view, this independence would include a state's right to govern itself and the right to maintain the institution of slavery.

Southerners with slaves often wrote in their diaries and letters of the impudence of their "free" slaves and the fear they felt as some of these slaves asserted their freedom. With the increase of slaves leaving plantations as runaways or as "freemen," the North's Negro population continued to grow. Jefferson Davis ordered southerners to forget about planting cotton and tobacco and replace them with "food crops" as food was becoming increasingly difficult to provide-for soldiers and citizens alike. Morale, especially in the south, was decreasing daily and in both the south and the north many expressed their heartfelt longings to be reunited with their families.

On November 18, 1863, President Lincoln left Baltimore by train heading for Gettysburg, where the next day, he would deliver what has become one of the most well-known and memorized speeches in our nation's history, the Gettysburg Address. Prior to his arrival, crowds of people had formed, most still mourning lost friends or family members; some were officers who were reliving the battle they had fought almost five months earlier. Some present were self-serving citizens seeking to sell relics of the battle from little stands they'd set up in the streets.[2]   Contrary to the part of Lincoln's "little speech" that proclaimed "the world will little note, nor long remember, what we say here," the Gettysburg Address has long been remembered and immortalized for all time. The ten sentences spoken in just five minutes "will live among the annals of men," wrote one reporter from the Chicago Tribune. Words that had been written only three weeks before and rewritten less than twelve hours before were added or omitted and in the end Lincoln gifted at least four "copies" to some who were present that day with the first two of his drafts eventually being given to the Library of Congress.

Also in the month of November, the wily Morgan, "the Thunderbolt of the Confederacy," had tunneled out of his Camp Chase confines and along with Basil Duke, was back in action. A lesser known fact is that Lincoln, just one month earlier, had declared that Thanksgiving Day become a National holiday.[3]

Julia and the children were most likely with William on that first official Thanksgiving Day in 1863. Because of references in their letters of 1864, it is clear the family were together for about nine months - the longest time they had spent together since the beginning of this war - almost three months into its fourth year at the time Julia wrote hers of "July 1st." The first of her fourteen letters from 1864 seems to be soon after she and the children returned from Kentucky and also after William made a brief visit home. She ends her letter with "give my love to Anna,

George, and Mrs. Scott, and a big kiss for yourself" and with her most frequently used closing, "Affectionately, Julia."

Mrs. Scott is mentioned in several more letters of both Julia's and William's; in Julia's of July 7, she asks "who does the little spit-fire have to scold at now our children are out of her way?" Mary Scott was one of the largest landowners whose land was confiscated by the Union army for the construction of Camp Nelson. Her house, built around 1850 by her son-in-law, Oliver Perry, was commandeered by General Burnside in 1863, and used to house Union officers and occasionally their families.

The Oliver Perry House circa 1855. This two-story frame Greek Revival style house is the only building from the Civil War that remains at the Camp Nelson Heritage Park, now a National Historic Landmark. It is currently the focus of restoration and preservation efforts. (www.campnelson.org accesssed November 2014)

In June, 1864, three months after Lincoln gave General Grant command of all Union Armies, Grant began the ten month campaign often known as the "Siege of Petersburg." Grant had given control of the western theatre to Sherman and pressed him to take Atlanta while he, Grant, sought to engage Lee in a campaign that would lead to the surrender of Lee's Army of Northern Virginia and ultimately to Appomattox Courthouse. With supply lines being constantly interrupted by one side or the other, morale of citizens and soldiers decreased even more but especially in the south where most of the battles were fought. After the death of John H. Morgan in Greenville, Tennessee, in September of 1864, the morale of the Confederacy plummeted to an all-time low as so many in the south saw him as their "Robin Hood."

William writes Julia of Morgan's death and continues to tell details of his responsibilities as quartermaster, even sharing details he was asked not to share! In his letter dated September 13, William writes he is going on a "raid after the rebels" that "will continue from one to four weeks" and that "the thing is being got up on the sly." He implores Julia to "please bear up like a brave woman until I return" …"that Gen McLean said yesterday he did not wish men to tell their wives." Apparently William's battalion was going to be heading across Kentucky and into Virginia "over mountains and very picturesque valleys" and into "the most desolate country you ever heard tell of." In many of his letters from 1864, William writes with passion of his devotion to Julia and his desire to be with her. He even seems to be pushing her to have another baby and asks for something else with which she does not seem comfortable.

From what can be gleaned from the letters, it seems William is not able to get home until November. At the National Archives in Washington, D.C., is a copy of a letter from William, written in more elaborate script than any of his other letters in this collection. This letter addressed to the Regimental Quartermaster at Camp Nelson for a "leave of absence of thirty days" (in November) "for the purpose of attending to my private business," explains why there are no letters from either Julia or William in November 1864. There is only one letter (in this chapter) from someone else, Julia and William's brother-in-law, D.E. Gardner (married to Julia's sister, Sarah) settling "accounts."

Paper continued to be a precious commodity as supplies of all kinds became increasingly scarce. In one letter (July 17 Sunday), Julia writes of medicine her doctor prescribed that she might not want because it would make her "want to eat all the time" and "it was such a bad time to get any thing to eat." Although the shortage of writing paper did not stop the flow of letters between Julia and William, it is evident in their writing. More than in the previous years, their letters of 1864 have whole paragraphs with writing above, below, and in the margins of what was first written. William's letter of July 31 written on four pages of paper is the epitome of thriftiness as he wrote *perpendicular to what was previously written on three of the four pages!* This is William's longest letter and interspersed between news of his work as Post Quartermaster and advice about their business at home are some of his most sentimental words to Julia.

Unlike today, where we may communicate more frequently but lack quality and style in some of our forms of communication, William's letter - like others in this collection - is like much of the written communication of the 19th century - more expansive and formal. What today might be expressed in a short text, email, or note with copious abbreviations, people then might have expounded on in four or five paragraphs! The social mores of the time dictated discretion and sexual matters were not openly discussed. There were very few "advice" books for young couples, newly married or otherwise. Two that William or Julia might have read though, did talk some about "the birds and the bees." They were *The Ladies' Medical Guide and Marriage Friend*, written in 1859 and *The Lover's Marriage Lighthouse*.

The latter written in 1858 by Harmon Root was said to be a "guide for the perplexed."[4]

Not only were there few books of any kind on reproductive health or sexual matters, but many of those in print at the time had what we now know is *mis*information. Women's menstrual cycles and even childbirth were often referred to as a time of being "unwell" or "sick" and most adults alive then and for several decades after had heard of the "dangers of self-stimulation." In spite of this pre-Victorian view of anatomy, there were materials available to soldiers and private citizens alike that contained graphic drawings (some could even be called pornographic). However, most of these have been secreted away in private collections or purged through the decades by embarrassed family members. As Dr. Thomas Lowry writes in his book about sex in the Civil War, "…probably 90 percent of all sexual information has been deleted from the public record of personal lives." As a matter of fact, William and Julia's letters of 1864 contain more references to letters *not in the present collection* than were "lost" in previous years. To assume that Julia herself or perhaps one of "the children" destroyed them later, due to their intimate content, is not far-fetched at all.

Clearly the men and women of the mid 1800s had the same physical needs and longings as those of both genders throughout the ages. Multiple hospital records from the Civil War as well as newspapers of the time and surgeons' statistics show there were a large number of soldiers ill from a variety of venereal diseases; as one soldier wrote, "…a good many sick now mostly caused by imprudence."[5] Also available today are pictures and records of hospitals just for "female venereal" patients and records of prostitutes, or *'filles de joie,'* following regiments in both the south and the north. As James Robertson wrote in *Soldiers Blue and Gray,* "The Civil War had its seamy side, to be sure, but the evidence is overwhelming that a majority of soldiers North and South displayed fidelity through words in a letter, longing in the heart, and hopes for the future."[6] Julia and William seem to be among those who were faithful to each other, as each wrote the other of their hopes and dreams and their remembrances of "'coosy' (cozy) times together."

Monroeville July 1st {1864}

Dear William,

Your letter written the 29* came through yesterday being only two days on the road and I thought perhaps the road was repaired from Covington through. Ed Angell wrote that you did not leave Cincinnati 'till Monday but I thought he was wrong. Dora's clothes came yesterday. They are very handsome but he sent no pieces so I think it would be economy to send by some one going there from where you are and get a quarter of a yd. I will send a sample. You will probably think it is "small potatoes" but I don't. You will have many more chances than I and I wish you would not forget it. Betty has been quite puny, one of her bad sore mouths, and Dora has had a very bad time with his lungs, kept me awake most of two nights. We had such a sudden change in the weather Monday that the children all felt it, although I tried to guard against it. Sunday it seemed as if we would melt, and Tuesday we sat by a fire. You have left your shawl here and I am afraid you will want it as you have nothing with you. You are a <u>goose</u> that you don't send to Cincinnati and get your overcoat. Frank came over (though before you left I believe). Father made quite a call Wednesday. He probably knows I have no favors to ask and therefore dares to come. Old Major has never come back and I am sure I don't know where he can be. I sent for the girl, or rather I got Scouton to send for her.

She seems to be a clever yankee girl but she cannot milk, so that is a <u>bother</u>. It has been raining for nearly two days and it will do much good. Mr. Corwin set 150 cabbage plants for us this morning and some tomatoes. I wish I could have a basket of vegetables from Cincinnati. I have just been curling Betty's hair and she said "Mama does God put our hair in, does he just light a candle and stick it in? Let's ask God when we go up to Heaven. Mama, Mama how will we ask God and will we say God, God how do you put our hair in?" and I said "yes" and changed the subject. I believe I did not get my cool dress from Cincinnati. I know you did not have much time but I thought it might come in the package with Dora's clothes. I sent Mr. Corwin after them. The Express man said he did not know what the charges were but he could take them and I could pay him when he found out. I guess he thought he had shown off enough to you. I expect the Ladies make themselves very agreeable. Perhaps you are lonesome when you go to your room at night. Do you keep that same room? I would not have the one below on <u>any account</u>. I hope you will write very often for you don't know how lonesome I am and how forlorn I feel. I have been much the same in health ever since you left and quite miserable. I have done nothing towards fixing up, and don't have any heart to undertake any thing. You know William I could not bear to have you leave me. It seems very dull here and I have not seen papers since you left.

Give my love to Anna, George, and Mrs. Scott, and a big kiss for yourself.

Affectionately, Julia

*No letter from William dated June 29, 1864 was found.

Monroeville July 7th {1864}

Dear William,

Your letter {of} Monday night* found us all quite well. The children went to the office and expected to see some fireworks it being the evening of the fourth but there was only a few rockets. Mr & Mrs. Scouton drove up here in the afternoon of the fourth and wanted me to go up to Lyme to a pick nick for the Aid Society. We went about noon and came home at five. They had a very nice table, and a most lovely day. They also had a platform for dancing that would accommodate three sets of cotillion, two violins, and they played old fashion tunes; they all seemed to enjoy it hugely. I danced once with Mr. Jamison. He told me to say to you that he sold the horse that you thought would do to go into the Cavalry for $475 in Toledo. I have not got Billy home yet for I cannot get any grain and there has been such nice rain I thought Clary would be more willing to keep him. It is awful dry living. I cannot get hold of anything good. Major has never come back. The box of fruit you spoke of ought to be kept in a cool place. The jars I brought home I had to heat over. I have not seen a paper since you left but I conclude I have not missed much for there does not seem to be much news. Our army does not seem to get along very fast and it makes me feel very blue.

Flour is eleven dollars and every thing in proportion-hams from 25 to 28¢ a pound. I wish you could draw some in Cincinnati and a box of candles. The potatoes came, and are a great comfort-the children won't eat h{ominy}. It is uncommonly dull in town no where to go to and I am dreadful lonesome. Write to me every thing you can think of, for it is all the news I get. People were quite surprised to hear you had left so suddenly. Your mother has been in Cleveland for three weeks. Let me know whether you send Caroline the money or if I shall when I get some. You ought to send about eleven dollars as she made Birdie a dress and a shirt. How are you situated? I hope just as you were when I was there. Have any more of Mrs. Scott's men enlisted and how does she get along? Who does the little spit fire have to scold at now our children are out of her way? How soon will the road be repaired. I don't expect to come over it right away but I would like to know {if} it was in running condition. I hope to get another letter to night. Don't fail to write very often. I have to write in such confusion there cannot be much sense to it. You must thank Mr. Saffle for me when the right time comes and tell him I appreciate his kindness and hope I may have it in my power to repay it at some future time. The bird came and I pay'd for it. I did not like to spare the money just now. It is almost tail less and a tail is a very pretty part of a ~ ~ bird. The children are as cross as murder this hot weather.

Remember me to all that cared for me and were kind to us. Love to Anna, George, Mrs. Scott, etc. and a big kiss for yourself.

Your affectionate wife, Julia

*No letter from William dated Monday (July 4) was found.

Monroeville July Thursday 14 {1864}

Dear William,

I wrote you a long letter yesterday* and will again to day to let you know the package came all safe. I went to the depot this morning and found it there. I am very much obliged to Mr. Hutchison for his kindness. I always thought he was a gentleman and now I am sure of it. I was much pleased with the dress. It is beautiful and altogether different from anything I have seen this season. I guess you had to pay for it. You spoke of getting me a lace mantle. It would be very acceptable for I have nothing comfortable for a hot day. If you should get one, I would prefer one with a lace fulled on around the edge like a deep lace flounce.

There is much difference in the quality, and several cheap ones are worn around here. We have had very warm weather ever since you left. Dora had a bad time with his lungs again last night. In the night I woke and felt the bed wet. Betty was asleep, but I said "Ma{y} Ann, you wet the bed" "Oh that's only sweat" and went on sleeping. She is looking anxiously for her "five cents". I see there is just an even amount of the Treasury notes so I will try and not use any of them. I had not used any of the other ones, but have had to run in debt some to save these. I will make the $30 go as far as I can. You must be having a good time without the rebels. I should like to be with you. You may depend. Do you think it would pay for me to get a riding dress? Delia will be up here to make my silk and the dress you sent me week after next. Webb painted the three stoops, the dark closet and the but{er}ry floor to day. Jane has cleaned the pantry and it looks much more like living. I wish you were here to enjoy it all with me for "home is no home without you".

Affectionately Julia

*No letter from Julia written July 13 was found.

✦————————✦

Monroeville July 17th Sunday {1864}

Dear William,

William how bad I do want to see you. It seems to me time never did drag so slow and heavily as it does now. And yet I have to keep very busy. Yesterday I white washed the bed room and papered it too, with Jane's help. Now don't scold or think scold for I could not get any body to raise a finger for me and the old paper did look so bad. I succeeded very easily although the old paper was very thick and tore easily. The new carpet I did not make. I thought I could wait till you got the new furniture and could be at home to enjoy it. We are all clean now but the kitchen part and dark closet. We shall get through this week. I got a nice bottle of medicine from Martains. It is called "Elixir Peruvian Bark, with Protoxide of Iron". It is very pleasant to take. I was in the drug store getting it. Prentice said after I had taken it a few days I would want to eat all the time. I told him then I thought I would not get it for it was such a bad time to get any thing to eat. He said that was the reason he did not recommend it more generally.

George Clary is very low with dysentery and typhoid fever. It is a bad combination of diseases and his case is a very critical one. Their distillery run three days or till the first of this month and stop{p}ed. Harkness lost his little girl. The town is duller than I ever knew it and the price of every thing so high and the gardens all so late. I feel most starved for vegetables. My garden is coming on but will be very late. Betty just came in with a pocket-full of goose berries and saw me writing to you and she said "Mama tell-tell-tell Papa I've got a pocket and want him to send me five cents right straight". Birdie says in her slow way "tell Father if he is so home sick he might resign and come home". Fannie says "tell Father send me something for sore toes".

Why did Platte leave? You never wrote me the reason. I hope Ross will stay with you. I feel much better to know he is there. You know he is a young man that I respect very highly. Remember me to him. If Annie comes home I wish she would come through here on her way back. I think you and George will be two forlorn men. William I do feel very sorry for you. I guess I know how to as well as any body can for it has seemed to me at times as if I could not have it so any longer as if it was wrong, and almost wicked for us to be separated as we are. I know you feel as if you did not know what to do with yourself. I used to think many times before I came away how desolate it would be for you to go into the room at night and find it empty and William the tears come while I write about it. I thought and knew you loved to have us with you. I think it rather annoys some people that you don't resign and come home as so many here have done. Several have asked me why you did not, and I feel very proud now that you have not.

Father makes frequent calls here and I think he feels greatly relieved. I treat him in a friendly way as if nothing ever had happened. He often asks the children why they don't come over and says they have been expecting them. We have none of us been. I shall let the children go this week if Fannie's toes are well enough. I gave him Sherman's letter to read.[7] He was much pleased and said it was a much better thing than John could have written. I don't know when I have read any thing that pleased me more and the best of it was I got it before any one in town got it. The next night after I had the pleasure of reading it, it came out in the Toledo Blade. I miss the papers awfully.

Dora has had another bad time with his lungs. Friday morning I sent for Prentice. He said it was asthma and left Dovers powders for him. It troubles him much. Do you remember he only had one attack while he was in Kentucky? I think the climate was favorable for him. I think he is as handsome a boy as I ever saw of his age. His hair curls more than ever it did, and he has sweat off a good deal of the black. The truth is you need not be ashamed of any of them. As soon as I get through with the big work I shall try to have them attend to their studys some. Fannie and Judy read a great deal and seem to be very fond of it. I think I shall be in favor of having them go to Sandusky again this Fall. The rest I can bring with me to Kentucky or wherever you are. Don't that make you feel good? It is getting toward the last of July and I tell you I count the days. I had got the gingham before I knew you could send me a dress but paid for it by letting my girl have a dress that was too short and too small for me. I guess I should have roasted if I had not got it. It has been so very warm, I have gone almost equal to the Greek Slave. Would you like to have seen me?

How does my carriage progress and are you going to send it home or keep it there for me to ride in? I have written twice a week ever since you left and three times last week. I will close with a big kiss and think how I would like to be with my head on your bosom and sleep this night, for then I could sleep.

Your Julia

Monroeville July 20th Wednesday {1864}

Dear William,

Since I received you letter last evening* I have felt worried and unhappy, I hope you will not have to leave your Post. The weather continues so warm that we are all getting worn out with it. I have been abed all the afternoon. I am so wakeful nights. I get but little sleep till day light and to day I was thoroughly used up. I had a most confused day yesterday. It was on this wise, in the morning I had to go to market for meat for dinner which was enough to tire me out for the day. I got some nice mutton and got back home and was dusting the parlor and getting up clean white curtains up in my bedroom when there was a buggy drove up with Mary Martain, Maria Hylliar and Lillis Williams and all the rigging to make ice cream. Jane was in the midst of ironing and it was almost noon. The dime circle was to meet here in the evening and they felt determined not to have such a failure as they had before. Well as I said before it was most noon and they all stay'd to dinner we were baking and the kitchen all in confusion, but I got them a nice dinner and Lill stay'd the rest of the day to see to freezing the cream as I know nothing about it. They had no cake the evening before and I thought it looked like slim fare so about four O C I went into the kitchen (by the by I had not been out of it much) and made those nice large jelly cakes. They were beautiful and they all seemed much pleased. One thing certain they were <u>fresh</u>, the cream froze very hard and the evening was splendid and they all seemed to enjoy themselves. Mr. Bishop and his wife were here. He has preached here several times and will continue to now 'till the minister comes that they gave a call from Kansas. He married Birdzei's daughter near Norwalk. The rooms were full. We play'd some charades, which were ridiculous. One word was "Quakers", a terrible quaking and trembling for the first scene and Henry Roby and Wilson play'd cats admirably with some old furs tied around them for tails, and we had a quick Quaker meeting for the tableau and with some Quaker talk that I got off. They guessed the word and said it was acted well. They broke up about eleven then we washed all the dishes and I got to bed about one O C and I was so tired and nervous that very little sleep I got till after four. So I concluded to do nothing to day but write to you. When I was asleep this afternoon I dreamed you came home with a new suit of military on with the greatest quantity of gold lace and trappings on, and I was so overjoyed I rushed out into the yard to meet and kiss you and you had a <u>great</u> <u>pipe</u> in your mouth, and how sad and disappointed I felt. Oh but I do want to see you. Among the rest of the confusion of yesterday Father made a call and while he was here, Calligan and the ladies were in the cellar making the cream, (but I dont think he knew it and) Mr Ellers came to give the girls their first music lesson. Well I lived through it like a great many others of my stormy days. I think Ellers will get along with the girls very well. He is very pleasant and says he would rather teach them from the beginning. Betty went into the parlor to talk to him while the girls were getting ready. He asked her how old she was she said she was three (he was telling me about it). "I said -oh no that cannot be", well then she said I am six and will be five next winter. He was very much pleased with her, but thought she did not understand figures.

George Clary was better yesterday morning. I have not heard from him to day. They had succeeded in putting him asleep, he had been very delirious. I have not heard anything from Toledo. If Delia comes up here I think I will go up and spend a day. I have not been to Norwalk yet. Perhaps I will go over the last of this week. I think Mr. Bronson and Louisa will get home next week. What shall I do about using any of these notes?** I don't want to, for they won't allow any thing for them. I have a chance of getting two tons of hay at $20 a ton, had I better get it. Your letters come through very straight. If you should have other money you might enclose me a little at a time so I would not have to use any of the other. I hope the communication will not be cut off as it is all the comfort I have, getting your letters and you are very kind in writing so often. I have so many ways to turn or I should write oftener, but mean to write every other day. I write every thing I can think of, and a good deal of nonsense with all.

I hope you will get my letters as they would be very uninteresting to any one else. I will close with much love and hope the time will soon come when we can live together again and not have to depend on letters as the only way in communication between us.

Yours affectionately Julia

P.S. Betty says if you don't send her five cents she will cry.

*This letter that Julia referred to was not found.
** Julia is probably referring to Treasury Notes.

Dear William,

I received your letter last evening with the pleasing intelligence that the raid was played out*. I had felt quite long faced about it but on the strength of it wrote you one of my longest letters. I went to Norwalk yesterday afternoon and took Dora. I sat down on one of the first seats I came to and in a few minutes the gentleman sitting behind me spoke and asked me if Mr. Jackson was with me. I looked surprised and said no. He then asked me if you were at home. I said no. He then said well he has been home. I said yes. And then I asked him what his name was. He said it was Finn, Tom Finn. And then I recognized him. He said he knew the boy first. He told me there was no truth in the raid and I felt quite relieved. They were all very glad to see me at Mothers and stop{p}ed all their work to entertain me. Theodore took me all over the new house. I think it will be a very complete and comfortable home. The chambers are ready for the painters, and the lower part, all but the Parlor and hall. I spoke of getting some furniture at Hoyt's. He said he wanted to get some too, so we went over. He had a very fine lot on hand. It did not look much like the Sandusky shops. I bought a very nice mahogany bureau with marble top and dressing glass for $35 and wash stand with two drawers and marble top for $18, and a bedstead to match for $22 with head and foot board alike. He had no others and they would have been twice as expensive. All I am afraid of is that it is not quite wide enough for our mattress. I think I will take the measure and go over tomorrow and see about it. I thought his prices were very reasonable. If the bedstead is not wide enough I shall not take it. He had one of the same style that I know was big enough but it was more expensive. Theodore is getting all of his furniture of him. I came home on the 9 O.C train went to bed at my usual time, had one little nap and laid awake all the rest of the night. It was good and cool and I did feel so provoked I could have spanked myself, but if I get the least bit excited I cannot sleep. Louisa and Mr. Bronson are having a fine time. The day after they got to Georgetown Mrs. McMeans who is boarding at Henry D. Cooks and spends her time in the hospitals, went to the tent where the supplies are kept for the sick to get some thing she wished and she found the lady who had charge of things asleep. She woke her up, and during their conversation she asked Mrs McMeans where she was from. She told her from Sandusky. She said I have a cousin living there who married the clergyman there Mr. Bronson. Mrs. McMeans said, why she will be at our house to night. It proved to be Clara Thomas. Wasn't it a strange meeting? Clara told Louisa where to find Mary Ramsy (she is another cousin) and living in Washington City. Her oldest daughter has been quite a heroine during the war. When the first sick and wounded were brought to Washington she took a very active part in taking care of them, and would read and sing to them. She is a very fine singer and gave two concerts at Willards Hotel for the purpose of getting a library for the soldiers. Many saw her zeal and contributed to the cause and erected a small building costing $1500, to contain the books. At the time of the defeat of Bull Run she went around the City and gathered up food and her and her lover (now her husband) rode all night to get to the battle field. When they came up where the guards were they told them they had orders not to let any ladies pass. She jumped up off the seat and said what! Not let me pass! And the guard knew her voice and said oh you can pass. They sent out a wagon load of bread from Washington and she blistered her hands breaking it up for them. I think if the history of this war is ever written her name** should be mentioned. She is now married and living in Brooklyn. I hope I have written something that will interest you for a little while. William I do feel real sorry for you and I expect you do for me. It is not a good way to live, is it? I wish you could get leave of absence and come home in a month or two. I think there are some things you would do before winter. I think it would be well to sell the young cow she milks so hard. And feed will be very high. Perhaps Clary would keep Billy again this winter, for you know if you stay away I must come to you. I could not think of staying here alone. Wood and every thing will be so awful high I think it would be cheaper. It seems as if you might come as your business is somewhat lessened. Dora got Dan's picture. The children were all much pleased. Tell Mrs. Scott that if I ever get through with my hurry and work I will write to her. Clary is getting better slowly. Molly looks very well I think she has grown tall. She looks upon Ed with perfect disgust she met him face to face on the side walk but took no notice of him, and so did I yesterday. I must stop writing my side aches so. Oh I wish you were here. You don't know how lonesome I am and how I want to be with you.

Affectionately, your Julia

Betty got the 5¢ and says she is going to buy soap blubers

*This letter of William's was not found.
**Indeed "the history of this war" WAS written and there were *many* women who helped nurse the soldiers on *both* sides of the conflict! It is uncertain just who Julia is referring to in this specific instance.

Monroeville July 24th {1864}

Dear William,

It is Sunday and I have just come from Church where we are now having very good sermons preached by our Bishop. He will continue here for some weeks yet. I paid $5.00 last week towards our Church matters. I got two letters* from you last night. One was a good long one. Now William supposing I should say yes to your proposition what is a going to "be did"! And how are you going to proceed! You are there and I am here, and I don't see how that is going to consumate matters. I guess I will not decide 'till I see how things can be arranged, if satisfactorily most likely I might consent but as to the other request, I hope you will not urge it as there is no inclination on my part unless I am with the one I love. Can't you come up before long and then perhaps we can make some arrangements for the Fall and winter. I feel every day as if I could not live so I don't mean to complain or wish to make you feel, or think, that I don't take the proper interest here, but if you are homesick and lonely, you can make allowance for my feeling so too. We were very happy together for nine months and I guess it has spoiled both of us for living separated by so many miles. My health is much better in some respects but I don't think my nerves are any stronger. I don't sleep only as I get worn out to it.

I went to Norwalk again to see about the bedstead and found it six inches narrower than our mattress so I did not take it, but instead of it I took a nice large mahogany stuffed chair for you. It is on casters and I think it is real nice. It will be very gratifying to me to see you enjoy it, and hope it will suit you. It was $20. I had heard you speak of getting one. Perhaps you will see a bedstead in Cincinnati of the style you are sleeping on. You know I have got my ideas up for a mahogany one. It ain't a bit too good for a man that has done what you have for three years past, and where you sleep of course, I shall. I expect <u>Georganna</u> is quite as long-faced as you are so you are not much comfort for each other. I want to see Anna. Is she expecting to come here before she goes back? Jane went home to day so I am busy getting supper. I have got a nice little roast of beef in the oven and some vegetables Theodore gave me from his garden, and oh, how I wish you were here to eat with us and stay with me. Jane is a real good reliable girl and a great comfort to me. If it was not for her I should be back in Kentucky in two weeks. It has been four long weeks since you left us and you may depend I have counted the days and hours. I <u>dressed up</u> to day for the first time since I have been home. I put on the nice muslin you got for me in Lexington and I really felt thought that when I looked in the glass that I looked <u>very</u> <u>well</u>, and you know I don't often flatter myself as much as that. Calligan has gone to Buffalo on the NY & Erie RR. I think the family are pleased with his situation. Mrs. Colton is here. I think the family will leave next month. I should feel real sorry if I thought I was going to stay here for he has been as accommodating and his family as neighborly as any body in town since you left. I suppose my box and jug will be at the depot to morrow morning. I shall write again Tuesday. I have to write in such confusion I am very glad if you can read my letters and you can thank your Stars if you can make any sense to them. A part of the entertainment since I have been writing this is to bring in grasshoppers for the kitten to catch. Betty does take the most comfort with her. Mother had a letter from Louisa last week from New Haven Ct. They will start for home next Wednesday. I suppose they have had a splendid time. It is six weeks to morrow since they left. Ellers has given the girls two lessons. I think they get along very well he seems to be very patient and pleasant.

I believe I can't stretch this any longer. I got a ton of hay for $16; had I better get any more? Peggy will have an increase very soon and hogs are so scarce they cannot be bought. Shall I keep the gentleman or have him fixed? There is only one in the four. It is most night. I must close and take this to the office.

Affectionately Julia

*These "two letters" from William were not found.

Monroeville Tuesday 26th {July 1864}

Dear William,

I shall have to write you a short letter this time for I have been in such comotion all day that I could not write till now and it has got to be nearly six OC. To begin with yesterday I went to the express office and there I found the box, which had come Saturday but no jug. I went again this morning but still it had not come. The man here said they would not bring jugs through unless they were packed or if they were broken we would not get any pay. I told him the express man at Nicholasville was a particular friend of ours, and then he said most likely it would come through. But I had better write to you to know if it had been certainly started with the box. Theodore and John just brought my furniture over. I am very well satisfied with it. He said Mrs. Sawyer had just got a letter from her husband saying Lieut. Williams was drownded in the Rappanhouk while crossing it. There were two Lieut. Williams in that regiment and I am in hopes it is not Dayton. It seems to me the family would have got a dispatch before this time if it had been him. I hear Gen. McPherson of Clyde is killed at Atlanta. I have not seen a paper but Mr. A____ was telling me of the desperate fighting there. Don't you believe George Clary was up to the distillery this morning? A week ago to day his life was dispaired of. Martain was riding with him & of the two looked much the worst.

It rained here a little all day yesterday and towards night very hard and in the midst of it I put on my things and went down to the office, and then did not get a letter. Wasn't it to{o} bad, but you are real good William about writing and I look forward in the morning when evening will come and I shall get a letter from you. Perhaps you can make some enquiries about the jug and I will continue to here. Betty has a little sore on her face. Last night she followed me into the bedroom and said mama "I wish

Mr. Ballud would put a plaster on it he ought to come up and do it, write to Papa to tell him too". It seems Lem Ballard put a plaster on her face in Kentucky and she remembered it. Jule & Fannie have gone to Norwalk in the waggon with Theodore. They will be back to morrow. I think they are going to get along with their music very well. They have taken only two lessons and are beginning to count time. I have not had time to open my preserves yet but think they came all safe. I must close with much love for my friends and a big kiss for my husband.

Affectionately Julia

Office A.A.Q.Master
Nicholasville, KY July 28, 1864

My dear Wife,

Your precious letter of Sunday last came to hand and I have read it about six times.

You seem to see some difficulty in the way of your acceding to my proposition in having a baby. Since the war I have heard of several instances where the thing has been done by proxy or sent in a letter but I don't think I like that way.

I rather insist upon the other proposition or request and want you to think of me and write to me all about when it was and the time of day and just say Oh! How good because I was thinking of you and the pleasure we might have if we were together and will have when we are permitted to be in each other's embrace.

I don't want you to think I am foolish about you. It is my privilage to love you and be happy with you and my family.

And I know you are equally devoted to me. As soon as an oportunity offers I am bound on taking a french and visiting home upon the plea of going to Cincinnati~

I am remaining here very close for the time being so as to get a good ready for it and then won't I have a comfortable time in the new chair you got me.

I shall draw for commutation of fuel and quarters for the year. Which every person says I am entitled too and it will amount to 300$ or more.

Write Mrs. Scott a letter when you have time. It would be very gratifying to her to get one from you.

Keep using the hops and your other medicine. It is so gratifying to hear that your health is improving.

Your devoted
Wm

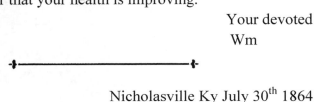

Nicholasville Ky July 30th 1864

My dear and devoted Julia,

I went to Lexington yesterday and purchased a <u>Lace Point</u>.

I concluded it was quite as genteel and more economical than a Lace Mantilla in as much as the points are always fashionable. If you are not pleased with {it} I'll try again.

I saw what pleased me there yesterday. Gen. Burbridge is collecting the Rebels according to Gen. Sherman's order and sending them south. I saw a car load leave yesterday - men, women and children. The family by the name of Pettis living in the large brick house two miles this side of Lexington was arrested and sent south together with about 25 other men, women and children. The order is being enforced throughout this district and they have a list for each county (Jessamine included) in all about 500 names that are to be <u>sent up</u>. When they arrest the man they send the whole family & Negroes if the family wants them to go along. Jo{s}e Cole is still here. Upon my telling her and Mrs. Scott last evening of what was going on, they manifested a good deal of distress and uneasiness and I would not be surprised if some of Mrs. Scott's family was elected and I am quite confident <u>Cole</u> <u>is</u>. There will be hot times here for 3 or 4 weeks to come. The Gov. and Gen. Burbridge have locked horns on the coming election. The Governor says they shall & Gen. Burbridge says they shant. I'll bet on Burbridge.

Well, my pet wife I am in hopes you will be pleased with your point. I want you to do as I wanted you too & tell me. I do love you so much and so very much & send you only a kiss for the present.

Your Wm

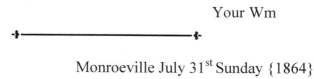

Monroeville July 31st Sunday {1864}

Dear William,

I have just come home from church and am so near roasted that I have set myself down to write to you with nothing on but my shoes and stockings and chemise. I look cool and feel cool and it is the only way one can be comfortable. Friday I was sick abed all day with dreadful pain in the pit of my stomach and bowel complaint and it still continues but not so bad. I had just got off of the bed Friday evening because it was so warm I could not be there any longer when there was a cry that Aunt Louisa and Mr. Bronson were coming. I had taken a Dovers powder and felt some better. I was very glad to see them. Theodore had started from Norwalk with them to take a man to enlist as a substitute, but when he got off of the cars here there was a woman grab{b}ed him, and by the time the Southern train come in the man had gone, so Theodore came back here and stayed here all night. Jane got a real nice supper for them. Louisa said they had not been in the habit of seeing as much for tea in some time. How I wished you were here. They inquired particularly after you. They thought my furniture was very nice and the prices very reasonable. You speak of coming. If you could come right away it would be the nicest time. If not wait till I write to you for <u>certain reasons</u>. I think when the weather gets cooler I shall feel quite well again. I think the medicine Prentice gave me has helped me, at any rate I am all straight. I think I have lost flesh since the warm weather it has been so very warm all the week I could not even sew. I don't think the pastures are suffering. We had a very nice rain last Monday. John Sargent is very busy in his ware house. They got their elevators up last week. I did not go up to Clyde, for that was the day I was sick and it was fortunate that I did not for they did not get through with the services till three OC. Mr Hildreth preached the sermon. When I get hold of it I will send it to you, as it is to be printed. Those that heard it said it was very fine. Wilson said he didn't know but the copperheads would almost take him off of the stand for he did give it to them so hard. Fannie is getting supper and I will stop and help her. Jane has gone home to see a brother that has just come from the war. Betty comes in while I am writing and says "did you tell Papa I was half dead to see him!" They all seem to enjoy themselves. Yesterday they went with nothing but their dresses on. Old Mrs. Gill died last week. I felt sorry for I think she was a most amusing subject and a great wit. I often met her on the rail road and always made it a point to stop and talk with her and I was always amused with her Irish wit. I must try to get up to Caleb's this week. It seems they have been looking for me. I do feel so very sorry for them. It seems Dayton was swimming the river and while in it was shot through the head back of his ear and Henry Stultz through the neck. The rebels got their bodies out of the water and strip{p}ed them of everything and left them lying in the sun for three days when some of our boys went and buried them without any coffins. I don't think William you can compliment me any on this letter, either the composition, or the writing. The flies are so troublesome it keeps one fighting them, and three of my front teeth are aching ever so bad. They trouble me very often after eating. I guess I shall have to stop for I am getting so nervous. I wrote to Mrs Scott this morning but I could not find much to write about. When does George expect Anna back? I had not heard from her since she came up. Oh William how I wish you were here at home this evening. We could have such a cosy time here in the woods and it is very lonely for me. The jug was all safe. I paid $1.50 for it and $1.75 for the fruit. Good bye for this time. I do hope I shall see you soon and imagine a sweet kiss for to night

Julia

This letter below was a FULL four pages long and then William wrote across (perpendicular to) what was already written! CJB

Nicholasville Ky
Sunday July 31st 1864

My precious Wife,

Yours of Thursday* last come to hand and I as usual read it about four times before I was satisfied to lay it away.

How very sorry I am to hear of Dayton William's death. I sympathize deeply with his mother and the family and pitty his poor wife very much. They were appearrantly so happy with each other and seemed to enjoy life so well to gether.

You can hardly imagine how we are suffering for rain. There has been scarsely a drop of rain since I returned and the corn is very seriously damaged already by the drouth. The thermometer has stood at 96° in the shade for two or three days past and you can imagine about how warm it is in my room with a low ceiling and no draft through it.

Jose Cole is with us yet but seems rather down cast and quiet since they have commenced sending Rebels South. They sent another batch from Lex{ington} yesterday and it is to be continued from day to day until we get relieved of them. There is to be a Negro Regiment of Cavalry organized at Camp Nelson which will draw heavily upon the Negroes in this state. I have the 47th KY infantry (one company) here for Provost Guard and I act as commander of the Post and Quartermaster. They seldom do anything without first a{s}king me. Day before yesterday a man from Woodford Co. had two darkies on their way to Camp Nelson to enlist and he overhauled them near my stable and threatened to shoot them unless they returned home with him and by threatening them severely he started them towards home. I heard of it in about 20 minutes and sent three of the Provost Guards on horseback after him and took him and his Negroes to Camp where he is now locked up for discouraging the enlistment of Negroes in compliance with Gen Burbridge's orders on the subject. He has all outlaws and guerillas shot after they are taken. There has been some 6 or 8 shot already - It is very difficult to determine what the end of his order in opposition to Bramlett's proclamation respecting the elections about to take place in this state will be. But I am inclined to think that Gov. Bramlett will re{scind?} his future policy and back down. Bramlett and his party announced the name of one of the most notorious rebel copper heads in the state for Judge of the Court of Appeals and Gen Burbridge has issued an order ordering the arrest of any set of trustees that open a poll and permits votes to be cast for him and the arrest of those voting for him. Rather square <u>toed</u> <u>isn't</u> <u>it</u>.

Geo sent the carriage to Wellington day before yesterday where I want it to remain all quiet until I get home without having anything said about it. It will cost $25 to send it there.

I wrote to Tom Cone asking him to look to McMillan for me and keep him close to work at the buggy. You speak to him and ask him to see that is made complete in every respect and the work well done ~

I will send you 100$ by express which is the amount of my months pay less $27. I have a little coming to me here that I can't get in case I get short~ I am not spending much money myself. You had better let Webb do about as he thinks best about painting the house. Can't you get Corwin to whitewash our old fence? I don't see why Theodore should think we are all going to pot unless it is the heavy taxes he has to pay. You know what my wish is about matters and I know you will be governed by it.

It is so gratifying to me to be able to make you comfortable with means and to gratify every want of yours as far as in my power. I so often think of your unrelenting <u>devotion</u> and kindness to me and your saying so many times to me <u>I don't want to but you may</u> a secret to my affection that you did not understand during the first five years of our married life but the <u>bliss</u> we now enjoy more than compensates for the time lost in learning. The <u>pet{t}ing</u> that you require from me comes gratefully and cheerfully and I want to devote my future life in living for you and my family and content myself with their happiness. I know it is a study with you to please me and that many times you fail to consult your own comfort and I may say health in doing it. I am never as well pleased as in pleasing you and my affection for you knows no bound & may we be permitted soon to give each other a more satisfactory proof of our love than by mere mention on paper. I long to have your head upon my bosom and press my lips to yours and receive your sweet responses. I asked one little thing to please me and I expect every letter I get from you to hear of it being complied with or that you will say it was <u>so good</u> because I was thinking of you but would have been better had <u>you</u> been with me. I think of you so much & so often.

My dear do be careful of your health and avoid being drawn into hard work and the confusion of work and use the medicine prescribed for you and use it regular and try and get stronger.

You had better pay Dr. Prentiss 13$ dollars or something on his bill against us~

It has been sprinkling a little on us to day with every appearance of rain but still it comes not~

Be as cheerful and happy as you can and I will make a detour home before many weeks and do more than sending a kiss as I do to day. I got the childrens letters and will answer them~

Kiss all of them. Mrs. McF. is in a fix already~

Cook has gone East to Washington, N.Y. Boston, Phil. & Baltimore on a pleasure trip.

McQuitty is here from Nashville on a visit. I send you a fancy photograph and will send you one every time I write. The one I send may induce you to want another baby. I have several others. I guess I'll send you two to day. I know you would consent to have another baby if I wanted it. I mean when I can be at home with you.

I am just hearing an ambulance started to take a Negro teacher to camp. I don't mean a Negro but a man to teach them.

I hope you went to the funeral of Maj. Gen McPherson as you expected too. It was a great loss to the country.

The news to day is that Grant is moving on Richmond and that he has captured three entire Brigades of rebels and that Pennsylvania is invaded again. I think we will have very stirring news for a week to come. I wish you had a paper. Have Frank Taylor leave one someplace at the Depot for you so you can send one of the girls & get it or have it left at the P.O. and then you can get it when you get my letters. You can then read the paper first and my letter afterwards. I am writing with a 10$ pen & holder presented to me as usual by Will Saffell. He tells me he is to be married in about six weeks & I bet he will not get as good a wife as I have.

Your affectionate

Wm

*This letter of Julia's from "Thursday" (28th) was not found.

Dear William,

I am reduced to a half sheet of paper but thought you would rather get such a letter than none at all. We have had a fine rain all day and heavy showers last night, which will help everything very much. I went down to the P.O. in it last night but did not get a letter. The Cincinnati mail did not come or else went on through. It has got to be so sure a thing my getting a letter every night that I miss it very much. I have been sewing hard to day. I have made two pair of drawers for the girls. Ellers gave the girls another lesson to day. I think he is starting them just right. He has forty two scholars and has a fine instrument at Wilson's where he gives some lessons and it would be much out of his way up here. I saw Harrison Terry Saturday. He looks very well. He has bought a farm of 40 acres in Wood county for his father and sister. I slept good last night for the fourth time since I came back which is eight weeks to day since I left KY. I dreamed I turned over in the night and found you in bed and I was so glad. I gave you such a hug and kiss as I know you have not had in one while. Birdie dreamed you were sick which I hope is not so. I am feeling better to day for it is cooler. I wrote you a long letter Sunday. I hope you get them all for I should not like to have any one else read them. Grant has done a big thing at Petersburgh and I am so anxious to hear the news to night. William are you coming soon? Do let me know. Excuse this short scribble for it is car time.

Affectionately Julia

Nicholasville KY "Wednesday"
Aug. 3, 1864

My Dear Wife,

I received your letter of Sunday. It would have afforded me the greatest pleasure in the world to have seen you in your nice clean sundress with that red gold stud in front. I send you a phot{ograph} which is rather an improvement upon your stile for a summer dress and exactly my stile of beauty tall and graceful like my pet wife & much her stile of beauty. I purchased it because it was and I hope you will not think it vulgar as I think it is not. I am obliged to you for your sudjestion about the time of making my visit home. I shall be compelled to wait until I hear from you again owing to my anxiety about getting all of my papers up before I come. I think next week will clean {clear?} them all up & then Geo will not have the least trouble in keeping them up all the time. I told him he could go home when they were up snug & he is hard at work at them.

Intimate to me in your next the time you expect to be unwell so I can vary the time to suit matters here. I{t} seems that you think of coosy times as well as myself and I hope we may have one soon. I think of you OH! So good once or twice a week. Do be careful of your health and strength. You are the most precious prize I have. Do have the girls read and spell and have them at it every day & never mind their geography & arithmetic. Let them spell the most-I sold my Grey mare and have got my pay for 150$ cash and a buggy worth about 75$ to 100$ covered and in good running order. Now if you come in the fall I have a buggy. You remember she cost me 115$~

Anna will call and see you before she returns which will be in about 4 weeks- I don't want you to get nervous writing to me notwithstanding I like {a} nervous woman. I am not feeling atal bad to see some of this at home stir{r}ed up about the draft. I got a letter from Sam{uel} Jackson to hunt him up a negro substitute, but cant do it- He says he thinks Beach will want one and it seems Theo{dore} is also in search of one. It's nothing to be in the army - I want you to use some of that whisky regularly-

I must close with a kiss~

Wm. R.

Nicholasville KY
Aug 4th 1864

My dear Wife,

Yesterday was a quiet and pleasant day with about the usual amount of business to do here at the post.

I will say while I think of it that I wish you would send Caroline ten dollars to square up Birdie's Bills at Mansfield and Belleville.

Anna is at Bellville and will visit you in turn after going to Mansfield. George's health seems to be very good at present. I pay him 125$ per mo.

No ladies at Mrs. Scott's only Miss Moore & I think she and Blackburn would do to be called rebels. We have seen some curious figuring about there and they always seem to be in the secret.

I cant write you a very good letter this morning. I have no news neither have any letter to answer. Geo received a letter from Kennedy upon a recommend{ation} I gave him. It seems he has got a place as operator at Chilicothe Ohio. I got Dr. Train to have him discharged from the service.

How I enjoy the cool nights we have had for a few days. If you had been here I believe I should have spent much of my time in bed. I dreamed last night that you was laying on my arm and was sadly grieved when I realized that it was not so, and I mean that it shall be so before many weeks. An affectionate kiss and I must close.

Wm

—————————————————

Nicholasville KY
Aug 6th 1864 "Saturday"

My dear,

I{t} is cloudy and pleasant this morning with a fair prospect of rain. I had a fine serenade last night which I enjoyed very much. The party consisted of Graves and three Schaffers brothers and all accomplished german musicians with two violins, Guitar, and Bass viola. I invited them into my room and had quite a treat on music inasmuch as they were fine performers. Oh if I could have had you laying close to me to dream away the <u>first surprise</u> Piece when they commenced 'Oh delightful'. Miss Moore is going to Covington to day with Blackburn. I say Moore will not do she is a Rebel and is trusted by them.

Captain Morris is as usual spending one half of each day and night with Molly Butler a flirting but desperately in love. It requires a good deal of research and patience to find a union man or woman in Kentucky.

Geo has been presented with a yearly pass over the K.Y.C. Rail Road ~~

Let me know about <u>things</u> and I will then make some calculation about my visit home to see my <u>most precious old gal</u> and devoted wife & children. You have never complied with one of my requests. Cant you to please me.

Theodore has never sent me a description or a deed made out for the Iowa law for me to get signed by Sayer ~

I must close my <u>sweet one</u> wishing that I could inflict upon you a kiss.

Your affect{ionate}
Wm. R.

Nicholasville KY
Tuesday Aug. 9th/64

My dear good Wife,

8 O'clock and breakfast over and I am at my usual task and my pleasure of the day.

It bids fair to be an extreme warm day as it was yesterday and last night. How warm it was in my room.

I have just been telegraphed to come to Lexington. I expect it is to represent to Gen. Burbridge about the movements of the Rebels about town. I have no news and I declare I don't know what to write to you about. Only to say you are so dear and precious and you are as constantly in my mind as if I was desperately in love with you. I expect to get a good long letter from you to day. You must excuse short ones from me until I can accumulate some news. A good kiss and a sweet embrace & I close.

Your affect{ionate},
Wm

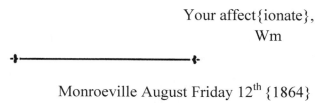

Monroeville August Friday 12th {1864}

Dear William,

I have set down to make an effort to write to you but whether I shall succeed or not is yet to be tested, for oh! It is so oppressively hot that one's ideas are all cooked. I have been miserable all the week with my face and teeth, but no other cause until to day. And now I shall feel badly for several days from another cause. I shall try and keep as quiet as possible that I may feel better soon, at any rate in four or five days. I think it was the hottest night last night that we have had this summer. It was very little sleeping that I did. I got up at 4 OC this morning and opened all the out side doors but it was almost as bad on the stoops as in the house. The children were crying and we all seemed uncomfortable. I expect you have had a smothering time in your room. There was a smash up on the southern road at Shelby Tuesday evening so we got no mail, and for some reason there was no mail Wednesday night, so I did not hear from you from Saturday till last evening, when I got four letters. The children were very much pleased with the pictures. I gave Dora the "first lessons on the flute". I thought it was the cunningest of all. Dr. Beach took dinner with us Wednesday. He was on his way west and did not make connection. He has sold the mill and bought a small farm for your Father up towards the widow Halls. Your Father thought it was best. I spoke to Theodore about sending you a description of your land and thought he had done it. Mary told me he was going to Iowa this week and I should think likely would go and see it. He did not say anything to me about going. She said she should come and stay here part of the time. It is queer how they all like to come here.

You ask me how I like the lace point. I think it is very nice. But I think perhaps a mantle would have been larger for me, you see, I have to lay several plaits in the neck behind to make it fit in the shoulders and that takes up the length of it. Perhaps the merchant where you got it would let you bring a mantle up when you come and then we could decide which looked the best. And you could take the other back. I hope you will not think me difficult to suit. You have a good linnen coat here that I expect you need. It was new last summer. I wish if you go to Lexington you would get Betty another pair of shoes such as I got her at the place where you had the rings put into my gaiters. They were thick soled kid 9½. They have been very excelent shoes to wear and the half size makes them just fit her. I think she feels better. She is not so dreadful cross. If I was in your place I would let Blackburn and Miss Moore both of them know just what I thought of them and I would give them all down the banks if there was much figuring about the house. Don't you suppose Bob Scott is around somewhere! Or what are they trying to do? I think William you deal in pictures of pretty females. They are pretty to be sure. But I am afraid you will get your ideas so exalted that you will be disappointed in the real live one that you have at home and then you will expect to have the deficiencies made up in some other way and dear me! What will I do. You will have to bring some paint and powder along for you know I don't keep any and your eyes have feasted on the pretty women of Kentucky so long that do use it, that I shall look very inferior to them. You know if you bring the powder you will have to get some body's <u>old stocking leg</u> to put it on with. I believe that is the approved plan of getting on. But please don't get a "niggers". It does seem so comfortable not to have any of them to scent up the house this hot weather. You speak of bringing Will. I have no objection. There is a good deal he could do but what would he do this winter. You know I don't expect to stay here. I think if you could keep him till next year it would be a very good plan to get him here for then I suppose you will be coming home for good. But I want you to do just as you think best.

And now William you wished I would write you a love letter. How will I begin! Where will I begin! Well now I will tell you I love you dearly, <u>yes that's sure</u>. I love your good, true, and noble heart for it loves me. I love your curls for I can make them curl just as I want them to. I love your forehead for it is my sweet place to kiss. I love your eyes for they betray more love than words can express. I love your lips because they press sweet kisses on my cheek. I love your arms because they press me to your bosom and I love your bosom because it is my own, <u>own</u> place to lay {my} head and sleep and the union of all these yea more - makes the man I love, and <u>I love the union for the sake of the union</u>. Now William I fancy I can see the corners of your mouth jerk with a sort of nervousness and your nostrils distend.

~ 179 ~

And then you think if I just dared to show that to some body. But now William it is my love letter and you must keep it <u>secret</u>. When shall I look for you home so I can tell you how much I love you and will you stay long enough so that you will feel that you can have some time to stay with me and will not have to hurry and attend to business so as to get through to have to hurry back. I don't think either of us would be satisfied with such a visit and I know your time for the last three years has been spent as closely for the Government as any other mans and you might have a few weeks rest. I think when Paramore comes home a party will go over to the Islands. You know they went last summer and had such a time. William when will you come. Tell me so I can be thinking about it. It is so dull and lonesome for me here. I wish you could get a house and take us all with you. I would try and get you such good things to eat and try to make it seem like home to you. I should have written yesterday as usual but the mails had been so irregular I did not know as my letter would get through. My face is swelled and is very sore and with all of my ailments I am almost a used up woman. I think if I should see Capt. Morris I should hardly speak to him for he must be destitute of all honor and void of all feeling to practice the deceit he is practicing. As for the Butlers I never saw anything to love in any of them. I was asking Theodore about Gay. He says he is a most thorough <u>scamp</u> and rogue and that his oldest son has been in prison for all sorts of things. So I thought we would not extend our acquaintance with them any farther. He seemed to think she was a nice woman. Delia has not got along yet. Darwin wrote to me last Saturday to come up and bring all the children. I have thought of going but now I will wait till you come home. Oh I will be so glad to see you and I hope it will be cooler so I can fix up and look pretty. I never went looking so in my life but I can't wear any thing decent. This is a long letter and now I will close with all the affection of a devoted wife.

Julia

Monroeville August 30 {1864}

Dear William,

I suppose you are anxious to hear how the birds got through. They came yesterday morning. Fannie had left word for them to let us know from the office when they came and they did. They had feed and watter but bathed freely when we gave them a dish. I got the box Monday morning and I think I shall send the hand trunk tomorrow with your clothes. I put up a few cling stone peaches off of our tree yesterday. The chickens were eating them so bad and there was so few I thought I would make sure of them. I saved four on the top of the tree for you. I never saw finer or larger peaches. There is just one pear on the tree which I am saving also it is turning yellow. I hope you will come in time to get them. They will be ripe in a week. I am still very miserable hardly able to crawl about the house, and this morning I am aching all over again. I am taking pills to act on my liver and to quiet my nerves for I have suffered more than I could tell. My head troubles me very much. If I could have some rest from the noise and confusion of the children I should be glad and to cap all Jane is going to leave Saturday.

I close with many affectionate kisses Julia

Nicholasville, KY
Aug. 30th 1864

My dear Wife,

We have had unusual pleasant weather since I last wrote to you. Business goes on smoothly and every thing is quiet respecting the raid and much anxiety expressed here to have McClellan nominated at Chicago.

My health is quite good and I hope yours has improved since I left you.

The mare I sold McQueen run a race Saturday again and beat winning from 3 to 5000$. I have an inquiry almost every day to know her stock and how fast she can run, &c, &c. McQueen has promised me her picture.

Mrs. Scott has been suffering very much with her face originating from cold and decayed teeth. Mrs. Moore is yet in bed but is improving slowly.

I have made out my account for commutation of fuel and quarters amounting to 330$ and Cap{tain} Hall says he will recommend that they be allowed if they are allowed my pay in future will amount to about 150$ per month.

You must excuse short letters for there is no news. I have not heard from you since I left home.

Remember me to the children and a good kiss for <u>you</u>.

Wm

Nicholasville, KY
Septem 6, Tuesday {1864}

Dear Wife,

I am very sorry to inform you that the bridges that were burned by Morgan on the K.Y. Central RRoad was carried away by high water on Sunday night and there will be some delay in my letters reaching you. I{t} will take from two to four weeks to reconstruct them. Consequently our supplies for camp will come from Louisville via Lexington. There has been nothing but confusion for a week past in smashups of one kind or another on that road.

Syle just says to me that John Morgan is dead but can give no particulars ~ only that he was surprised by Gen Gillem and had six hundred killed and wounded. Sherman has taken about 50,000 prison{ers} at Atlanta.

The death of Cara Mignor was very melancholy. She was at her uncle's visiting who lived in Ill{inois} and was <u>unwell</u> at such times was flighty and quite insane at times for a day or two. Such was the case with her while there and they called a Dr. who left medicine for her. Her aunt went into the room to see her and found her much better and up and she had just taken what she supposed to be the medicine left for her and instead of that she took some <u>arsenic</u> they had got a few days previous to kill rats & had left it on her dressing table. She only lived about six hours ~

I think I can arrange with Mrs. Scott about renting her house and if I do Hutchison, Todd & Carlisle are very anxious to stay where they are. She wants to leave sometime in October. I will write more particulars as soon as she concludes what she is agoing to do.

McCampbell is quite sick again and thinks he is going to die. I think it is only nervous for he was here at the office yesterday morning and was only complaining of his back and now complains of <u>seeing</u> <u>double</u>.

I want to see you very bad and I am again in hopes that some good may arise for our success at Mobile & Atlanta & of the late victory on Morgan & Wheeler.[8] So that we can all live together -

You may wonder at my blind way of writing to you by Geo{rge} but I will explain when I see you. I will send you some money as soon as I get my pay, or sooner if you want it.

You are so good and so very clever to me.

A kiss and several other good things and I close.

Your affect{ionate},
Wm

Monroeville Thursday Sep 8th {1864}

Dear William,

I have but very little of importance to write about, but as I have written but once before this week you will be anxious to know how we are. Julia is quite well again. Fannie's feet are so she can wear slippers and the rest are well. I got the letter last night that you wrote Friday*. It was mailed the 2nd and got here the 7th. I've had no others. It was a very short one. I have felt very gloomy for several days and was in hopes to have had a letter from you that would raise my spirits. I had to stop writing as there was a lady called for me (I was up stairs writing). It proved to be Mrs. Dr Tifft. She had been over all day and was going home on the cars to night so of course I flew around and got tea for her. She has just gone and I have but few minutes to finish my letter. The copperheads have had a convention here today, and I heard a dinner was given at Crippins old Hotel. If McLellan accepts the nomination I hope he will come out flat footed, for they will make a fool of him if they can. I guess you are more contented than you were and are not so home sick. I told you in going to the cars how I felt, and I still feel as if it would be a long time before we were together again. School does not begin till week after next but then the children can go. There is no Cincinnati mail about every other night so I get your letters very irregularly. I believe Theodore got into his house Monday.

They are looking for a lot of company to night. I am glad it aint me. Mine comes without looking for. George & Anna have not got along yet. I hope she has got some money for me. I dont think the girls can go to Sandusky. Ann has left. I don't know what help they have got. William I love you just as well as ever and wish I could see you this lonesome evening.

Affectionately Julia

*No letter from William dated Friday September 2, 1864 was found.

Acting Assistant Quartermaster's Office,

Nicholasville, Ky.

My dear Wife,

I am fearful you may feel grieved at not hearing from me oftener this week. In the first place I have had but very little to write about and the confusion with the mail has been such as not to offer much inducement to send letters to you expecting that you would get them in any reasonable time. I omitted writing to you on Saturday because I went to Lexington Friday evening on the cars after dark and stayed there until Saturday evening attending to some business and getting some printing done.

Capt. Hall and Santmeyer was here this a.m. and spent several hours with {me}. Hall made me a present of a very good buggy harness and is very pleasant and accommodating generally.

I have him looking around for rooms that you and I and the children Birdie, Dora and Lillian can spend the winter in. If I can get two rooms I shall rent them. Mrs. Scott claims to be very much disappointed because I did not get her house and says Blackburn pressed his claim every day for it so she was compelled to let him have it. I hope him and his wife will have a good time with so large a house for him and so small a family.

Col._____ allowed my commutation for fuel and quarters amounting to over 300$ and in future my pay will be about 150$ per month. McDowell sent me work that he expected to be here in a few days and I think he will bring his wife. How I wish you could be here. May be you will think you can leave the children a week or two and come down and see how we can arrange for the winter. My buggy is all newly painted and Mr. _____ gave the painter orders to stripe it. He would pay the expense of it. I have no desire to ride unless you are here and it will probably stay in the shop until you or McDowell and his wife comes here to use it. I have a great mind to buy Mrs. Scott's carriage and fit it up for I know I can make something on it.

I want to see you very very bad and have a good cozy time.

Santmeyer wife and family are at camp to remain a week or two. The R{ail} road will run through again by Wednesday when we will have a rush of business again, for a time.

Will you think of me and comply with an old request. And write to me about it. I think of you so much and grow to be a real baby about you. I love you so dearly. A good hug and a sweet kiss for you. I will answer my charming Julia's letter to morrow.

Your affect{ionate}
Wm

━━━━━━━━━━━━━━━━━━━━━━━━━━━━━

Acting Assistant Quartermaster's Office,

Nicholasville, Ky.

Sept.13, 1864.

Dear Wife,

I was ordered to report to Gen McLean for temporary duty which will continue from one to four weeks. Every thing to remain unchanged and go{es} on as usual at Nicholasville. I think he and Gen. Burbridge are contemplating a raid after the rebels beyond Mt. Sterling and may only be gone a few days and may be out two or three weeks. I sent all of my teams to assist in hauling stores from Paris to Mt. Sterling for a few days. The thing is being got up on the sly and may be a brilliant affair. I shall have but little labor and no responsibility & am not necessarily in any unusual danger and shall avoid it as much as it is possible on your account. If very successful Gen Burbridge will probably go further and be gone longer than he would otherwise. Now please bear up like a brave woman until I return for during my time out I shall make an effort for a Furlough and let Probert continue to run my post. Gen McLean is Judge McLean's son. I was at Lexington again yesterday and while there heard Dr. Breckenridge speak. He is very much the character of a man your father is. And no better speaker.

I shall send you some money by Express in a day or two. Now keep up courage. I am not going a very great way but over very rough roads where we are compelled to travel along and will see pretty rough times but I expect to go through all O.K. and perform my duty creditable to you and myself. It is being got up so secretly that Gen McLean said yesterday he did not wish men to tell their wives. The Gen is a very pleasant man. As soon as I return I shall come and see you or send for you. Now please don't worry if you don't hear from me very often. I will write to you again tomorrow.

Your ever affectionate
Wm

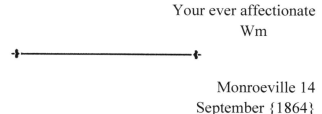

Monroeville 14
September {1864}

Dear William,

Why don't you send me some money? You wrote two weeks ago that you would send me some. I have had $50 in five weeks just what would keep me two. And found them out of every thing when I came home but flour and that I had to pay for. And it does seem with your salary as if I need not have to be pinched in this way for means. And I knew my claims ought to come in before any one else. It would be hard enough to contend with poor health and have plenty to do with without having it to worrie about it. I have been to the Express office till I am ashamed to go any more. I put your sheep papers in the hand trunk with some others. I hope you have got it by this time. Sarah and her children are here while Darwin has gone to the State Fair.

Affect{ionately} Julia

———————————————————

Hd. Qr. 1st Divis. D.K.
Prestonburg Ky~
Friday 23^d Sept/64

My dear,

We arrived here all in good shape and fine spirits at 10 O.C. a.m. to day and will probably stay here during to morrow and start for Pound Gap Sunday distants 46 miles. We are 95 miles from Mt. Sterling over mountains and very picturesque valleys. Scouts report but a small force at the gap where we expected the fiercest resistance. We have not suffered any for a good living. Water and forage and I never was in better health than I am now and improve upon it every day and thus far am pleased with the trip. The road from here to the gap I am told is no worse than that which we have come over. There are very few inhabitants in the mountains and they are a different people from any you ever saw. Many of them go 40-50 miles to get their groceries and necessaries of life. There is seldom more than 15 or 20 acres of level land to be found that can be tilled and that is on some small stream or creek.

This place is on the big Sandy River which is a very large stream at high water being fed by ten thousand small streams from the mountains. Every thing we have got to continue our journey come to Louisa 45 mi below here on the river by steam boat and was brought from this in flat boats pushed with polls and pulled over the shallow places with oxen and hauled from the river up into town on a sled drawn by 4 yokes of oxen.

There is no mail that comes this far up and I send this by a currier that leaves here in the morning. If you have written here I probably will not get your letter.

My only anxiety is about you and the way you will get along until you hear from me again.

We have very good accommodations at a private house and strange as it may seem we have not layed out either night yet. Four of our party is in the parlor with me playing whist* while I am enjoying a greater pleasure writing to my precious wife & companion. All I have to do is give general directions about camping, the issuing of grain & the movements of the pack mules. I am almost as familiar with the Gen. as I am with Col. Garrard and am treated with all of the consideration I co{u}ld expect and a general good feeling seems to prevail with the officers of the whole command.

Gen. Burbridge is expected here to morrow with another Brigade making 4 Brigades in the Divis{ion}. We are also told that there is only about 800 old men and boys guarding the salt works in Virginia when {where?} we may possibly bring up~

Our animals are all in good condition yet. We have only left 5 mules out of 700 and not more than 6 or 8 horses. I have not seen a slave since I left Mt. Sterling.

I must close expecting I can write to you again in a day or two. Remember {me} to the children and kiss all of them. A real good one for you.

Your affect{ionate},

Wm. R.

* Whist is a card game played with a full deck of 52 cards, usually by two pairs of players and similar to bridge, of which it is the forerunner. (Webster, 1962)

H Qr 1st Divis D.K.
Saturday Sept 24
Prestonburg Ky
8 OC P.M.

Dear Wife,

Expecting an oportunity to send you a letter to morrow I write to you again.

If Gen Burbridge arrives to night as expected we will leave in the morning. We are ready to move any moment. I have been very busy to day superintending arrangements in general and my experience as Q{uarte}r Mast{er} saved the command great trouble and confusion to day and Ross and Fry were just the men I kneeded to assist me and I think the Gen was much pleased with my management He has thus far yielded to my wishes in everything I asked and Gen Hobson and I are on the very best of terms.

I think the expedition will be a very successful one. If it is and I return again I shall never regret the trip - I can ask and get them almost any thing I want at H{ead} Quarters. I have an understanding now with Cap Butler the Rgt Guard about a leave of absence when I return before I was relieved from Gen McLeans staff so as not to be compelled to apply through the Qr.M. Dept for it. If I only knew you was happy and getting along well I would go along easy with every hardship I may have to encounter on any duty I have to perform and I do want so much to hear from you but cannot -

We have enjoyed the music of two very good bands of the 12th Ohio & 11th Mich. Regts this Evening - We have our Negroe Rgt of Cavalry with us and Negro Infantry to lead the Pack Mules -

I will have the pleasure of again sleeping in a good clean bed again to night and if I could only have added to that the greatest of all other pleasures, your company, how delightful it would be in the desolate valley of the Big Sandy. I can only enjoy the next greatest that is to think of you and the children. I know you think of me and maybe worry about me but I dont want you {to} yield to any unreasonable trouble with me & trust you will not --

My candle is about played out and I will close for to night with a kiss .

25 Sep-Evening

Gen Burbridge arrived last night and found the River to{o} high to cross and could not reach us until we sent him a boat in the morning to cross. It rose some 7 feet in a few hours and is falling as fast almost as it rose -

We are all well fixed for a move at our H{ead}Q{ua}r{ters} and I think I can say Gen B. is not fixed atal <u>owing to the difference in Qr Mas -</u> unless the River falls to night we keep on this side of the river and take a different road from what we expected to, no differ{ence} in the distance only not so good -- I see by the papers of the 21st that there has been trouble on the Lake{Erie?} - We are living very well here having sugar and coffee to furnish the family we board with.

I have no certainty that I can send this in the morning but hope I can -

I hope my dear wife is getting along well. My health is very good and I think it will continue so - We have picked {up} 6 rebel deserters to day and two citizens fleeing from Va and all tell the same story of the condition of things where we are going and I think we will not make a failure of it-

How I would like to see you but must close by saying good bye with a 100 kisses for you & the children -

Yours affect{ionate}
Wm. R

~ 191 ~

H{ead}Q{uarters} 1st Divis. D.K.
In the mountains
19 miles Pound Gap
Wednesday Sep 28/64

Dear Wife,

At five OC a.m. and raining hard I sit under a paulin {tarpaulin} between two mountains writing to you. I am unusually well and every thing move{s} along slowly. We scared up 16 Rebel scouts yesterday about one mile from here. They fired at the advance guard and took to the mountains but hurt no person.

We move to the left of Pound Gap to day into Virginia. This is the most desolate country you ever heard tell of.

The pack mules return to day & I try and get this to you by the Lt. in charge of them.

We move in a very few moments & I must close with a kiss to you & the children.

Your affectionate,
Wm R. J.

+————————————————+

Acting Assistant Quartermaster's Office,

Nicholasville, Ky.

Oct 25, 1864

My dear Wife,

I have two more rooms in tow and am going at once to see about them and as usual will let you know my success in the morning--Geo. goes to Henrys to morrow, and I guess Hutchinson too.

The rooms I am trying to get are up stairs oposite the Court House in the building that is occupied by E{d} Peckover{?} what L_____ occupied for an office and sleeping apartment.

I got two letters from you complaining sorely about my not writing. I have written almost every day and if the letters have not reached you in time you should not place suspicion on me for neglect.

Your affect{ionate}
Wm. R

-╂─────────────────────╀-

Toledo,
Nov 30th 1864

Wm R. Jackson, Esq.
Dear Sir,

Julia's letter is just recd and Sarah will report. You have my statement of your affairs in full. The accounts paid by me for you last winter were: McCollum, Brunderhoff & Brewster, $150.00 Bostisick, H_____ , $100.00 which I shall need during the coming month.

The matter of Mr. Hillyer you can as well settle yourself and I have not recd any response from Vandusen, B_____, Bergen. We are all well. Wm started for Chicago last night.

Yours truly,
D. E. Gardner*

*Brother-in-law Darwin Gardner married to Julia's sister, Sarah.

-╂─────────────────────╀-

Acting Assistant Quartermaster's Office,

Nicholasville, Ky.

Dec 9, 1864

My dear Wife,

I arrived here Thursday morning. I reached Newark at 12 OC and had quite a visit with Beach. My expences from home to Lex ~ was 2$~ I saw Gray a few moments. There is a good many changes taking place about Camp Nelson. There is another effort being made to reduce the importance of that place. We are sending a great deal of stuff to Louisville. Anna & Geo. are well. I have not settled upon any place to board. It is very dull about the town and junction. They stripped me of all of my best horses again to send them to the front. I did not see McDowell when I was in Cincinnati. I was only there about two hours. Hutchinson has gone to Cin to take charge of the office there. I will send you some money in a day or two.

Remember me to the children & a kiss to my dear wife.

Your affect{ionate}
Wm. R. J~

———————————

Acting Assistant Quartermaster's Office,

Nicholasville, Ky.

Dec 11, 1864

My dear Wife,

There is about 6 in. of snow on the ground here and it is tolerable sleighing.

I have found no place to board yet unless it is at the Hotel. Every thing is as dull as the grave about town except what little business we are doing. I spent last evening at the Shaffers' rooms and was entertained with good music.

I have not seen Mrs. Scott or any of the family yet. Blackburn's folks are all alone except Moore. I have only seen him yet.

Have Barney put a stake to the evergreen at the end of the back porch to keep the wind from killing it & have him fat one or both of the sows. Feed them corn.

I expect to be very homesick here this winter. There is no guard here and I expect I cannot get one. Tell the girls to be good girls and apply themselves to their music.

Remember me to all of them & a kiss to your own dear self.

from your affect{ionate}

Wm ~

-+--------------------+-

Acting Assistant Quartermaster's Office,

—Nicholasville, Ky.

Thursday <u>Dec 15,</u> 1864

My dear Wife,

The weather is more mild and muddy. I have not seen Mrs. Scott. She has been at Lexington ever since I returned.

Miss Moore is at Blackburn's and I tell you it looks rough and cheerless about there.

I send you Darwin's letter showing the amount I owe him for claims he has adjusted for me. I want you to go to Theodore and have him settle it and interest with Darwin. Don't fail to attend to it soon and write to Darwin.

I feel very much unsettled here and am really discontented here but still I say nothing to that effect. Matters are rather squally throughout the State. Theaves and robbers reign supreme in many parts of the state. ~~

I have received nothing from home. I sent you a memorandum of David's yesterday. Let me know when you receive it.

A kiss to all of you.

Your affect{ionate}

Wm

Acting Assistant Quartermaster's Office,

Nicholasville, Ky.

Dec. 16th, 1864

My dear wife,

I have not heard one word from you since I left.

Sherman has taken Savanna and we all feel pretty good over the news. You probably know that Will Wilmore married one of Buford's girls and they were living in Wilmore's old house. It was set on fire as they suppose by the Negroes and they bearly got out alive saving nothing.

It seems the old man had some trouble with the Negroes a few day{s} ago. I have not seen Mrs. Scott yet. I would like to see all of you but can only send a kiss to all.

Very affect{ionate} husb{and}

Wm

Acting Assistant Quartermaster's Office,

Nicholasville, Ky.

Monday <u>Dec 19,</u> 1864.

My dear Wife,

It has been raining here almost constantly for three days and every thing is afloat here & very gloomy ~

We have cheering news from every quarter now & I hope it will continue. Sherman at the Coast probibly in Savanna. Hood badly defeated by Thomas his communication with Mobile cut and Stoneman & Burbridge within ten miles of Saltville & will probibly take it and another fleet leaving City Point for some place on the co{a}st.

I may get a chance to send the girls some prayer books.

Morris is going to Cint. to day and I will try and get him to get them and send them by Exp{ress}. I am not settled to live at any place yet and Oh! how lonesome and dreary it is.

Mrs. Scott is still at Mr. Clark's ~ I have not seen her. I wish I could see all of you Christmas. a kiss to the children & a sweet embrace to you.

Your affect{ionate} husb{and},
Wm. R.

•————————————•

Acting Assistant Quartermaster's Office,

Nicholasville, Ky.

Thursday <u>Dec 29,</u> 1864.

My dear Wife,

I have not heard from you in several days*. Yesterday Geo., Anna, Rob & myself went out with Mrs. Scott to Mrs. Barkley's to dinner and we were very well fed and entertained~

I expect McDowell and his family here from Lexington on the cars to day. They will remain over night and then go to Danville.

Ross returned from Ripley yesterday where he has been making a visit for ten days. The folks there all wished to be remembered to us.

McDowell & Maj. Jones' clerks are in and about my office making up pay rolls so I have plenty of company. There was an order from the pay Dept. not to pay any more officers until the privates and men to be discharged were payed off. I don't know whether I can get my pay now or not by some informality on the part of McDowell.

I have some persons waiting to see me so I must close with an effectionate good kiss.

Yours,
Wm

*No December 1864 letters from Julia were found.

Chapter Five Notes

1. Rhodes, Robert, *All For The Union, the Civil War Diary and Letters Of Elisha Hunt Rhodes*; New York: Orion Books, 1985, p. 136 (diary entry of Dec. 31/63).

2. Nevins, Allan, *The War for The Union: the Organized War 1863-1864;* New York: Charles Scribner's Sons, 1971, p. 447; Sandburg's *Abraham Lincoln*, Ch. 44, pp. 452-77.

3. About Lincoln's proclamation to observe Thanksgiving Day as a National Holiday: While Lincoln issued the proclamation, at least one source states that credit for making Thanksgiving a national holiday should go to Sarah J. Hale, the editor of *Godey's Lady's Book*, a popular magazine for women in 19th century America, *http://history1800s.about.com*, (accessed in June, 2014).

4. Lowry, Thomas M., M.D., *The Stories the Soldiers Wouldn't Tell: Sex In The Civil War*, Mechanicsburg, Pennsylvania: Stackpole Books, 1994, (Introduction) pp. 1-10, tells of these and other books that were available to doctors and/or the public.

5. Robertson, *Soldiers Blue and Gray*, p. 120 quoting from a letter of Perry Mayo's of the 2nd Michigan (from *Civil War Letters, 170*) referring to what today are known as S.T.D.s or Sexually Transmitted Diseases.

6. Ibid., p. 121.

7. Julia is probably referring to the July 9, 1864 letter of General Sherman's written to his brother, Senator (John) Sherman of Ohio. This letter can be found on pp. 300-301 of *Home Letters of General Sherman, ed. by M.A. DeWolfe Howe.* The entire book can be found through a search at http://bgsu.summon.serialssolutions.com. (accessed November 2014).

8. On August 10, 1864 General Joseph Wheeler attacked the Western & Atlantic Railroad below Chattanooga, then began to strike at the railroads south of Nashville, and finally to return to Atlanta with almost 3000 men, again hitting the Western & Atlantic, en route. His hope was that if these railroads were ruined, Sherman's army would be faced with starvation, and "either be forced to retreat or make a suicidal frontal assault on Atlanta's strong fortifications." Wheeler's plan was initially successful, ripping up more than 30 miles of track near Marietta, Resaca, and Dalton. However, he was driven away from the Western & Atlantic by heavy concentrations of Union infantry causing him and his army to flee, contrary to orders, into East

Tennessee. Moving westward, he destroyed a few miles of track south of Nashville, then fled into Alabama with his troops so exhausted and demoralized that they did not resume active operations until October.

For more on this particular raid of Wheeler's, see: http://www.civil-war-tribute.com (accessed October 2104) and http://www.mycivilwar.com/campaigns (accessed June 2014) and http://www.nytimes.com/1864/09/04/news (accessed June 2014).

Chapter Six

The War's End
January - December 1865

"How I long to hear the announcement that the thing is at an end."

William Jackson, April 8, 1865

While William and Julia continued their letters of devotion to one another throughout the conflict that had now been going on for almost four years, much was happening militarily and politically toward bringing it all to "an end." After the capture of Atlanta in September, 1864, Sherman and his army continued trying to disable that part of the south as Union forces destroyed more and more railroads and warehouses. A month later, Jubal Early, "Old Jube" to his Confederate troops, would be defeated by General Phil Sheridan in the Shenandoah Valley. Confederate General John Bell Hood, not one to give up, hoped to "bait" Sherman into changing his direction and heading toward Tennessee. Instead, Sherman was granted permission to ignore Hood's bait and it was General George Thomas who Grant sent to Nashville in anticipation of Hood; it was Thomas' troops who would ultimately crush Hood's army by mid-December of 1864.

Sherman had waited until after the presidential election as Grant had asked him to; this election could make or break the Union's attempt to remain a Union. However, after Lincoln defeated his Democratic opponent, former General George B. McClellan, Sherman moved forward with his plan and focused on finding a route through Georgia to either Charleston or Savannah. Sherman chose to go southeast to Savannah for a route that would hopefully provide more food for his troops.

Thus began his "March to the Sea," which in Sherman's own words inflicted $100,000,000 worth of damage.

This 250 mile march must have been similar to a plague of locusts to the poor citizens in the small rural towns of Georgia through which these troops passed as they killed just about every animal they could find and looted pantries and barns along the way. One New York soldier wrote that only one fifth of the slain animals were used for their advantage; "the remainder is simple waste and destruction." Some soldiers told of "putrefying carcasses" that lined the roads and the accompanying stench that filled the air. What the Federal forces didn't take or destroy, the Confederate deserters and other stragglers seized. Just three days after William R. Jackson wrote to Julia his "cheering news from every quarter now" and three days before Christmas Day, 1864, William T. Sherman was presenting the city of Savannah and its 25,000 bales of cotton to President Lincoln as a Christmas present.[1]

On the first day of January, 1865, Elisha Rhodes, a private in the 2nd Rhode Island Volunteers, wrote in his diary, "The war drags along, but we feel that we are gaining all the time, and when Petersburg and Richmond fall, as they must soon, the war will end."[2]   Two days later, William wrote to Julia from his camp in Kentucky of Hood's defeat and that the "gurillas have I think concluded they are not safe here and have almost disappeared." He goes on to speak of how "wonderful to see the change in sentiment on the subject of slavery. Every person I talk with seems to have simultaniously given it up." No doubt both William and Julia had heard of the controversy surrounding the Thirteenth Amendment. Although passed by the Senate in April, 1864, it would not be passed by the House until January 31, 1865. It was almost a full year later in December, 1865 before it was finally ratified and slavery formally abolished as a legal institution. Ironically, it was Congress who passed and Lincoln who approved a very different thirteenth Amendment four years earlier, one that specifically stated that the Constitution could never be changed in such a way as to permit interference with the institution of slavery.[3]

There are only six letters from William and one from Julia before the war officially ended, however there are a total of 18 from William and 11 from Julia included in this final chapter because each has something of interest to those who have followed the Jacksons thus far.

Julia writes William (May 5) of "the goods and chattels" and how they arrived "all safe the next morning after they left you." Apparently, William had responded to not only Julia's request for more help at home, but neighbors who had similar requests such as one from a Mr. S.A. Harkness written "Mch 21/65.....I wish to ask a favor of you to send my wife a good collard Girl that understand doing house work such as cooking, etc." Perhaps these "chattels" were some of the "freedmen" who now were seeking jobs. The only other letter in this chapter written by someone other than Julia or William is "C. C. Kellogg," William's sister, Caroline.

Rankin and others write of Columbus, Georgia, being the "last battle of the war for the preservation of the Union." However, most would agree that the last battle of the war was the one that Catton recounts in his book, *A Stillness at Appomattox*. It was on the road to Lynchburg, the road to Appomattox on Palm Sunday, 1865. The starved rebel soldiers in their diminished regiments faced the larger numbers of Yanks; one Yankee officer noted that it almost seemed the tattered battle flags of the rebels outnumbered the soldiers. The large numbers of troops in blue had also missed breakfast but were prepared to fight as they had been ordered. However, just as the soldiers on both sides were drawing their sabers and muskets preparing for yet another battle, a lone rider emerged, "a young officer in a gray uniform, galloping madly, a staff in his hand with a white flag fluttering from the end of it."[4] The troops would live to see another Easter and as William wrote to Julia (April 8, 1865), "I illuminated my room on the occasion and the next day I had the satisfaction of hearing one hundred guns fired at camp."

Although the war's official end was General Robert E. Lee's surrender to his Union counterpart, Ulysses S. Grant, there were still troops to be notified - on both sides - of this good news. When Richmond fell, Jefferson Davis reportedly fled with a small group of trusted advisors and military escort; he was reluctant to give up the fight and was hoping to continue the Confederacy in Texas. Rankin recounts in his book that the Seventh O.V.C. "was ordered to send out scouts in every direction to apprehend Jeff. Davis." But it was ultimately the Fourth Michigan and the First Wisconsin Cavalries who surprised Davis in the pre-dawn hours of May 10 at his camp in Irwinville, Georgia and the Seventh O.V.C. who "took charge of him and guarded him to Augusta, Ga."[5] The story is different from one source to another, but one popular story is that Davis fled from his tent wearing his wife's cloak and the rumors flew! The Northern newspapers especially had fun with this as they printed cartoons of Davis fleeing in "his wife's clothes." Even Julia and William's own preschooler picked up on the news as Julia quotes Lillian in her letter of May 15: "aint papa coming home now Jeffs tooken with his wife's dress on."

All but the most remote troops on both sides were celebrating soon after the surrender at Appomattox; however, there were still more deaths from disease and skirmishes here and there, even after Davis' capture, as evidenced in Julia's letter of July 9, 1865. Neither Julia nor William mentions anything about the assassination of our sixteenth President, Abraham Lincoln, on April 14, 1865.

William writes of his work, paying the troops and other tasks related to *de*-construction of Camp Nelson and in late June he begins writing on The Adams Express Company letterhead: "it would surprise any person as it did Gen Rossiaux yesterday to see the amount of business we are doing."[6]   In October, William's search for a house large enough for his family ended and in November, 1865, the William R. Jacksons were among those fortunate enough to be reunited at the end of our nation's tragic Civil War.

Jany 3^d/65 Tuesday

My dear Wife,

I received yours and am very sorry to hear that the girls are unwell and that you are compelled to have so much anxiety ~~

You continue to speak about the prospect of my being stationed at Cincinnati. There is no object now in being there now as the prospect is that there will be no more appearances of War in Ky than there is in Ohio owing to the enemies lines being so far removed from here and since Hood was so completely thrashed the gurillas have I think concluded that they are not safe here and have almost entirely disappeared ~~~ It is very wonderful to see the change in sentiment on the subject of Slavery Every person I talk with seems to have simultaniously given it up

I went with Mc_____to camp and helped him pay off the 1st Ky. I payed them myself about 80,000$ and Mc_____about 120,000$. They are all discharged, and this morning I ordered all of the saloons and whiskey shops to be closed on account of them. I don't know as I told you that I am commander of the Post and give orders to the Provost Guards. I sent you 100$ by Express yesterday, which I expect you kneed ~

I want 240 acres of land that I understand is for sale in Wood Co. Jones the a Pay Master from Wood Co is well acquainted through that county and says it is a good bargain at the price asked $4.10 an acre and I shall send some person to examine it first to know what the quality of it is.

With a good coozy embrace I am

Your affect{ionate}
Wm

———————◆——————————————————◆———————

Tuesday <u>Jany 10,</u> {1865}

My dear Julia,

Yours of the 4th* come to hand and I was glad to learn that you had arranged to settle Darwins matters ~

It has rained here almost incessantly for about fourteen hours and there was a heavy snow upon the ground before it commenced so that every thing is afloat.~

I wish you could arrange matters about the house so as to make a visit here sometime so while I have but little to do. It will relieve you of care while you are here and give you an oportunity to rest. Caroline will stay with the children & take charge while you are here. I have a good quiet room. I think I would leave all of the children at home. I want to send Toby back with you for Theodore.

Graves acted very wisely in not calling upon you. He had been exposed fairly and squarely to the small pox by shaking hands with the man that died with it at Norwalk.

I am not going to Camp Nelson. Santmyer has been ordered there.

Capt. Hall is going to Washington and proposed to make {Wm goes to second page without finishing his thought here...}

~ 206 ~

If you conclude to come I should let Beach know when you will be at Newark and he will put you on a sleeping car that comes through to Cint. And by that means you will have no anxiety or trouble in changing cars. You will reach Cint. in the morning & leave in P.M. for here. It may be so I can meet you in Cint.

Yours with a kiss
Wm

*This letter from Julia was not found in the collection.

━━━━━━━━━━━━━━━━━━━━━

Acting Assistant Quartermaster's Office,

Nicholasville, Ky.

"Monday" Mar. 6, 1865

Dear wife ~

I continue to have neuralgia in my head but am some better I have been taking quinine and iron for three days past. It rained almost without intermission for three days the last of the week but it is very fair and pleasant to day. Things are going on about as usual only I am rather more lonesome~
I have not heard from you since you got home. Neither have I recd your photo from Cint yet ~
Probert has been confined to his room ever since he returned but is better to day.
Ross is going to Cint. to day & I will send Hoag & _____receipts by him for your picture. I close with a kiss~

Your affect(ionate)
Wm

━━━━━━━━━━━━━━━━━━━━━

Monroeville Mch 21/65

Wm Jackson Esq
Dear sir,

I wish to ask a favor of you to send my wife a good collard {sic} Girl that understand doing house work such as cooking etc. Since our Catholic Church has bin in Monroeville it is imposable {sic} to keep a good girl every time and if you can assist us in getting a good girl you will ablige us much -- I was talking with you{r} collard man som{e} time ago about his daughter and had a talk with your wife to day and she ses the{re} is a god {sic} girl in your camp and his partner ses he will give you an order for him to go north or if the old mans girl could have wood like it - but I am willing to trust you in getting me a good girl you no what I want as well as I do.

I will pay good wages say from 12 to 16 and what ever it cost to get her threw I will pay and remit to you.

Please answer. Wood like to have the old mans oldest Girl if I could get him if not some other one

Yours Truly
S.A. Harkness

Acting Assistant Quartermaster's Office,

Nicholasville, Ky.

Wednesday <u>March 29,</u> 1865.

My dear Wife,

It is a calm pleasant morning and every thing is moving along quietly ~

Susan, Anna & Geo went to Lexington yesterday and she seems very much pleased with her trip. She was at Camp Monday~ She returns Friday ~

I wrote to Fannie & Julia yesterday have them write to me often and I will answer them.

We are constantly getting rumors and reports of gurillas but I dont take any stock in any of them. ~

Gen Fry is relieved at Camp and Lt. Col Carpenter supercedes him of 5th U.S.Col{ored}Cav.

I wish I had some news to write that would interest you but I have not. Unless I tell you how bad I want to see you and that I love you more dearly every day I live and how I look forward to our being together soon. I close with a pile of kisses and an affect{ionate} hug.

Your affect{ionate}
Wm

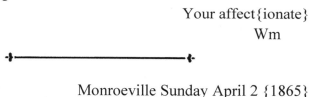

Monroeville Sunday April 2 {1865}

Dear William,

For ten days past I have only received one letter from you 'till last night when the stop{p}age seemed to be removed and, I got three, and the girls each one which pleased them very much. the grape cuttings came, three sacks but no trees and I sent again last night to the Depot but Mr. King said there was none. I think I will have him telegraph and find out where they are. I suppose the tag had been torn off and they are either at Clyde or Cincinnati. Fannie had a dreadful night with her teeth and ears. I think it began with a chill for she had a very high fever nearly all night and it went off with perspiration. she is feeling some better this afternoon but I have not been to church on her account and I feel dreadful achey myself full of sharp pains and was awake and up and down all night. A great many of your friends enquire when you are coming home. I tell them this month. you dont tell me how soon you expect to come. I went out yesterday afternoon to make some calls as a matter of duty. I went to see Mrs. Scouton whose recovery is very doubtful and I suppose hopeless. She enquired particularly about you, she has a constant diarrhea and cannot retain any thing on her stomach, she looks dreadfully. I went also to see poor Ad - I found him much better than he had been. Reed is his physician now and has relieved him very much. his complaint was heart disease and dropsy. he was very glad to see me and called me right into his room and told all about his sufferings. Reed told him his case was a very bad one and he had four ways of treating it. The first did not relieve him but the second which were pills relieved him directly. he said the first day he passed 2 gallons of clear yellow water and threw a great deal from his stomach. he said he felt like another person. he has taken them three times and thinks the bloat has all gone. Reed said his case was not as bad as he at first supposed, that he mastered it eiser than he thought he could, and he did not think it would be necessary to visit him but once more. Linus Ward got back Friday. he says he would not go back East to live. Every thing has been so high there this winter. he saw a turkey weighing 15 lbs sold for $6.00, eggs 70¢ dozen. Philip's folks are mooving into Roby's house. Linus says they are having smashing times in New York but the merchants here are holding their goods clear up yet, and none have gone East yet. I am glad you went to the wedding but I think I should not have taken much pains to have treated Miss Brown with much attention for she has never shown me any civility. I saw some neck ties at Shillito's{?} I wish you would get me & Jule & Fannie one if they are not too expensive. they were way back in a glass case and were like the one Mrs. Saffle wore on her hair. I shall have to get them something to wear to Mary's wedding. it is to be in the evening and a full dress affair, and I think it would not hurt you or your business to come now, and then too.

I suppose you begin to get vegetables from Cincinnati. it is a dry time here. the markets have both been closed since I came home till last night. I got some steak and a soup bone. Our hams are nice and Barny hunts all the eggs and I dont know but he lays some when he cant make out the number. I believe the mare at Cones has a colt, the children said he told them so. I asked Scouton yesterday but he said he didn't know. He told me to write to you to send him a nigger to tend his stable. I never go down town but I have an application of that kind.

How I should like to be with you this afternoon. it is such a lovely day. the sun shines warm and the air is so quiet and so many more Sundays I have got to stay alone and I begin to conclude I am not good for much. I came home yesterday with a nervous headache because I had walked too much. Betty has gone to Sunday school with the rest, she is awful hard. When Caroline was here Dora got provoked at something and said "consarn it". Caroline said Oh Dora that sounds bad. Betty thought a minute and said "well the Bible says we can say so," Caroline said if Dora said that she was afraid he would say something worse. "well Betty said, it wasn't half as bad as to say go to hell". Caroline concluded she wasn't making much {sense} and stop{p}ed the conversation.

If I dont write as often as you do, I think I write longer letters and close this with a big kiss.

Julia

Acting Assistant Quartermaster's Office,

Nicholasville, Ky.

Tuesday April 4th, 1865.

My dear,

The news was glorious yesterday and for the 1st time in three years the stars and stripes were flying from the Court House Cupulo {cupola}.

I am waiting anxiously to know where Lee is since he was compelled to rush out of Richmond. You will hear of the capture of Mobile in a few days and then they are closed out, whipped, disgraced and will be compelled to lay down their arms and bring this war to a close. ~

Did you hoist your Flag yesterday. I was in extacie all day yesterday at the thought of my seeing the rebellion crushed and I yet in the Army. ~

No person has been designated to relieve me. As soon as there is I will arrange to be at home soon after.

Your affect{ionate}
Wm

Acting Assistant Quartermaster's Office,

Nicholasville, Ky.

Saturday April 8, 1865

My dear Wife,

Your letter of Tuesday* come to hand and it added to my discontent in staying here and I think we can expect the war to end now very soon. There was but little more feeling or excitement here when we received the news than there usually is on Sunday.

I illuminated my room on the occasion and the next day I had the satisfaction of hearing one hundred guns fired at Camp.

The men were again cheering yesterday and I think we will get the most of Lees Army before many days.

How I long to hear the announcement that the thing is at an end. I am very anxious to get my matters so as to come home a few days and have a good time with you and the children and get matters arranged for Spring. With six kisses I am

Your affect{ionate}
Wm

*This letter was not found in the collection.

-§————————————§-

Monroeville Friday 5th May {1865}

Dear William,

I suppose you are anxious to know about the "goods and chattels" you started they arrived here all safe the next morning after they left you. they had no difficulty in getting through. I think Vina is the choice of the lot and shall keep her here for the present. I don't know just how the rest will be disposed of I saw Mrs. Harkness yesterday she thinks she would not like Ann because she is married. I got a dispatch from Gray Monday saying Gaither wished to see you in Columbus on your return to Kentucky. I answered it immediately that you had gone, and then wrote to Gray that I thought you would meet Gaither at any place he wished if he would let you know by telegraph. I hope my money will come soon for I am clean out and there is a good many ways I want to use it. I have done nothing for the wedding yet in the way of getting the girls or myself ready. I write in haste with love, Julia

Monroeville Monday night 15 {May 1865}

Dear William,

I just received your letter written Thursday, you ask if you shall get me a bonnet, do just as you please. I have had an old one done up for a common wear and should like something for Sunday if convenient to get it, if you wish to bring Jule & Fanny something I think a summer dress would be nice they never have had a nice lawn, and would be much pleased with such a dress. be sure and get something that will wash, pink is the surest. If you can, get Dora two of those linen jackets such as you got last summer in Cinat {Cincinnati} & a Sunday hat. Betty says you promised her a doll. She sat pulling off her shoes & stockings to night and said "aint Papa coming home, now Jeffs tooken with his wifes dress on". I think the war would be over.

Perhaps you will have started before this reaches you. My letters are a long time getting here. I dont think I shall write again but hope to meet you soon <u>at</u> <u>home,</u> <u>here</u> <u>at</u> <u>home</u>.

Affect{ionately}
Julia

Acting Assistant Quartermaster's Office,

Nicholasville, Ky.

June 2, 1865

My dear Wife,

I am still at work Endeavoring to close up my business here. I see by the Papers that the 7th is on its way back.

Aunt Jennie Ridgely died very suddenly this morning. Martha Ridgely some better. Mrs. Wilburn about the same.

I saw Mrs. Scott yesterday. She is very anxious to see you. Will not probibly visit you for some time yet.

It is very warm here now and getting warmer every day. I left my linnen pants at home which I want the most.

With many kisses. Your affect{ionate},

Wm R.

LOUISVILLE HOTEL.

Rebuilt 1856. Enlarged & Refurnished 1859.
Keen, Steele & Judge proprietors
Cor. Sixth & Main Str.
Louisville, KY

"Wednesday" June 7/65

My dear Wife,

I am still sweating it out in Louisville I think I never suffered more with the heat than I did yesterday.

I am becoming quite well acquainted with the numerous Employees about the office and I am inclined to think I am agoing to get along smoothly with them.

I was over to Jeffersonville this morning on business for the company It looked quite natural there. The present Agent Mr. Rose lives there but after I get located he goes to Nashville Tenn. You must not complain about my irregularity in writing because I am compelled to suit myself to circumstances, and can not be very regular in my doings.

Many kisses to all of you

Your affect{ionate}
Wm

Monroeville June 8th Thursday {1865}

Dear William,

I think your letters are getting few and far between. I have got but two since you left.

Dora's sick proved to be measles and he has been real sick. I have had but little rest for three nights with him and was a good deal worried about him yesterday noon but he rested better last night under the influence of Dover powder. How I wish you could come home till you are mustered out and we could get straightened out. We had a little rain last evening and it is cooler this morning. We need much more. I took my bonnet to Sarah Chapin she thought she could fix it easily. Mr. Bronson will preach here next Sunday. I have not time to write longer as it is mail time. I hope I shall hear from you to night, it is so forlorn.

Affect{ionately} Julia

On stationary from

The Adams Express Company.

Louisville, _____ Jun 29th 186_

Thursday 6 OC a.m.

My Dear,

I am up and fortifying myself for another very hard days work. It would surprise any person as it did Gen Rossiaux* yesterday to see the amount of business we are doing Lew Bonar** has just this moment come in upon me. I assure you I am glad to see him. I shall set him to work in about an hour. I had not time to get out yesterday to get you the dress -

I send you my most affectionate regards but wish I was not compelled to send them but could take them.

Your aff{ectionate}
Wm

*William was most likely referring to General Lovell Rosseau.
**William's brother-in-law married to youngest sister, Julia.

Louisville

July 2nd, 1865 "Sunday"

My dear Wife,

After a very hard weeks work Sunday is usually a very welcome day. But to day has been spent at this office in transferring and taking care of over 600 boxes of goods which arrived by the mail boat this morning. Our teams and men have had to work hard all day. My oversight has been comparatively light because but few of the clerks have been at work.

I many times think my wife is a man of better judgement than myself. Have young Scudder you write about write to me and I can then soon determine whether I can set him at work some time soon.

I am now going it alone here. Mr. Jones & Ross have both left me to myself. I shall have a chief clerk in a few days who will relieve me of considerable responsibility in looking after the business of the office.

I have put Dick in the cashier's office as his assistant. It is a very nice place, but I am afraid he will trouble me some about increasing his wages. I think I can give him 75$ dollars which I think a very good salary. I am also afraid he will assume to take liberties I deny to other clerks. It might be well for some of you to caution him about it. With so many clerks it is very necessary for me to keep a restraint upon all alike.

I think Mr. Jones will get me a pass for you over the CC&C & CX & LW R Road so you can make me a visit before long. I should like very much to get my buggy here for many times the Co{mpany} Buggy is in use & I like to feel independent ~

We have fire works and flags ready for the 4th and will not receive any freight on that day & will not have much from Cint. it being Tuesday our easy day here ~~

We move into our new office Wednesday. I have a new desk the Co. paid 50$ for and will have things in good style. Business is constantly on the increase so much so that we have been compelled to get four or five new teams. We are doing more at this time than Cint. I settled their bills for damage to goods yesterday, the largest $36.00, the smallest $3.50. I am now compelled to meet all questions as they come up myself.

How I wish I could see all of you this Evening. Remember me to all the folks~

Many kisses-
Your affect{ionate}
Wm

-+————————————————+-

The Adams Express Company.

Louisville

July 5th, 1865

My dear Wife,

I received a good long letter from you to day*. I like such letters because I like you and would write just such a letter if {I} could but you know I write often.

I am entirely upon my own hook now. Rose & Mr. Jones both gone. We have had an uncomfortable mixed up day moving into our new office. It is not entirely completed but much pleasanter than the old one. Dick has got fairly at work and has a good place if he will only appreciate it and keep steadily about his business.

E{d} Peckover came yesterday and has been hard at it to day. he is agoing to be a valuable man for me. Dan Ridgeley came with him and I set him at work driving a wagon in the city. I guess he will do well He has shown a disposition to change his habits for some months past and as long as he does well I shall keep him on Ed's account and give him some encouragement. I have four men constantly employed just in receiving money, and they cant do the work. Lew has about pigged out to night receiving boxes and bundles.

Oh! Oh! How warm yesterday and to day not one about the office pretends to wear a coat or vest~

My a/c at M{onroe}ville Peck tells me are all square and nice nothing short ~

Probert is going to Cint. with Gray at $100 per mo. as soon as he can leave M{onroe}ville. He boards at Bufords. Blackburn & folks also. Mrs. B. came perty near using herself up by avoiding reoccurrence of a year ago last Spring. She looks very bad. Mrs. Wil____ is no better.

Many, very many kisses.

Your affect{ionate}

Wm

*No "good long letter" from Julia dated early July or late June was found.

~ 220 ~

The Adams Express Company.

Louisville

July 8th, 1865

My dear Wife,

We continue to be pressed with business. There is an order to muster out all of the Army of Tennessee* that are here and when that is done I am in hopes our business will be easyer to handle ~

Many of my men are getting sick but not serious. I am quite well myself but I tell you this extreme warm weather is rather heavy on me.

I am not writing you a very good letter but the best I can to day. T. Allen was here this P.M. & I expect Col. G. to night or in the morning. Won't we have a good time.

If Scadden was here to day I could set him at work.

Many Kisses.

Your affect{ionate}
Wm

*William was probably referring to the Army of *the* Tennessee, not to be confused with its Confederate counterpart, Army of Tennessee. Union armies were typically named after rivers and Confederate armies after states or regions.

Monroeville Sunday July 9th {1865}

Dear William,

I don't know as this letter will find any thing left of you if it has been as warm in Louisville as it has been here. it has seemed as if we could not stand it. to day it is comfortably cool and we are all glad of it. The new minister was here to day. I turned out a host of children but was not well enough to go myself. Jimmy and Sarah Gardner are here to spend some time. I wrote for them to come now for I should probably go to see you before long and they had been anticipating a long visit for some time. Ella Goodnow has been here since the fourth and I have had a kind of a fretting time entertaining her. there is very little she can eat for it does this, that or the other to her, and I didn't know what to get and she is the hardest person in the world to entertain in conversation. she was to have gone home last evening but it rained and they did not come for her it makes me twelve in the family. M____ has left Harknesses and has been here. She is going into the country this afternoon. Word came the fourth that Sam Clock was dead and his remains would be in Nashville the fifth on their way home at the same time word came that Lester Cone was shot in the hip. Yesterday we heard he was dead also.[7] I don't know any of the circumstances.

It has been very rainy here during the week it is making bad work for the farmers harvesting. I think I shall tell Theodore to write to Dick, but if I was in your place I should speak to him without the least hesitation he ought to have sense enough to know how you are situated and do as the rest do. I got a letter from George Probert Friday saying he had just sent me a bundle by Ex{press} containing one Parlin. Seems to me that is a queer thing to send here. it has not arrived yet. He says it is <u>lonesome</u> there. William I have thought of you more for the last two days than I ever did. Friday night it seemed all night as if you was with me and in the morning I really looked to see if you wasn't in your old place and all day I could not convince myself that it was not so. I could feel your face on my cheek almost as if it had been pressed against it and you may be sure I felt very very teary ever since. It is so forlorn and lonesome here. I hope you will be able soon for us to moove you have never written any thing about it. I sent you Friday your hand trunk with five shirts, three collars, two sheets, two pillow cases, and flannel shirt which I suppose you have received all the quilts I had were too large, the sheets are marked and I put a 'J' on the pillow cases as well as on your shirts. I would rather have you send your new ones home to be done up than to have them muddled up as your washing used to be. I should have written a note with them but I had to hurry to get them off in the morning and it was so hot. I wish I had something good to eat. We have had a few new potatoes and that is all. You have been gone six weeks last Friday and oh how long it seems. I wish you would send the girls some little thing, a ribbon to tie around their hair, or some thing you may happen to see it would please them very much. I wrote you my dress pleased me. I have not got it made yet there was just enough for a dress but not for a sacque. If you had been with me the fourth, you would have been quiet <u>sure</u> <u>enough</u>. I was the only person on the place in the afternoon. Just before noon Miss Mason and I went up to Dan's where we had been invited for a picnic but it proved to be a dreadful little one. Mary Martain, Fred Minor, and a young lady, Dan's girls and us were the party.

Fred sat and made milk punch, his wife has just been confined, lost her baby, and came near dying herself, but is smart now. We stay'd about two hours and came home. I unlocked the door and came in and oh how lonesome. I just wandered till Barny came from Sandusky. Dick was in the barn when I drove Billy away {was} very uneasy and when I came back he had jumped through over his manger without braking his halter. You wont believe nor Duly nor I did till we took him out and saw where he had a scratch on his hind leg. I wonder he did not break every bone in his body. He had pushed the big box against the buggy wheels so he had not enjoyed that. Now again I close with a good kiss while you are reading this long letter from your Julia.

Dear William

I received your letter last evening saying you had got your trunk and contents. It gives me a great deal of pleasure to comply with any such request or to do any thing that will make you more comfortable, and that too, as soon as I know you have any wants, for I know from experience that it is very uncomfortable to have necessary wants unheard or <u>unheeded</u>. It rained here all day yesterday and all night, and so far to day, and makes it gloomy enough. The two girls went to Church this morning but I concluded not to go in the rain. Sarah's two children are here yet and Father & Toby was here yesterday. Caroline has been confined to her bed for over a week with several ailments. I did not get your buggy off as I expected this last week. Drake was away. I will attend to it as soon as the weather clears up, tomorrow if I can. I shall expect Delia up tomorrow. I shall have to get several things for the children for there has been nothing made for them this summer and I have altered over about as long as I can. Sam Clock's remains arrived here Wednesday morning. The funeral was at 2 OC. The members of the band were dressed in deep mourning with badges on their arms and playd a dirge from the house to the church and from there to the knoll on the farm where he was buried. There was a great many present. His mother is very much composed but his Father seems to feel very bad. Andy got home Friday. I have not seen him. I shall go to see the them {sic} and tell them what you did for I know it will please them. Mr. Ellers spoke to me again about the piano. Mrs. Hamilton is figuring to get it and I know he would rather we would have it. I told him you had promised in one of your letters to write to me what you would do and I had been expecting an answer for four weeks, but had got none yet. I told him also that I did not think you had the money just now and that I had given you what I had. He said that would make no difference for a month or two. You can do just as you please. I told him to say to Mrs. Hamilton that it was engaged. The girls will not be able to use the old one but little longer. There were two dampers drop{p}ed off last week so the keys don't sound at all, and it is all out of _____

Dick has written home that he has lost seven pounds of flesh in two weeks and has to pay $40 a week for his board and he thinks he cannot stand it but there is one comfort about it. If he does not stay it will stop his _____ and writing to you about finding him a place and that will be so much gained. I don't like your Dan Ridgely arrangement. If you have felt friendly enough to Ed Peckover to give him a situation it is all that he ought to expect without your taking that <u>scape grace</u>, and we are not <u>at all indebted to the family</u>. We all feel anxious to see you and the children fret about your not coming home and all that I can say to them is I don't know when you will arrive. It takes your letters four days to get here and that seems to{o} long. I must close for I have written a long letter although there is not much in it.

Affect{ionately} Julia

Monroeville Sunday July 23rd {1865}

Dear William,

I sit down as usual Sunday afternoon so lonesome I dont know what to do with myself to write to you. my head feels confused and bad, and will probably wind up with a dreadful head ache for I am not feeling well. We all went to church this morning. It is the first time I have heard the new minister I guess he will do. He looks very much like Date Williams* used to. The Bishop (Bedell) was here Tuesday night and he certainly had a splendid sermon and a full house to hear it and I never saw a more attentive congregation - Well at the close of the sermon he called for the candidates for confirmation to come forward there were six ladies, and just as they got to the altar who should come up but <u>Toot</u> <u>Conklin</u>. I thought when I saw him I should go through the floor. our seat was nearly full of ministers, just room for Delia and I. I wondered so how he would be disposed of, but Wilson finally come up and took him by the arm and said. 'Toot they aint ready for you yet' but he objected to going and said he wanted to join the church. but Wilson said, they aint ready for the men yet so he went back with him. It seems when he first came into church Sargent, Roby and Wilson had all they could do to keep him from going into one of the front seats but finally succeeded by staying with him, and when the ladies went forward he turned to Roby and asked what they were going to do, and Roby told him and he asked again. And Roby told him they were going to join the Church and he said I want to too and started off so fast they could not get hold of him. After they got him away I would have given the world to have laughed. I cram{m}ed my handkerchief in my mouth and did not dare look up. Altogether it was the most ridiculous thing I ever saw. We have had such a rainy time all last Wednesday and all night and then Friday and Saturday all day. I think it must injure the harvest. Sarah's children went to Norwalk yesterday evening they will be back in a day or two.

Mr. Ellers brought the Piano up last evening it seems Frank Hamilton was going to pay the difference between the old one they had and this one so I told him to do just as he was a mind to about bringing it up. last week two more of the most important keys broke so it made four that would not sound at all, and the girls had to either stop taking lessons or have something they could play on. Mr. Ellers has acted like a gentleman about it. I dont know whether you will blame me or not, but if you do, you must blame yourself too. You would not write to me what to do, but now it is here I should like to know that it could be paid for before long. I got the money and the trunk. The girls could not have been better pleased with any present than with the fans. the satchel I supposed was for Birdie and the toy for Betty and the boat for Dory, with which he was delighted as were the other two with their presents. My dress is a sweet pretty thing but I am afraid that kind of pink will not stand washing. Delia made up the first one you sent and I think I shall like it very much. The beets and cucumbers come nice but the tomatoes were too ripe and had soured and decayed. We are beginning to get some things from the garden our potatoes are very nice. I saw David Benedict at the cars last evening. He said he had seen you frequently. Matild thinks Dick will be back soon. Theodore only offered him $4.50 a year so he told me. It seems a long time since you went away, eight weeks last Friday, and I never felt more unwilling to have you go than I did the last time.

How bad I want to see you. But it seems to be doubtful yet when that will be.

<u>With all the love in the world</u>

Julia

*Julia is probably referring to Dayton Williams who she'd mentioned in her letters of Tuesday (July) 26 and July 31st, 1864.

Monroeville Monday Morn August 14 {1865}

Dear William,

We arrived home all safe Saturday at five OC. if you had only been with us I should have enjoyed the trip on the river. the Capt. was very polite the boat very comfortable and the weather fine. Dora took a heavy cold, I think, the night before we left and has had a bad time with his lungs. I found them all well at home. Caroline was still here. Perhaps Julia will come up with her baby and go home with her. Barny is going to cut his grass to day. James' brother says it looks very fine and he has raised a great deal. My first <u>easy job</u> is to shoe them all around and it is a job. There is no delay in the morning train except at Shelby we got there about one OC and waited till nearly four. I suppose you found your bed much more comfortable when there was not so many to sleep in it.

You remember I let George Clary take your old long double gown* and told him why you had it made and Mary Martain plagued him in her _____ way and sure enough a few days ago he was presented with a pair of twin girls he says he is going to send the gown home he has no more use for it. I must close and get this to the office.

Affect{ionately} Julia

*Unable to find anything about "double gowns", the editor assumes that William created a double gown-much like a double sleeping bag-so that he and Julia could sleep in a "cozy" embrace in the winter months. It appears to have had benefits beyond mere warmth!

‑•———————————————•‑

The Adams Express Company.

Louisville

<u>August 17,</u> 1865

My dear Wife,

I received your letter this morning hurrah for Clary.

Jim Norton says it {is} his especial request that you send the Double Gown down here and he will pay all Expenses. How Jim laughed when I told him.

I am very glad that you made your connections through so well I was fearful that you might be compelled to go by way of Grafton.

Business remains about the same every thing going south. When our fall business commences from N.Y. we will be overrun with business.   Payne, the agent of the America Ex{press} wants to sell me his furniture and give me possession of the house he has It never was occupied until he went into it and he was in it only 22 days and that is all he used his furniture says it cost him $700. The house I think is to{o} small It only has four rooms and a large kitchen~ Isn't to{o} small rent $360 ~ Another house on Main Street rent $1000 ~ too much rent. The small house is up near Norton's. Jones left here Sunday and very wonderful for him he had no fault to find about business~

Your affect{ionate}

Wm. R.

Shall I send you a box of sweet potatoes -

-∦————————————∦-

𝕿𝖍𝖊 𝕬𝖉𝖆𝖒𝖘 𝕰𝖝𝖕𝖗𝖊𝖘𝖘 𝕮𝖔𝖒𝖕𝖆𝖓𝖞,

Louisville

September 7,186{5}

Thursday Evening

My dear Julia,

Yours of the 4th is at hand* I was so glad to get it. I have not been very well and have been pressed to death with business and have been very low spirited ever since yesterday and feel weried but I guess a good nights sleep to night will help me. It is raining and not quite so sultry as it has been for several days~

Pray don't ask me to send letters by Express when it takes over a week to get a Hand Trunk It is not here yet but may come in the morning. How I wish I could be with you to night & have you comfort me. You are my only real comfort ~

Jones has not been here since you left I have to take it all alone.

Many kiss{es}, sixteen hugs & a big squeeze & every thing else that is comforting.

Your affect{ionate}
Wm

*This letter was not found.

The Adams Express Company,

Louisville

<u>September 21</u>, 1865

My dear good wife,

Yours of the 18th come to hand* I am very sorry the money has not reached you yet. I sent you $215 and will send more when you want it ~ ~

I have nothing to write about only to say how good you are and how badly I want to see you and all of the children

I should think with help I sent from KY that you should not do your own work Vina is your girl and you should get her whenever you want her and I insist on it. It was not my object to supply help to any person but you

I have had a severe bilious attack for a day or two & have felt very bad but I manage to keep moving. With many kisses -

Your affect{ionate}
Wm. R~

*No letter of the 18th was found in this collection.

Monroeville Thursday Oct. 5 {1865}

Dear William,

I wrote you a long letter Sunday and have not much to write to day. I have looked for you very hard for a few days past and hope we shall see you soon. the children get very impatient it is over four months since they have seen you. The weather is cold, cloudy and blue. Barny has dug 35 bushels of potatoes and thinks he will have ten more. he is going to cut up his corn to day and by the time he gets through with that his sorgum will be ready to cut. We have had no frost yet and every thing is out of danger. I got down to see Hellen last evening for the first time. she wishes very much we could all go back together. she has a nice baby but it looks like an awful job. I am feeling some better but not well by a good deal. I think Father must be very miserable. he has not been over for nearly two weeks. he is very feeble at best. hoping to see you very soon. I will close with an affectionate good bye

Julia

Ad Clock says you wrote him a long letter and will answer it as soon as he gets stronger he was very much pleased.

The Adams Express Company.

Louisville

My good wife,

In luck again I rented a house today such as I wanted and am to have possession 10th Nov a plan of which I inclose. It has 4 Rooms two up stairs and two down stairs 15 x 15 just the size of our rooms and each room has a grate in it and then a kitchen and room over it 12 x 15 ft. Also a very good stable 2 stalls & shed a coal house and a shed for a Buggy ~ All on a nice clean lot with a yard front and back with a Cistern, located in a good neighborhood and a clean part of the city about as far from the office as from our house to the P. Office at house. Rent $360 per year, and it will require but little furniture, if we bring the Piano for the front room, and our carpets. I will buy some chairs & B{ed}stead & stove & furniture. Also bring some few common dishes, &c & buy others. You can tell pretty well by looking at the plan what we want. We will require an extra lodging room out if necessary. I can keep my bed at the office for an emergency - It is one half of a double building but no connection whatever between them. It is at the extreme end of Market Street towards Portland -- near where we drove the grey horse ~ The stairs to the room over the kitchen are outside and a door from the room up stairs into it also ~~

I got your other letter - I think Mr. G was a little stupid to open the other one ~ With many kisses -

Your Wm

The Adams Express Company.

Louisville

<u>Oct 18th</u>, 1865

My dear Wife,

It has been cold and gloomy for two days and we have had no fire in the office. I have a stove in my room and have kept near it much of the time.

Jones left for Nashville to night and has been in unusual good spirits ever since I returned.

Business goes on smoothly only I am very lonesome after business hours but the 10th of Nov will soon be here and then I will have company ~ With a kiss

Your affect{ionate}

Wm

Monroeville Sunday evening 22nd Oct. {1865}

Dear William,

I wrote you a letter by Hellen which I suppose you got and sent you some pillow cases. How relieved I was to hear you have a house for us and one that suited you and with a moderate rent. I want you to write to me immediately how I shall send the things shall I send them all the way by Express or shall I send them by freight to Cincinnati by way of Newark, and have Beach hurry them or from there. Had not I better send the Piano all the way by Ex? How many barrels of potatoes had I better send. I think I had better get some more winter apples of Charlie Williams at

~ 233 ~

$1.00 {per} bushel. Barny will have <u>nine</u> loads of sorghum. he has taken six and will take the rest Monday and they will make it up the same day. I shall have to get another barrel. shall I send one barrel to you. I should like to send your big cushioned chair and the little card table that is up stairs. Had I better? shall I bring all the carpets or leave the front parlor on the floor here? I have had the girls old winter hats fixed over and they look very well but I tell you I shall have to have some more money. I paid $10 on Church matters and by the time I pay for the making of the sorghum I shall be out, with my other expenses. Do you think you can get papers for us to come through now and cant you meet us at Cincinnati? Don't forget to answer <u>all </u>the questions I have asked for it is a big job for me and I want all the advice you can give me. I have written this evening for Vina to come and keep house for Barny. If it is so you can, I think you had better send the balance of Mr. Eller's money before I go away and I met Dr. Prentice and he said he wanted to have seen you to get some money before you left so I should be glad to pay him some. You remember I spoke of it while you were home. In haste and with much love Julia

—◆———————————◆—

The Adams Express Company,

Louisville

<u>October 23</u>, 1865

My Dear Wife,

Where are all of your letters I believe I have only heard from you once since I returned.

I spent the day yesterday in company with Gray and his wife at the Louisville Hotel. She is very pleasant but not very pretty she looks very much like Molly Butler only not quite so tall, rather sallow and no better looking than my wife.

I only received Eleven letters from Jones Saturday evening and Sunday that are to be answered this morning. I expect I shall get a letter from you this A.M. Gray will remain here to day to attend to business for his line. I have plenty to do to day so I'll close.

With many kisses
Wm

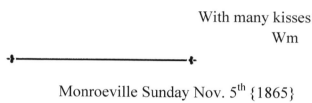

Monroeville Sunday Nov. 5th {1865}

Dear William,

I wrote you a short letter Friday and thought the box left that day but they did not send it till the next day which was Saturday. I hope it will get through safe for there was a good deal in it. I want to get another started this week and would be glad to get as far as Bellville and go on from there Monday but I wont know as it will be possible. I will let you know when I shall start. Jane was here to day and said she would come Tuesday and stay a few days. I am so tired out it seems as if I could not go any longer. Barny is not willing for either of the girls to go back {to} Kentucky. I hope we shall find some one there. Mr. Ellers is giving the girls four lessons a week till we go. I think I shall have him pack the Piano the last of this week. Oh how bad I want to get there and get settled. I thought the chamber carpet would do for the sitting room and I will make the new one for the parlor, the bedroom carpet will go up stairs and the old one in the back parlor can go in one of the chambers. I will send it and the new one in the next box. I have got one large enough to put the chair in and will pack beds in around it. I wish you would subscribe again for the "Atlantic Monthly" and "Our Young Folks". there will be only one month more for this year, it ought to be done right away so they will continue to come. I think they are very good. Father was over last Monday and was very miserable, so much so that he asked to lie down.

Louisa came up yesterday and spent the day her health is better. Delia is getting along with the sewing but there is a good deal to do yet. I am having some of my old scissors fixed.

Don't neglect to send Barny's boots for he needs them. I hope the apples, Sorghum, and potatoes have all got through safe. I had started the potatoes before you wrote not to send so many, but I still think I did right for in the winter they might freeze. there were five barrels left here and three of apples, forty six gallons molasses and this week I sent another barrel of apples. you can be on the look out for them. Theodore has got home. I have not seen him. I believe I have not heard from you but twice this week. I hope to be with you next week and not write letters. Good night.

With a long sweet kiss Julia

Belleville
Nov. 30/65

Dear Brother,

Enclosed you will find your note. If you can make it convenient I would like what is due on it. I feel some hesitancy in calling on you just now knowing you have been to a good deal of expense settling your family there and if it is not convenient or is going to discommode you in the least don't send it for I can do without it for awhile yet, but let me hear from you so I can make my arrangements accordingly.

We are very busy making preparations for our "family reunion dinner" to be eaten December 7th at three o'clock. We are expecting all the family to make a desperate effort to get here. When Julia was here on her way to Kentucky she said if you and herself could make arrangements possibly to come you would do so. Can you come? Then our family will be complete.

We are about as usual. Mother is better than when Julia was here. Dr. has been East for about two weeks but we are looking for him home to day.

Give my love to Julia and the children. Tell the girls to write to me.

Excuse haste as Sister Lib is calling me and I must close with much love to all.

C C Kellogg

-+--------------------------------+-

Chapter Six Notes

1. Catton, Never Call Retreat, pp. 415-416.

2. Rhodes, p. 205.

3. Catton, Never Call Retreat, pp. 418-419. For more on the Thirteenth Amendment and the involved slavery issue, see Sandburg's Abraham Lincoln, Vol. 3, War Years.
Also see http://www.greatamericanhistory.net/amendment.htm (accessed November 2014).

4. Catton, A Stillness At Appomattox, Garden City, NY: Doubleday & Company, Inc., p. 379.

5. Rankin, pp 26 & 27. Soon after, they received a telegram from Grant to "cease hostilities," that Lee had surrendered, Richmond was captured, and that Sherman and Johnson had agreed upon an armistice…"   Rankin incorrectly gives credit to the Second Mich. Regiment for being part of those who captured Davis. The last actual battle of the war has been claimed by several regiments or locales. For more on this topic, see: http://freepages.history.rootsweb.ancestry.com/~bellware & http://thomaslegion.net/lastshot.html (about the "last shot" being near present day Waynesville, NC) (accessed October, 2014).

6. (William's of June 29, 1865) see Adams Express Company and General Rosseaux in Persons of Interest Appendix.

7. For more on Sam Clock and Lester Cone, see Persons of Interest Appendix.

Epilogue

William, and others who were with the "River Regiment" to the end of the conflict, formally mustered out on July 4, 1865. R.C. Rankin probably spoke for many in the Seventh when he wrote, "while we would not deprive any regiment of her laurels, we believe the 7th O.V.C., for the services rendered and the number of times she was under fire, stands second to no regiment from Maine to California."[1]   Sadly, some men lost their lives even after the agreement at Appomattox; Julia writes in her letter of "Sunday July 9th"(1865) that "word came the fourth that Sam Clock was dead…and Lester Cone was shot in the hip…and he was dead also." Samuel Clock apparently did die of his "wounds received while in discharge of his duty" in Macon, Georgia.[2] Julia's information on the soldier named Lester Cone, however, was inaccurate as he lived into his sixty first year, dying in Grand Rapids, Michigan in 1905.[3] In late summer, 1865, the Third O.V.C. also mustered out and the men began to return to their homes, all no doubt expressing the same "extacie" that William told Julia he felt (April 4, 1865).

William continued to work in Kentucky for all of 1865 and the family remained with him from November 1865 into 1866. Apparently William was still living in Kentucky and Julia at home in Ohio, when he wrote (December 1, 1866), "My Dear Wife" about the newest addition to their family. Included here in the epilogue, it mentions the baby's weight but no "particulars only that it is a sweet little girl" and since William apparently was the one who liked girls and Julia the boys, he expresses his happiness "about our good fortune." Whether or not this baby died early or her birthdate was later changed will always remain a mystery as the records about the Jackson's youngest, Anna, indicate that she was born in *1867 not 1866*. Her death records as well as William's pension records list Anna's birthday as November 27, *1867.*

The exact date of William's (permanent) return to his home and family in Ohio is uncertain. Although this collection contains post war letters throughout both 1865 and into 1867 they are fewer in number which most likely indicates that Julia and William were able to travel to each other more frequently and to enjoy longer "cosy times." There is one letter of William's from Cincinnati but most of his letters continue to come from Nicholasville until early June 1865 when he began work with The Adams Express Company in Louisville. Local records from Norwalk, Ohio show that once William returned home, *for good*, he became active in his church and community; records indicate that he was a trustee of Monroeville in 1868 and also an active member of Norwalk's St. Paul's Episcopal Church. *The Norwalk Experiment* article about William's death (dated Sept. 24, 1877) said "he had long been a resident of Monroeville and was regarded as one of the most respected and influential citizens of that village." He died of apoplexy only four months after his 54th birthday, twelve years after the end of the Civil War.

Julia lived another nineteen years after William's death; according to one newspaper article, she died at "age 72 after a lingering illness." The same article in *The Firelands Pioneer* states "she leaves three children to mourn her loss, Theodore W. of St. Augustine, Fla., Mrs. E.O. Friend of Norwalk, and Mrs. Walter Brown of Monroeville." Her only son, Theodore (great-grandfather of this editor), her daughter Florence, and youngest daughter, Anna, are the three named above.

All but Fannie married. Her twin, Julia, married Reverend George W. Williams; they had three children and she died in 1884 at 33 years of age. Fannie died two years later, in 1886.

Florence married Emil O. Friend and between 1879 and 1887 they produced four children. Florence lived until 1926. Her granddaughter, Florence, and this editor's Grandmother (Eve) Jackson corresponded in the 1940s and their letters are among the Jackson records.

Theodore (Dora) married Georgia Logan Kennedy and they had two children, Marguerite and William Richard (later changed to Randal) Jackson. Later the Theodore W. Jacksons moved to Florida, eventually moving to Palm Beach County (which in the early 1900s was known as Dade County). Particulars about Theodore's death including date of death and where interred are unknown to date. According to his grandson who was the editor's father, Georgia divorced Theodore and after that Theodore William Jackson has been difficult to trace!

Lillian, known as "Betsy", or "the baby" in so many of William and Julia's letters, married Ed Homes (or Holmes) and they had one daughter, Grace, who reportedly never married. Lillian died in 1889 and along with her father and all of her siblings (except her brother, Theodore) is buried in Norwalk's Woodlawn Cemetery.

Anna C. Jackson married Walter Brown and they had no children. "Aunt Daisy," as she was known to the editor's father and his cousins, lived in the old home place until her death in 1945. As mentioned before, Ray, (third cousin of this editor) and his wife now live there and have been gracious enough to share his family's notes on the history of the William Robinson Jacksons.

There are many more letters in the collection besides William's of December 1, 1866, the one chosen as the last for this book, but most are from someone who appeared to be the family's financial advisor. There are also several letters from the children to Julia and William written in 1866; perhaps these will be included in the "next book," one that someone from the *next* generation will write in the future. William's letter of December 1, 1866, as well as another written the same day by a relative, "B. Jackson" from "Belleville," reveals that the William Robinson Jacksons seemed to be getting along well at the end of 1866.

Because these letters were saved and passed down through the years, we are allowed a glimpse into one couple's lives - William Robinson Jackson and Julia Williams Jackson. They were two of many separated by a tragic war but so in love and dedicated to each other and the hope that they would, in the end, be together again. They were among the fortunate ones who were reunited as a couple and as a family. Because of their foresight, *we* now have the good fortune of holding evidence of that generation's tenacity and endurance during one of the most tumultuous times of our nation. These letters are a testament to their lives; like us, they had good days and bad, sorrows and joys. As Samara O'Shea (*For the Love of Letters*) so aptly wrote, "we must make arrangements for our descendants to discover us in such a candid way."[4]

The Adams Express Company.

Louisville

Louisville, <u>December 1st</u>, 1866 "Saturday"

My dear Wife,

I am delighted to learn from Julia's letter recd this morning that you are comfortable with a prospect of getting along well.

Her letter don't say when the baby was born nor give any particulars only that it is a smart little girl weighing 8½ lbs. Well I <u>like</u> <u>girls</u> and you like boys so that I am the one to feel pleased about our good fortune.

Julia if it does fret you to remain in bed and have them perambulating about the House in confusion, remain as quiet as you can in bed until you are strong beyond a contingency and the necessary quiet at this time may be the means of your health being greatly improved by your confinement.

Many kisses for you and one for the baby if there is a chance to get one in for the children who I expect monopolize most of them.

Your affect{ionate}

Wm

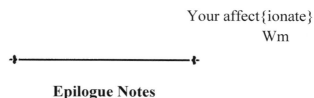

Epilogue Notes

1. Rankin, p. 27.

2. Crofts, Sergeant Thomas, *The History of the Service of the Third Ohio Veteran Volunteer Cavalry in the War for the Preservation of the Union 1861-1865*; Columbus, Ohio: Stoneman Press, 1910, p. 286.

3. *The Daily Norwalk Reflector,* September 13, 1905.

4. O'Shea, Samara, *For The Love of Letters, a 21st Century Guide to the Art of Letter Writing*; New York: Harper Collins Publishers, 2007, p. xi.

Glossary

Alterative - Also known today as "blood purifiers". They are used medicinally to favorably alter disordered metabolic and catabolic processes.

Artillery - Large guns such as mortar and cannons; also name of the units armed with these guns.

Battalion - Operational unit composed of two or more companies or (in the case of artillery battalion) batteries.

Battery - The basic unit of organization in the artillery that typically consists of four or six guns and the accompanying personnel and material.

Bilious - Usually means some ailment of the bile or liver; however in the mid-1800s this term usually meant having a lot of gas, digestive problems or diarrhea. When William talks of "bowel complaint," he is probably referring to this.

Brevet rank - An honorary rank that did not include an increase in pay.

Brigade - In the Civil War, an operational unit consisting of two or more regiments. Union brigades averaged 2000 men and Confederate brigades averaged about 1850 men.

Butnub (butternut) chaps or butnub britches - Homespun cloth died with brown juice from hulls of butternut or walnut trees often making the cloth a yellow-brown color, used when the imported gray cloth became scarce. "Butternut" was also a slang term for a Confederate soldier.

Buttery - Pantry.

Camp Ella Bishop - Near Lexington, KY, this Union Camp was reportedly named such to honor a girl by this name who bravely waved a Union flag in the Rebels' faces, then wrapped it around her body and refused to give it up.

Cavalry - Sword carrying troops who rode horses into battle.

Company - The basic operational unit in the Civil War era army. In the Union Army, it consisted of 30-60 officers and men, including one captain, one first lieutenant, one second lieutenant, four sergeants, eight corporals, two musicians, and one wagoner. The remaining men were privates.

Copperheads - Often called "southern sympathizers," these Northerners, usually Democrats, were against the war, preferring "negotiated peace" instead, so often called "Peace Democrats."

Corps - An operational unit consisting of two or more divisions commanded by a Major General.

Cotillion - A brisk lively dance of the 19th century characterized by many intricate figures and variations and the continued changing of partners.

C.S.A. - Confederate States of America.

Dime Society or Circle - A Soldiers' Aid Society that in Huron County, Ohio met "once a fortnight on Friday evenings at 7 ½ o'clock" Several weeks of the *Norwalk Experiment*, and other papers, had ads for these meetings. Interestingly admission was five cents, not a dime as one might expect. On the intervening Fridays, in the afternoons, the women often met for sewing circles, to prepare necessary items for the soldiers or to prepare small sewing kits, called housewives, for the soldiers to carry in their sacks.

Division - In the Civil War, an operational unit consisting of two or more brigades and consisting of, on average, 6200 officers and men, in the Union Army, and 8700 officers and men in the Confederate Army.

Dover's Powders - Named after Thomas Dover (1660-1742), an English physician. [1.] A powder of ipecac and opium that is now compounded in the U.S. with lactose and in England with potassium sulfate. It is used as an anodyne and diaphoretic (*www.dictionary.com* and *www.merrianwebster.com/dictionary*). [2.] A preparation of ipecac, opium, etc. used to relieve pain and induce perspiration. (Webster, p. 437)

Flat footed - (colloquialism from Webster) To take by surprise or to catch in the act of committing some offense.

French (Leave) - (mentioned in several of William's letters) An unauthorized, unnoticed or unceremonious departure; act of leaving secretly or in haste (Webster, p. 579). See also, Garrison, p. 87.

Gunboat - A small warship, fitted with a gun or guns in the bow or amidships, that was usually used in shallow water, such as inland waterways. (Nothing was found to support that Brigadier General Merritt, mentioned in Julia's letter of "Sunday Morning", actually invented the gunboat.)

Housewife - A small sewing kit made for the soldiers by women in various Soldiers' Aid Societies such as Julia's "Dime Circle."

Infantry - Troops organized, equipped, and trained to fight on foot.

Mite Society - Another of the Ladies' Aid Societies.

Oath of Allegiance - Also called a Loyalty Oath, it was often administered to prisoners and others who opposed the Union during as well as after the Civil War. It was a pledge that was often recited as well as signed (www.alexandria.lib.va.us).

Paulin (or parlin) - Thought to be short for tarpaulin - a canvas used to cover light wooden frames and produce pontoons. Although useful in many instances, these were unsuitable for fast-flowing rivers, but apparently worked well as a rain cover.

Plaster - Another name for bandage in 1860s.

Protoxide of Iron (elixir of) - Extracted from Peruvian Bark (and also known as Quinine) it was said to be "successful in treating dyspepsia, liver complaints, dropsy, neuralgia, headache, scurvy, skin diseases, bronchitis, diseases peculiar to females and more."(Seen in an 1860s ad and found on the website: *www.flickr.com* and www.chestofbooks.com/health/natural-cure.)

"Pidoplaline" or Podophyllum peltatum - Probably what Julia was referring to in her letter of "Sunday 8th" - Mandrake, also called May Apple, used as an alterative, medicinally. (See Pierce's Medical Adviser.)

Provost Guard - In the Army, an officer in charge of military police.

Quartermaster - In the Civil War, an officer whose primary duty was to provide quarters, food, clothing, transportation for troops and forage for their animals. The Quartermaster Department is now also responsible for burials of war dead and all National Cemeteries. For more on the Quartermasters Corps, see: www.quartermaster.army.mil or visit the Quartermaster Museum at Ft. Lee, Virginia.

Regiment - In the Civil War, infantry regiments were units consisting of ten companies and cavalry (as well as heavy artillery regiments retrained as infantry) had twelve companies.

The Experiment - One of Norwalk's weekly newspapers during the Civil War.

The Register - Sandusky, Ohio's newspaper that has been in production since 1822.

Rod - A measure of length equal to 5 ½ yards or 16 ½ ft.

Soldiers' Aid Society - The North's "Dime Circles" were just one example of a Soldiers' Aid Society that consisted mainly of women meeting to sew or prepare small sewing kits for the soldiers to carry with them in their sacks. Dances were held often as fundraisers for these groups or "Societies."

Squadron - Two troops of cavalry.

Square-toed - (from Webster) Old fashioned, narrowly conservative or formal; precise; prim.

"Sirsingle" (Julia's of "Sun. 27") - Correctly spelled, "surcingle," it is a strap passed around a horse's body to bind on a saddle, blanket, pack, etc. (Webster p. 1466).

Treasury notes - For more on U.S. Treasury notes as well as Confederate notes see: http://www.bloombergview.com/articles and http://www.qconline.com/archives.

Persons of Interest

Adams Express Company - Started by the ambitious Alvin Adams, it was formally incorporated in 1854. What began as "two men, a boy and one wheelbarrow," it soon became one of the fastest growing and our nation's leading independent express companies. It later became what it is today - known for being one of the largest closed-end investment funds. (For Andrew Carnegie's connection with Adam's Express Company and other stories about this company, see: www.adamsexpress.com/about. accessed October 2014.)

Allen, Theo - (William's of January 8, 1863) - Lieutenant/Adjutant and Capt. in the 7th O.V.C., Co. F&S.

Ashland - *See Clay, Henry*

Beach, Abijah, Dr. - Often referred to as "Dr." in Julia's letters - married May 1831 to Elizabeth R. Jackson, William's eldest sister. They lived in Bellville, Ohio, about 47 miles from Norwalk, Ohio.

Beach, Elizabeth R. Jackson - (1816-1875) William's oldest sister who married Dr. Abijah Beach, M.D. (above) and resided in Bellville, Ohio.

Ben - Probably the same "Bendigo" that William first mentions in his letter of February 9, 1863. William sent him to Ohio with Prince, one of the family's horses, to help Julia with chores at home. Ben may have been a runaway slave; his last name is unknown.

Betty, Betsy, Betsy Jane- *see Jackson, Lillian W.*

Birdie - *see Jackson, Florence.*

Boehm, Jacob - Neighbor who owned the mill where Julia bought her bran and other grains.

Bonar, Julia Jackson - (1842-1899) - William's youngest sister who lived in Bellville and Mansfield, Ohio with her husband, Lewis (Lew). They had three sons, two who died as infants and one son, James, who survived her.

Bonar, Lewis (Lew) - He was married to William's sister, Julia, mentioned above.

Bramlette, Thomas E. - ("Bramblett" as William spelled it in his letter of July 31, 1864) - (1817-1875) 23rd Governor of Kentucky, who was originally the Union Democrats' nominee for governor and appointed District Attorney of Kentucky by President Lincoln. However, a year after elected he decided he was against many of Lincoln's policies including recruiting Kentucky Negroes into the Union Army and proclaimed he would "bloodily baptize the state into the Confederacy." In early January 1864, however, he made a lengthier proclamation against guerillas in his state.

Bronson, Rev. (Henry) "Uncle Bronson" - married to Julia's sister, Louisa. They lived in Sandusky, Ohio, about 20 miles north of Norwalk.

Bronson, Louisa Williams - (1817-1879) Julia's older sister who with her husband, Reverend Henry Bronson, (above) lived in Sandusky. As mentioned in the introduction, she and brother, Theodore, were reportedly the first two children baptized at St. Paul's Episcopal Church in Norwalk.

Brown, John - Probably the father of Will Brown, author and neighbor (letter written to William on May 31, 1863).

Brown, Will - Author of a letter written May 31, 1863 to William.

Buell, Don Carlos - One of two generals in the West who Lincoln and McClellan wanted to move (Halleck being the other). According to *The Northern Generals*: "…when the prim general with the cold and chilly personality did arrive on the scene, for the second day's fighting, he saved Grant's army from disaster." (p. 43) "Not known for his speed, he seemed almost reticent to join a battle, even sending a message to Sheridan at the Battle of Perryville 'do not bring on an engagement'." (p. 75) Lincoln took Buell's command away from him soon after Perryville in October 1862.

Burbridge, Stephen Gano (General) - According to information accessed October 2014, this controversial Union general has often been vilified, even being nicknamed "Butcher Burbridge." His policies however, were often in line with Kentucky governor Bramlette as well as W.T. Sherman. For more on this man who began as colonel of the 26th Kentucky Union infantry, eventually becoming a Major General (by 1863). See: http://www.bryansbush.com/ - copyright 2006-2007 Bryan S. Bush).

Burnside, Ambrose Everett (General) - McClellan's replacement to head up the Army of the Potomac. Having fought in the Mexican American War and earning his first star during the Civil War at the first Battle of Bull Run, he was a failure by most accounts, especially after the Battle at Marye's Heights (Fredericksburg, Virginia in December, 1862). It was Burnside who was in charge of the "siege of Knoxville" in the fall of 1863 and winter of 1864.

Cain, Jim - *see Kain.*

Captain Flanagan (William or W.M.) - A quartermaster in the 3rd O.V.C., Company L.

Caroline Corwin - *see Corwin, Caroline.*

Caroline (Jackson) Kellogg aka C.C. Jackson - *see Kellogg, Caroline Jackson.*

Caroline (Williams) - *see Williams, Caroline.*

Carpenter, Lt. Colonel Louis H. - (William's of March 29, 1865) 5th U.S. Colored Cavalry, Company F&S. This was one of the eight Regiments organized at Camp Nelson in October 1864.

Carr, Lt. (Albert) - 1st Lieutenant, Co. M, 7th O.V.C.

Carter, General Samuel P. - (1819-1891) Born in Elizabethton, Tennessee, he was the first and according to some sources, only United States officer to have been commissioned both a general officer in the Army and a Naval flag officer. Carter, who along with his brother, William Blount Carter, made several raids into their home territory of Northeast Tennessee, was also commander of the cavalry division of the XXIII corps in the Knoxville Campaign. (www.civilwartalk.com, accessed October 2014)

Charly, (also spelled Charley or Charlie) - *see Jackson, Charles Benjamin.*

Clay, Henry - (1777-1852) Thought by many to be Kentucky's first significant national figure and known historically as "the Great Compromiser." The present museum site of his home, **Ashland**, is located in Lexington, Kentucky. It was built between 1854 and 1856 by Clay's son, James, and is said to be a replica of the original house. The tomb and monument of the senior Clay are located in the historic Lexington Cemetery where many Union and Confederate soldiers and leaders, including John Hunt Morgan, are buried.

Clock, Samuel or James S. - (Julia's of July 9, 1865). According to the Military History of Huron Co (p. 29), Clock was in the 3rd O.V.C. when he was killed. "Appointed 1st Lieut. from Civil life March 20, 1863; promoted to Captain Nov. 30, 1864; died July 2, 1865, at Macon GA, of wounds received while in discharge of his duty." From Croft's book, p. 208 "while we lay at Macon, Captain Clock of the Third Ohio, on duty as officer of the guard, was killed by a drunken soldier of the Fourth United States Cavalry, while attempting to arrest him."

Colver, E.M. or Elisha M. - (Will Brown to William May 31, 1863) - 3rd O.V.C. Co. BK; "appointed First Lieut. Sept 4, 1861, promoted to Capt. Co. K, June 16, 1862."(Croft)

Combs, General Leslie - probably the General Combs whose bio can be found at www.combs-families.org.

Cone, Lester - (Julia's of July 9, 1865)- A Private in the 3rd O.V.C. Co L. From *The History of Third Ohio Veteran Volunteer Cavalry…* "mustered out to date Aug. 4, 1865, at Columbus, O., by order of War Department." He actually died in Michigan, in 1905. (Obituaries from September 13, 1905 *The Norwalk Reflector* and www.ancestry.com).

Cone, Tom - Neighbor or friend mentioned often as one who picked up the mail from Julia to deliver to William or to take to the "cars" for Julia, may also be the father to above Lester Cone.

Cordelia - Friend of Julia who helped take care of the children when Julia went to be with William.

Corwin, Caroline - This young woman from Brady, Michigan was listed as 19 years of age in the 1850 Huron County census and probably was hired to help Julia. Her three brothers Dwight, John, and Mat fought in the 19th Michigan Infantry.

Corwin, Dwight - Age 23 when he enlisted in Co. K of the Michigan 19th Infantry in August 5, 1862, Dwight was the first of Caroline's three brothers to join the Union effort and the only one of the three to survive the war.

Corwin, John - The oldest of the three brothers of Caroline (above), he was about 31 when he died in March 1863 from illness. He is buried in the National Cemetery in Nashville, Tennessee.

Corwin, Mat - 26 years old when he enlisted, he also was a brother of Caroline Corwin. He enlisted at the same time that his brothers, John and Dwight did in August 1862. He died from disease in March 1863, nine days before his brother, John, and is also buried in the National Cemetery in Nashville, Tennessee.

Corwin, Samuel - (Also called "Old Corwin" in some of Julia's letters.) Thought to be father to the above mentioned Corwins, he also worked around the Jackson household and farm; he was listed as 65 years of age in the 1860 Huron County, Ohio census.

Crescent City Guards - (Mentioned in William's unsent letter to friend John- April 28, 1862.) May have been the "Crescent City Native Guards," an African American Group of 63 men from the New Orleans area, OR another of several militia from the "Crescent City."

Darwin Gardner - *see Gardner, Darwin.*

Davis, Jefferson - The President of the Confederacy, about whom much has been written. A historic marker in Irwinville,

Georgia indicates the spot where he was arrested at the end of the war, and the surrounding area is now the Jefferson Davis Memorial Historic Site, a thirteen-acre park that features a museum, hiking trail, and picnic facilities. Jeff Davis County, in central Georgia, is named in the Confederate president's honor. "The 7th O.V.C. took charge of him and guarded him to Augusta, Ga." (Rankin, p. 27)

Dayton Williams - *see Williams, Dayton.*

Dickinson, Capt. (John) - 3rd O.V.C., Teamster, Waggoner or Silas of 7th O.V.C., Co. I.

Dora - *see Jackson, Theodore William.*

Duke, Basil - A Confederate General in the war and brother-in-law of John H. Morgan. At the end of the war, when C.S.A. President Jeff Davis was captured, Duke was among the men acting as Davis' bodyguards.

Eells, Arthur D. - First mentioned in William's of January 8, 1863, he was a Captain in the 7th O.V.C., Co. H.

Eliza (Goodnow) - *see Goodnow, Eliza.*

Elizabeth (R. Jackson) - *see Beach, Elizabeth R. Jackson.*

Fannie L. Jackson - *see Jackson, Fannie L.*

Fern, Fanny - (Mentioned in Julia's of "Sunday 18") Born Sara Willis July 9, 1811, she became an American newspaper columnist, humorist, novelist, and author of children's stories in the 1850s-1870s. Fern's great popularity has been attributed to her conversational style and sense of what mattered to her mostly middle-class female readers. By 1855, Fern was the highest-paid columnist in the United States, commanding $100 per week for her New York Ledger column. A collection of her columns published in 1853 sold 70,000 copies in its first year. Her best-known work, the fictional autobiography Ruth Hall (1854), has become a popular subject among feminist literary scholars. She died on October 10, 1872.

Fernald, James - Julia's letter of April 17, 1862 - (also spelled Fernuld on www.itd.nps.gov website) Captain in the 72nd O.V.I.

Fish, Ed - Thought to be a family friend, he apparently was instrumental in delivering many of the letters between Julia and William and others of the 3rd and 7th Ohio Cavalries. He later came to work with William.

Flannagan, Capt. William M. - 3rd O.V.C., Co. L and possibly another quartermaster who worked with William.

Florence Jackson - *see Jackson, Florence.*

Fosdick, Wood - Battalion Adjutant entered service with the 3rd O.V.C. for three years of service on October 25, 1861. Wood was apparently a popular name; of the seven soldiers with the surname 'Fosdick' from Ohio, only two were not named Wood!

Foster, Major (John H) - In the 3rd O.V.C., Co. F&S. This MAY have been to whom William was writing in his unsent letter of April 28, 1862; also, William's May 11, 1862 letter to Julia talks of an investigation: "the impression in camp is that Maj. Foster is the responsible party."

Franklin, Arthur - He was listed as having been in the 55th Ohio Volunteer Infantry, Co A.

Fry, General Speed - (William's of March 29, 1865) William may have been referring to Brigadier General Speed S. Fry, about whom much has been written, especially concerning his involvement at Camp Nelson.

Gardner, Darwin (Also spelled Gardiner or Gardener) - Brother-in-law of Julia and William, married to Julia's sister, Sarah. They lived in Toledo and seemed to have kept the two older girls, the twins, at times, in order to help Julia while William was away.

Gardner, Sarah Williams - (1827-1906) Julia's younger sister, married to Darwin Gardner (above). They lived in Toledo at the time these letters were written. Sarah was also Julia's mother's name who was rarely mentioned in the letters, except as "mother."

Garrard, Israel - Colonel in command of William's company in the 7th O.V.C. and mentioned in many of William's letters.

Gaylord, Henry B. - (William's of May 17, 1862) 3rd O.V.C., Co I.

Gilmore (or Gillmore) General Quincy Adams - Saddler in 7th O.V.C., Co. B, he was from Lorain County, Ohio.

Goodnow, Eliza - Married to William Milton Goodnow, "Will." (See Goodnow, William.) They had a son, William Theodore, born February 27, 1862 (mentioned in Julia's of March 7, 1862) who Will apparently never saw. Eliza later remarried.

Goodnow, Mary - Married to Julia's brother, Theodore Williams.

Goodnow, Matilda -(1815-1889) Julia's sister who married M.W. Goodnow in 1837 and probably to whom Theodore W. was referring in his letter of June 3, 1862.

Goodnow, William Milton "Will" - (Mentioned in Julia's letters of March 7, 18, 28 and Theodore's to Julia of June 3, 1862.) Married to Eliza, he was a 2nd Lt. in the 3rd O.V.C., Co. I and died of typhoid fever in early 1862 near Corinth, Mississippi. Will and Eliza had a son, William Theodore, born in February 1862 who never met his father.

Gould, Amos - Father of Silas and good friend of the family (from Sullivan County) who wrote details of his son's death in his letter to Julia (June 1, 1863).

Gould, Silas - In the 3rd O.V.C., Co. F. He was a good friend of the family and died instantly after accidentally shooting himself, May 12, 1863. He was the eldest of ten and is buried in the Gould Family cemetery in Ashland County, Ohio.

Granger, General (1816-1894) - (William's of January 8, 1863). He is most likely Robert S. Granger who was a career officer. Born in Zanesville, Ohio, he was a West Point graduate and later assistant instructor there. He served in the Seminole War and the Mexican American War. Soon after the start of the Civil War, he was captured and then paroled with the agreement that he would not serve until after August 1862. In the fall of 1862, after being appointed brigadier general, he was placed in charge of camp and garrison duty in Kentucky, Tennessee, and Alabama. At the end of the war, he was brevetted as a Major General.

Grant, Ulysses S. - (1822-1885) His birth name being Hiram Ulysses Grant, he changed his name soon after reporting to West Point for he did not like the initials of his birth name ("HUG"). He replaced McClellan shortly after Lincoln's pronouncement of the Emancipation Proclamation. He was not given command of all the Union Armies until March of 1864.

Gray, D.S. - May have been the family's financial advisor as there are *many* letters to and from him about their accounts or the state of their finances. Many are difficult to read. He may also have been married to William's sister, Mary, as a marriage certificate of Mary L. Jackson to D.S. Gray dated December 27, 1858 was found through the F.H.S.

Hall, Capt. Theoron - Head Quartermaster at Camp Nelson. More is written on him in Richard Sear's book about Camp Nelson.

Hartsuff, General - (William's of July 6, 1863) Promoted to Major General on November 19, 1862, after having been severely wounded in the Battle at Antietam. He was later appointed to command the XXIII Corps in May 1863 and saw some duty in Kentucky and East Tennessee before ill health forced him to give up the position. He finally returned to field command in March 1865 in command of the defenses at Bermuda Hundred in the Department of Virginia and North Carolina. He was brevetted Brigadier and Major General in the regular army on March 13, 1865.

Hascall or Haskill, General - (1829-1904) Milo Smith Hascall who was in charge of a brigade in Thomas J. Wood's Division (under Don Carlos Buell). He arrived at Shiloh after the battle had ended but did take part in the Siege of Corinth. Later that month, he was commissioned as Brigadier General of Volunteers.

Henry - *see Terry, Henry.*

Hillyer, Asa R. - 1st Lieutenant commanding Co. F of the 101st O.V.I., he was mortally wounded in the Battle of Stones River (Murfreesboro, TN) and died January 4, 1863. He is buried in Riverside Cemetery, Ridgefield Township (Monroeville, Ohio).

Hood, John Bell - (1831-1879) Confederate General best known for his bravery that some say bordered on aggressiveness and recklessness. At Gettysburg, his left arm was injured so badly he never had full use of it again. At Chickamauga, his left leg was so badly injured that it required amputation.

Isbell, Elihu - (Amos Gould's letter to Julia June 1, 1863) 3rd O.V.C. Company FDC.

Jackson, Charles Benjamin - Referred to in some letters as "Charly" or "Charlie," he was the firstborn child of Julia and William. From *The Sandusky Register* dated May 6, 1853: "Charles Jackson, a lad of about 7 years of age, son of William Jackson and grandson of James Williams, Esq., of this place was drowned at Monroeville, on Friday afternoon last under the following stressful circumstances. He had accompanied his father to the back part of the garden-which extends to or near the bank of the river-where the latter was engaged in repairing the fence. They started for the house together, but the little fellow discovering some flowers, stopped to gather them while the father walked on. After waiting some time in vain, for the child's return, the parents became alarmed and went in search of him, and not finding him readily the conviction flashed upon the mind of Mr. J. that his son was drowned. He rushed to the river bank, and there discovered that his fears were but too well grounded. A bunch of wild flowers lay upon the water, marking the very spot, beneath which was the cold and lifeless form of his poor boy. Almost distracted the father plunged into the river, and it was with some difficulty, as we understand, that he was saved from drowning. It is supposed that while gathering flowers near the brink, a mis-step, or the caving of the bank, precipitated the poor boy into the water below. "

Jackson, Fannie L. - (1850 to 1886) One of the twins of William and Julia who was listed as 10 years old on the 1860 census and the only one of their children who didn't seem to have a nickname.

Jackson, Florence - Nicknamed "Birdie," she was the fourth born child of William and Julia and was five years old in the July 1860 census. She was also the great-grandmother of Ray Heck, the editor's 3rd cousin, mentioned in Preface and Epilogue sections of this book.

Jackson, Julia A. - (1850-1884) Twin to Fannie, she was listed as ten years old in the 1860 census records. Her mother, Julia, often referred to her as "Judy" or "Jules" in her letters to William. This daughter of William and Julia is buried in Norwalk's Woodlawn Cemetery; her headstone reads: "Julia A. Jackson Beloved wife of Rev. Geo. W. Williams died at Cleveland, O May 23, 1884 Aged 33 years, 3 months, 8 days."

Jackson, Lillian W. - (1859-1889) Nicknamed "Betty," "Betsy Jane," and "May Ann", she was the sixth child of William and Julia. Christened Lillian Walter Jackson, she was listed as 8 months old in the 1860 census and also referred to as "the baby" in the letters.

Jackson, Sarah R. - (1825-1874) - She was William's sister who married Samuel B. Jackson and lived in Bellville, Ohio when she wrote her letter of August 9, 1863). A child, Thomas, preceded her in death. (B: 1860 D: 1861).

Jackson, Theodore William - (1857- ?) Nicknamed "Dora" but christened Theodore William Jackson, he was the second born son and fifth child born to William and Julia. Theodore William Jackson was the editor's great-grandfather.

James Williams - *see Williams, James.*

John Sargent - see *Sargent, John.*

Jolly, Oscar (A. or J.) - In the 7th O.V.C., Private, Co. I. The handwriting being what it was, I was uncertain if William's letter of January 3, 1863 was referring to Capt. Jolly or Tally; also Alex Jolly was the author of a letter to William dated Feb. 21, 1863. The website www.itd.nps.gov had similar confusing data as they too have obtained information from original handwritten copies.

Josh - *see Waily, Josh.*

Julia (Jackson Bonar) - *see Bonar, Julia Jackson.*

Julia A. **Jackson** -*see Jackson, Julia.*

Kain, James H. - Waggoner in the 7th O.V.C., Co. D.

Kellogg, B.W. - Brother-in-law who was married to William's sister, Caroline (below).

Kellogg, Caroline Jackson - William's sister, Caroline, who was married to B.W. Kellogg and lived in Bellville, Ohio. She was mentioned in Theodore William's letter to Julia dated June 3, 1862 and author of November 30, 1865 letter.

Kimball, Calvin - "Kimble the clerk" (William's of August 15, 1862) William may have been referring to Calvin S., who enlisted into the 3rd O.V.C. (April 1861) as a private in Co. C. Later, as a 1st Lt. in Co. G, he was captured and imprisoned but escaped. He was promoted to Capt. in February 1865 and was mustered out with the company in August 1865.

Lee, Robert E. - (1807-1870) Renowned General in charge of the Confederate Armies during the Civil War who is generally seen as a hero by many Southerners and Northerners alike.

Libby Beach - May have been a nickname for William's sister, Elizabeth, who was married to Dr. Abijah Beach.

Lillian - *see Jackson, Lillian W.*

Lincoln, Abraham - The President of the United States of America from 1861-1865.

Louise or Louisa - *see Bronson, Louisa Williams.*

Lucy - Another girl who lived with Julia temporarily to help her with the children and household chores.

Magoffin, Beriah Governor - Kentucky's 21st Governor who took office in August 1859 and resigned from office in August 1862 after trying without success to keep Kentucky neutral in the War Between the States. He was instrumental in having Kentucky ratify the Thirteenth Amendment. He also pushed for the state to give more civil rights to African Americans.

Mary Goodnow - *see Goodnow, Mary.*

Matild or Matilda (Williams) Goodnow - *see Goodnow, Matilda.*

McClellan, George B. (General) - Appointed to replace Winfield Scott to lead the Army of the Potomac, he would find that he, too, could be replaced. In November 1862, President Lincoln chose to relieve him of his duties and replace him with Burnside.

McClelland, Thomas D. - (First mentioned in William's of August 23, 1862 and later in Will Brown's to William-May 1863.) Brown was probably referring to *this McClelland*, from Ohio. First Lieutenant Thomas McClelland mustered into the 3rd O.V.C., Co. A. Sept. 4, 1861 and was immediately promoted to Captain. (p.106, *History of Huron and Erie Counties, Ohio).*

McColgins, John - 7th O.V.C., Cos. F&S. Rank in: 1st Lieut./Comm. of Subsistence; Rank out: 1st Lt. /Regimental Commissary of Sub-sistence.

McCook, (Charles) - 2nd Regt. O.V.I. - organized at Camp Dennison, attached to 9th Brig. Army of Ohio; 3rd Division to September 1862, OR **Col. Robert McCook**, 9th O.V.I. killed by guerillas, August 1862 OR McCook, **Alexander** 1st Reg. O.V.I., Co. F&S, at the Battle of Shiloh (They may all be related to the McCooks in *The Fighting McCooks: America's Famous Fighting Family*, about how this family gave "seventeen men, four of whom lost their lives" toward the war.)

McEwen - (William's of August 15, 1862) Possibly Thomas L. of Cos. F&S, 3rd O.V.C. Corporal/ 1st Lt. /Regt. Quartermaster.

McPherson, (General) James B. - (1828-1864) From Clyde, Ohio, he was top of his class at West Point (that included his future nemesis, John Bell Hood.) Known for his engineering capabilities, he was chief engineer under Grant. He was killed July 22, 1864 in Atlanta while commanding the Union Army of the Tennessee against Hood's Army of Tennessee.

Miner, Henry - In the 3rd O.V.C., Co. M; 1st Lieutenant / Captain.

Morgan, John Hunt - The famous Confederate leader who eluded the Union Armies many times and is most famous for his raid into Southern Indiana and Ohio in July 1863. He and several of his men were captured and imprisoned in Camp Chase near Columbus, Ohio but escaped six months later. He was killed by Union Cavalrymen September 4, 1864 in Greeneville, Tennessee. There were two funerals for him, one in Abingdon, Virginia and one in Richmond, Virginia before his body was taken to its final resting place in Lexington, Kentucky.

Murray, Colonel Douglas A. - (William's of August 15, 1862) He is listed as having been a Lt. Col in the 3rd O.V.C., Co. F&S.

Paramore, James W. - Listed on the roster of the 3rd O.V.C. as having entered service on Sept. 27, 1861 and appointed Major; promoted to Col. January 5, 1863; honorably discharged July 1, 1863, Co. F&S, Major/Colonel.

Pillow, Gideon J. (General) - Appointed Brigadier General in the C.S.A. Army of Tennessee. After the war, he returned to practicing law.

Prentice, C.W. (or Obadiah) - The family's doctor.

Probert, George - Family friend, also in the 3rd O.V.C., he was listed as Battalion Quartermaster (1st Lt. /Adjutant). His wife, Anna, is also mentioned in several of Julia's and William's letters.

Rankin, R.C. - (Author of the *History of the Seventh O.V.C.*) - 1st Lieut. /Capt. in Co. E.

Reid, Dr. - Medical doctor in Norwalk (mentioned in Julia's letter of "Sunday Morning.")

Roby, John - One of the "Roby Brothers" well known in Huron County for their various businesses, mainly distilleries.

Roby, Rural or Ruehl - One of several Roby brothers, formerly from Detroit, he owned several businesses in Huron County.

Rogers, William R. - Friend of the family and a member of "Taylor's Battery" of Chicago who died of typhoid fever March 28, 1862 at the Mound City (IL) hospital, shortly after the Battle at Ft. Donelson. *The Norwalk Experiment* mentioned him in articles in March 31, 1862 and as late as May 5, 1862.

Rosecrans, (Union-Major General) William Starke - A West Point graduate and classmate of William T. Sherman, he was also from Ohio. When shelter tents were introduced to Rosecrans' army, the men took a great dislike to them, calling them "pup tents" and placing signs outside them saying, among other things, "pups for sale." Mistakes he made at Chickamauga caused Grant to relieve him of his command.

Rousseau, Lovell Harrison - (1818-1869) - (Mentioned in William's of June 29, 1865.) Pre-War Profession: Road worker, lawyer, politician, and served in the Mexican War. War Service: September 1861 Col. of 3rd Kentucky (Union) Infantry; October 1861 appointed Brigadier General of Volunteers; October 1862 promoted to Major General of Volunteers; he resigned in 1865.

Rust, Tracy - Son of R.T. Rust, Esq. of Norwalk, he was the Sergeant of his company and was killed at the Battle at Winchester (probably Battle of Kernstown, south of Winchester-March 23, 1862). First mentioned in Julia's of April 1, 1862. (Information found in *The Norwalk Experiment*-March 31, 1862).

Santmyer (Spelled Santemire in Rankin's history) - (Mentioned in William's of January 10, 1865) is probably J.P., Joseph or Joseph P. Santmyer of the 7th O.V.C., Co. B.

Sarah Gardner (also spelled Gardiner) - *see Gardner, Sarah Williams*.

Sarah (Matilda Hunt) Williams - *see Williams, Sarah.*

Sarah (R. Jackson) - *see Jackson, Sarah R.*

Sargent, John - (mentioned in many of both William and Julia's letters) assumed to be superintendent or head of schools in Monroeville at the time of the Civil War.

Scott, Mary Sappington - In Kentucky, a woman with whom William would board on occasion. Her house at Camp Nelson is still standing as the only building from the original camp. According to Peggy McClintock from the present Camp Nelson Heritage Center, "Mrs. Scott probably *was* a 'little spit fire' as Julia called her in her letter of July 7, 1864. Besides saving her family from Indian attacks long before the war, she petitioned the government for $85,000 for the destruction done to her property during the war. With the help of one of her sons, she was able to receive about 10% of that amount."

Scott's Louisiana Cavalry - William is referring to the 1st Louisiana Cavalry Regiment organized in September 1861 by Louisiana native, Colonel John Sims Scott. This regiment was known as one of the most heavily endowed, monetarily, and participated in more than 75 engagements during the two and a half years between November 1861 and April 1864. (See http://ehistory.osu.edu for more on this regiment's final year.)

Scouton, Charles - possibly Private in Co. L, 3rd O.V.C.

Sherman, John - (Julia's letter of July 17, 1864) - Younger brother of William T. Sherman and Senator in Ohio from 1861 until 1898. Responsible for the organization of the "Sherman Brigade", made up at one time of nine regiments. (For more on the Sherman Brigade, see www.archive.org/details/storyofshermanbr).

Sherman, William T. - (1820-1891) - Mainly known for his famous "March to the Sea" and the burning of Atlanta during the

Civil War. Later, when Grant was President, he was made Commander of the U.S. Army.

"Sidele" (Seidel) Charles B. - Enlisted in the 3rd O.V.C., September 7, 1861; promoted to Major from Capt. January 1862, taken prisoner in Kentucky in October 1862 and released on parole; promoted to Lieut. Col. June 1863, to Colonel August 1863; mustered out January 16, 1865 on expiration of terms of service.

Silas (*see Gould, Silas*) - first mentioned in William's of May 11, 1862.

Simpson, Wm. T. - 7th O.V.C. Co. F&S- Capt. /Major.

Smith, Charles F. or T. - (William's of January 8, 1863 and others) - Also referred to as "Lieut. Smith" - enlisted as a private in 7th O.V.C., Co. AMH, but mustered out as a 1st Lieutenant. He was listed as Charles F. and Charles T. in the online roster listed with the government website. There was another C.F. Smith (Charles Ferguson), a Brigadier General, who was mortally wounded at Shiloh and died within a month of receiving his injuries. Also in *Roster of Ohio Troops: A Compendium of the War of the Rebellion,* p. 376.

Sowers, Frank - Listed as Quartermaster in Louis Zahm's 3rd O.V.C. in *The Norwalk Experiment*, Sept. 16, 1861. He was a neighbor and friend mentioned in several letters. See also "nps.gov" website which lists him as Rgt. Quartermaster, Co. F&S.

Speer, James H., Jr - 7th O.V.C., Private, Co. C.

Stearns, Jo - (Julia's of March 23, 1862) - The government website site shows two 'Joseph E. Stearns' who were with the 21st O.V.I. and one 'Joseph Stearns' with the 33rd O.V.I.; both regiments were involved in "occupying" Nashville around the time of Julia's letter.

Stem, Leander - Colonel in the 101st Ohio Infantry regiment who was mortally wounded in the Battle of Stones River (Murfreesboro, TN) and died January 5, 1863, according to *The*

Norwalk Experiment article of January 22, 1863. His letters can be found in the book *Stand by the Colors: The Civil War letters of Leander Stem*, edited by John T. Hubbell, 24 pgs.; Kentucky Historical Society Quarterly, July 1975.

Stockton, Colonel - (William's of July 6, 1863) - Possibly John Stockton of the 8th Regiment Michigan Cavalry, Co. F&S.

Tally, *(See Jolly, Oscar A.)* - (Mentioned in William's of January 3, 1863). William was probably referring to this soldier who was later promoted to Captain.

Terry, Harrison - Store owner in Huron County and possibly father of Henry (below), a friend who Julia mourned in several letters of 1863. There was also a Harrison Terry in the 3rd O.V.C.

Terry, Henry - Friend of the family, (Julia's letters of "Sunday 18" and "March 7," 1862 as well as some of William's early letters) who was killed in the Battle of Stones River (Murfreesboro, Tennessee) December 31, 1862. In one *Norwalk Experiment* article (February 5, 1863) and in *A Military History of Huron County* he is listed as a Major but in another article (February 13, 1863), he is listed as a Lieutenant Colonel in the 24th O.V.I.

Theo (Allen) - *see Allen.*

Theodore (Williams) - *see Williams, Theodore.*

Thomas, General George Henry - (1816-1870) - Named as a "seasoned leader" in many sources; he was a Virginian who decided from the start to fight with the Union. Due to his stand at Chickamauga, he became known as "the Rock of Chickamauga," also known as "Old Pap."

Vallandigham, Clement L. - (1820-1871) - Best known as the famous Copperhead leader from Ohio, he was exiled to the Confederacy in May, 1863. He fled to Bermuda and then Canada where he campaigned to become Governor of Ohio. Although he lost that election, he did serve in the House of Representatives (after being pardoned and allowed to return to the United States).

He practiced law in Ohio until he died after accidentally shooting himself during a trial where he was defense attorney for an alleged murderer.

Waily, Josh - Mentioned in several of Julia's letters is thought to have been a neighbor who seemed to be a thorn in Julia's side most of the time!

Walter Kellogg or B.W. Kellogg - *see Kellogg, B.W.*

Washington Battery - (Mentioned in William's unsent letter of April 28, 1862.) He was probably referring to the "Washington Battalion" whose 5th regiment fought at Shiloh.

Wheeler, Joseph General - Born in Georgia but raised in New England, he returned to the South to enlist (as Colonel) with the 19th Alabama. He eventually became Commander of the Confederate Cavalry under Braxton Bragg. This general was often known as "Fightin' Joe Wheeler."

Will (Goodnow) - see *Goodnow, Will.*

Williams, Caroline - (1813-1898) Julia's sister who apparently never married and lived at her home at 55 E. Main Street in Norwalk until her death.

Williams, Dayton - (Julia's of July 26 and 31, 1864) - There were two soldiers named Williams from Ridgefield Township listed in the *Military Record of Huron County* (p. 29). Since Julia was referring to one killed in July 1864, it is probably "Lieutenant C.D. Williams, 123rd O.V.I. killed at Snickers Gap, July 1864." On p. 28, he is listed as having "mustered at Camp Monroeville, fall of 1862, Co. B, 123rd O.V.I." Not certain as to whether Dayton is directly related to Julia's (Williams') family.

Williams, James - (1787-1869) - Julia's father, a prominent lawyer in Norwalk. Details of Julia's father are mentioned in the introduction.

Williams, Sarah Hunt - (1791-1871) Julia's mother. As mentioned in the introduction, Julia's parents lived in nearby Norwalk. Several sources state she was a "devout Episcopalian." She remained an "earnest, devoted and exemplary member, and firmly Evangelical in her views." (*Firelands Pioneer*, Oct. 1874, pp. 116-117.)

Williams, Theodore - (1820-1907) - Oldest brother of Julia who is mentioned in many of Julia's letters and the author of one included in this book (June 3, 1862). He owned a store in Norwalk and was married to Mary (Goodnow). He and their sister, Louisa, were reportedly the first children baptized at St. Paul's Episcopal in Norwalk.

Wolford, Calvin (Sgt.) - 7th O.V.C., Co. L.

Wood, Brigadier General Thomas John - (1823-1906) - William's letter of April 28, 1862 written to 'Friend John' was probably referring to this man, from Indiana, who commanded a division of the Army of the Ohio and was present on the second day of Shiloh. Best known for his failure at Chickamauga, he commanded a division of the Army of the Ohio and later Army of the Cumberland. For more on this not so well known Union leader, see information in the Bibliography for Dan Lee's book.

Wooster, Lieutenant Colonel Moses Fairchild - Mortally wounded in the Battle of Stones River (Murfreesboro, Tennessee), he died of his wounds on January 1, 1863. He originally enlisted in the 24th O.V.I. and mustered out as a Captain. After resigning from the 24th (August 1862), he joined the 101st O.V.I. and was promoted to Lt. Colonel two months later, which was just a little more than two months before his death.

Wright, Major General Horatio G. - William may have been referring to this man (letter of January 14, 1863). Wright was commander of various departments, armies, or corps at various times. His commands included the Department of the Ohio and the Army of the Ohio. He took part in many campaigns, including one to force Bragg out of Kentucky in 1862. There was also a "Geo. B. Wright," but he was Quartermaster-general, Department of the Ohio.

Zahm, Colonel Lewis (in O.R. and Huron Co. newspapers) or Louis as some sources have written his name - Appointed Colonel of the 3rd O.V.C. when it was formed in Monroeville, Ohio, he was the subject of some controversy (William's of August 15 1862) and resigned in January 1863. The www.itd.nps.gov site listed another Lewis Zahm as adjutant, however in the December 23, 1861 listing of the organization of the 3rd O.V.C., the adjutant named Zahm was a 'V.J. Zahm'.

Zahm, Mrs. - wife of Col. Zahm (above) mentioned in several of Julia's letters.

Bibliography

Anderson, William, *They Died to Make Men Free, A History of the 19th Michigan Infantry in the Civil War*. Berrien Springs, MI: Hardscrabble Books, 1980.

Baughman, A. J., *History of Huron County, Ohio Its Progress and Development, Volume 1*. Chicago: S.J. Clarke Publishing Co., 1909. *Commemorative Biographical Record of the Counties of Huron and Lorain, Ohio containing Biographical Sketches of Prominent and Representative Citizens, and of Many of the Early Settled Families. Chicago: J.H.Beers & Co., 1894.*

Berry, Bertice, *The Ties That Bind, A Memoir of Race, Memory and Redemption*. New York: Broadway Books, 2009.

Blight, David W., *A Slave No More, Two Men Who Escaped to Freedom*. Orlando: Harcourt, 2007.

Catton, Bruce, *A Stillness at Appomattox*. Garden City, NY: Doubleday & Company, Inc., 1954.
Never Call Retreat, the Centennial History of the Civil War; Garden City, NY: Doubleday and Company, Inc., 1965.
Reflections on The Civil War, New York: Berkeley Books, 1981.
The American Heritage Picture History of the Civil War. Prineville, Oregon: Bonanza Books, 1960.
This Hallowed Ground, The Story of the Union Side of the Civil War. Garden City, NY: Doubleday and Company, Inc., 1956.

Commemorative Biographical Record of the Counties of Huron and Lorain, Ohio; Chicago: J.H. Beers & Co., 1894.

Crofts, Sgt. Thomas, *The History of the Service of the Third Ohio Veteran Volunteer Cavalry in the War for the Preservation of the Union 1861-1865*. Columbus, Ohio: Stoneman Press, 1910.

Davis, Burke, *The Civil War Strange and Fascinating Facts*. New York and Avenel, NJ: Wing Books, 1982.

Dyer, Frederick, *A Compendium of the War of the Rebellion*; Cedar Rapids, Iowa: Torch Press, 1908.

Foote, Shelby, *The Civil War A Narrative.* Toronto, Ontario, Canada: Random House, 1958.

Garrison, Webb and Cheryl, *Encyclopedia of Civil War Usage - An Illustrated Compendium of the Everyday Language of Soldiers and Civilians*. Nashville, TN: Cumberland House Publishing, 2001.

Gillman, J. Matthew, *The North Fights the Civil War*. Chicago: Ivan R. Dees, 1994.

Hallock, Judith Lee, *The Civil War Letters of Joshua K. Callaway.* Athens, Georgia: University of Georgia Press, 1997.

Hauck, Thomas, *Bellville, Defining an Architectural Identity in Ohio;* The Ohio State University Dept. of Architecture, Columbus, Ohio: Ohio State University Press, 1975.

Hubbell, John T., editor. *Stand by the Colors: The Civil War letters of Leander Stem*, 24 pages. Kentucky Historical Society Quarterly, July 1975.

Lee, Dan, *Thomas J. Wood: A Biography of the Union General in the Civil War*. Jefferson, NC: McFarland, 2012.

Leisch, Juanita, *An Introduction to Civil War Civilians.* Gettysburg, PA: Thomas Publications, 1994.

Leonard, Elizabeth D., *All the Daring of the Soldier: Women of the Civil War Armies*. New York: M.W. Norton & Company, Inc., 1999.

Livermore, Mary, *My Story of the War: A Woman's Narrative of Four Years Personal Experience*. Hartford, Connecticut: A. D. Worthington and company, 1889.

Lowry, Thomas M. MD, *The Story the Soldiers Wouldn't Tell: Sex in the Civil War.* Mechanicsburg, Pennsylvania: Stackpole Books, 1994.

Nevins, Allan, *The War for the Union: The Organized War 1863-64*. New York: Charles Scribner's Sons, 1971.

Ommert, Larry H., *A Military History Of Huron County, Ohio (Civil War)*. Norwalk, Ohio: Huron County Chapter O.G.S.(Ohio Genealogic Society), 1989.

O'Shea, Samara, *For The Love of Letters, a 21st Century Guide to the Art of Letter Writing*. New York: Harper Collins Publishers, 2007.

Rankin, R. C., *History of the Seventh Ohio Volunteer Cavalry*. Memphis, Tennessee: General Books, 2010.

Reeder, Col. Red, *The Northern Generals*. New York: Duell, Sloan & Pearce, 1964.

Reid, Whitelaw, *Ohio in the War Her Statesmen, Generals, and Soldiers*. Cincinnati: Moore, Wilstach & Baldwin, 1868.

Rhodes, Robert Hunt, *All for the Union, The Civil War Diary and Letters of Elisha Hunt Rhodes*. New York: Orion Books, 1985.

Robertson, James I. Jr., *Soldiers Blue and Gray.* Columbia, South Carolina: University of South Carolina Press, 1988.
Tenting Tonight. Alexandria, Virginia: Time Life Books, 1984.

Rodenbough, Brig. Gen. Theo F., *The Photographic History of the Civil War/ The Decisive Battles/The Cavalry*. Blue & Grey Press, 1911.

Sandburg, Carl, *Abraham Lincoln, The Sangamon Edition, Volumes Three and Four, War Years I and II.* New York: Harcourt, Brace and Company, Inc., 1939.

Scott, Captain Robert N., *The War of the Rebellion: A Compilation of the Official Records of the Union and Confederate Armies (O.R.)*. Washington, D.C.: Library of Congress, 1877.

Sears, Richard, *Camp Nelson, Kentucky: A Civil War History*; Lexington: University Press of Kentucky, 2002.

Trudeau, Noah Andre, *Out of the Storm: The End of The Civil War, April-June 1865*; New York: Little, Brown and Co., 1994.

Unknown Officer, *Annals of the Army of the Cumberland*, Philadelphia: J.B. Lippincott & Co., 1864.

Watkins, Sam, *Company Aytch Or A Side Show of the Big Show: A Confederate Memoir of the Civil War*; New York: Plume, 1999.

Webster, *New World Dictionary of the American Language, College Edition*; Cleveland and New York: The World Publishing Co., 1962.

Young, Rosemary, *The Civil War Diary Quilt 121 Stories and the Quilt Blocks They Inspired*; Iola, WI: KP Books, 2005.

Websites

All accessed during the months of June through November, 2014.

www.adamsexpress.com/about
www.alexandria.lib.va.us
www.ancestry.com
www.archive.org
www.archives.gov/exhibits/civil-war
www.bloombergview.com/articles
www.bryansbush.com
www.campnelson.org
www.chestofbooks.com/health/natural-cure
www.civilwar.org/education/civil-war-casualties.html
www.civilwararchive.com
www.civilwarhome.com-info on drugs/medicine during the Civil War.
www.civilwarindex.com/armyoh/rosters/7th_oh_cavalry
www.combs-families.org
www.cr.nps.gov/nr/travel/Lexington
www.dictionary.com
www.ebooks.library.cornell.edu (for the entire Official Records)
www.ehistory.osu.edu
www.familysearch.org
www.firelands.wordpress.com
www.firelandsmuseum.org/history
www.flickr.com
www.georgiaencyclopedia.org
www.history1800s.about.com

www.historynet.com/civil-war-nurses
www.merrian-webster.com/dictionary
www.nps.gov/anti/historyculture/freedom.htm (Antietam)
www.nps.gov/civilwar/soldiers-and-sailors-database.htm
www.ohiocivilwar.com
www.ohiohistory.wordpress.com
www.qconline.com/archives
www.quartermaster.army.mil
www.sunsite.utk.civilwar.com
www.thehuronhistoricalsociety.org
www.timeanddate.com/calendar
www2.bgsu.edu/colleges/library/cac/cwar

About the Author

Cheryl Jackson Baker moved from her South Florida roots to pursue a career in Special Education. After obtaining her B.S. from Florida State University in the Education of the Visually Impaired, she taught for two years in Virginia. She obtained her M.A. from University of Northern Colorado in Orientation and Mobility after which she continued to teach blind and visually impaired students (from infants to clients in their nineties) until her retirement in 2009.

Cheryl is an avid cyclist and hiker, having hiked all the trails in the Great Smoky Mountains National Park and ridden in several bicycle tours for various charities. When not traveling or substitute teaching, she enjoys cycling the roads in the foothills of the nearby mountains.

She and her husband, Phil, have lived in East Tennessee since their marriage in 1979. Their adult children, Matthew (and his wife and daughter) and Megan, live in Richmond, Virginia. When not traveling to visit their children, or other family, Cheryl has enjoyed traveling to various places mentioned in the book for research purposes. One of her next "projects" is to travel to all the National Parks across this expansive and diverse country of ours.

This book about her great-great-grandparents' Civil War letters is her first.

For more great stories, visit our website at
www.BadgleyPublishingCompany.com

49701113R00168

Made in the USA
Charleston, SC
01 December 2015